LEE, GRANT AND SHERMAN

LEE, GRANT

AND

SHERMAN

A Study in Leadership
in the 1864-65 Campaign

BY

ALFRED H. BURNE

INTRODUCTION BY DOUGLAS SOUTHALL FREEMAN

FOREWORD AND ENDNOTES BY ALBERT CASTEL

University Press of Kansas

Published by the University Press of Kansas (Lawrence, Kansas 66049), which
was organized by the Kansas Board of Regents and is operated and funded by
Emporia State University, Fort Hays State University, Kansas State University,
Pittsburg State University, the University of Kansas, and Wichita State University

Library of Congress Cataloging-in-Publication Data

Burne, Alfred Higgins, 1886–1959.
    Lee, Grant and Sherman : a study in leadership in the 1864–65 campaign /
by Alfred H. Burne ; introduction by Douglas Southall Freeman ; foreword
and endnotes by Albert Castel.
        p. cm. — (Modern war studies)
    Originally published: Aldershot : Gale & Polden, 1938.
    Includes bibliographical references and index.
    ISBN 0-7006-1072-3 (alk. paper)—ISBN 0-7006-1073-1 (pbk. : alk. paper)
    1. United States—History—Civil War, 1861–1865—Campaigns. 2. Lee,
Robert E. (Robert Edward), 1807–1870—Military leadership. 3. Grant,
Ulysses S. (Ulysses Simpson), 1822–1885—Military leadership. 4. Sherman,
William T. (William Tecumseh), 1820–1891—Military leadership.
5. Command of troops—Case studies. 6. Generals—United States—
History—19th century. I. Castel, Albert E. II. Title. III. Series.
E470 .B883 2000
973.7'36—dc21   00-043427

British Library Cataloguing in Publication Data is available.

Printed in the United States of America

10 9 8 7 6 5 4 3 2 1

CONTENTS

MAPS

On the maps in this edition, Northern troop movements are represented with the darker gray screen and Southern troop movements with the lighter gray screen.

FOREWORD

BETWEEN 1929 and 1939 three British army officers turned historians produced four books about the American Civil War. One was General J. F. C. Fuller, who in 1929 published *The Generalship of Ulysses S. Grant* and four years later *Grant and Lee*. Another was Basil Liddell Hart, whose *Sherman* appeared in 1930. And the third was Lieutenant Colonel Alfred H. Burne, whose *Lee, Grant and Sherman: A Study in Leadership in the 1864–65 Campaign,* published in America in 1939, now is before whoever is reading these words. Fuller's and Liddell Hart's works achieved a greater readership and influence in the United States than Burne's. Although understandable—Fuller and Liddell Hart already were much better known in America than Burne—this was unfortunate, for as this Foreword will endeavor to demonstrate, despite its defects (many of which stem from the defects in Civil War scholarship as a whole when he wrote), Burne's book is superior in its interpretations to the tomes of his compatriots, none of which has stood the test of time. Burne's was ahead of its time. But before examining the book, let us first take a quick look at the career of its author prior to his writing it.

Born in Shropshire, England, in 1886, Burne was the youngest of five sons of a British army officer. After graduating from the prestigious public school (as the English term their private schools) of Winchester he chose to become, as had his father, a professional soldier by entering the Royal Military Academy at Woolwich in 1904. Two years later he received a commission in the Royal Artillery and, following postings in Ireland and elsewhere, served as an artillery officer in World War I. During this war he participated in many of the greatest battles of the Western Front in France, obtained the rank of major in command of a battery of heavy artillery, and won the D.S.O. and a bar thereto for outstanding skill and bravery in action. Whenever he comments in this book, as, for example, he does on page 90, on the employment of cannons in combat, actual or potential, he assuredly deserves to be read with the utmost respect.

Following the end of the war in 1918 he became a "service lecturer," in which capacity he proceeded to publish the following books: *Talks on Leadership* (1921); *Some Pages from the History of "Q" Battery, R. H. A.* (1922); and *The Royal Artillery Mess, Woolwich* (1934). In 1934 he resigned from the service with the rank of lieutenant colonel. According to family tradition, he did so out of boredom with what he called "concrete gunnery" while stationed at

Singapore. But quite possibly he had decided to become a full-time historian, being inspired by the examples of Fuller and Liddell Hart, both of whom had cast aside their swords to take up the pen—or, if you prefer, the typewriter.

His initial post-resignation books, *The Liaoyang Campaign* (1936) and *Mesopotamia: The Last Phase* (1937), scarcely deal with subjects calculated to produce large sales, regardless of their intrinsic worth. Perhaps this explains why, also like Fuller and Liddell Hart, he found it convenient to supplement his income with journalism, becoming assistant editor of *The Fighting Forces,* editor of *The Gunner,* and the military editor of *Chambers's Encyclopaedia,* positions he held throughout most of the rest of his life. Furthermore, and again emulating Fuller and Liddell Hart, he proceeded to write a book about the American Civil War, a subject that would have a broader appeal than his previous works and one not limited to Britain. The result was *Lee, Grant and Sherman,* published in 1938 by Gale & Polden, Limited, Wellington Works, Aldershot.

How it fared financially in Britain cannot be determined—Gale & Polden closed doors long ago—but evidently the prestigious New York publishing firm of Charles Scribner's Sons concluded that it possessed sufficient sales potential to warrant reprinting it for the American market in 1939. It did so, however, without any indication of its prior British incarnation other than the English spellings in the text ("honour" instead of "honor," etc.). The sole differences between the Scribner's version and the original consisted of larger pages with bigger and darker type, a frontispiece (not included in this edition) presenting photos of the top Civil War commanders as of 1864–65, the transformation of a pocket map into a fold-out map in the back of the book, and—the most important change—adding a Preface by Douglas Southall Freeman, whose four-volume biography, *R. E. Lee,* published by Scribner's in 1934–35, had instantly raised him to the status he, in all likelihood, will always retain—as the greatest Civil War military historian of all (and their numbers are legion).

Freeman's Preface placed a stamp of approval on Burne's work, albeit with some qualifications having to do with the inherent problems faced by non-Americans writing about a subject so quintessentially American as the Civil War and its warriors. No doubt his endorsement helped, even though it was confined to what Burne wrote about Lee and Jubal Early and refrained from commenting on what he said about military operations in the West, a topic Freeman rightly declared he was not qualified to judge. Yet it did not help enough. *Lee, Grant and Sherman* attracted little attention, with most of it perfunctory, and soon it dropped from scholarly sight, little known by even highly

knowledgeable Civil War specialists and rarely referred to by the few
who did know of it. Among the probable reasons for its fate, these
are the most probable:

1. Nearly one-half of the book pertained to the Civil War in the
West. At the time of its publication scant interest existed among American historians in that phase of the "American Illiad" except as it provided a setting for the deeds of Grant, Sherman, and Nathan Bedford
Forrest—an attitude that long persisted. Thus, until 1992 the sole history of the Atlanta Campaign—surely one of the most decisive and
dramatic events of the Civil War—based on original research in primary
sources was Jacob D. Cox's *Atlanta,* published in 1882 and written by a
Union general who participated in the campaign.

2. Perhaps because of the paucity of scholarly works dealing
with the Civil War in the West all three of the only historical journals that in 1939 reviewed Civil War books assigned, incredible as
it may seem, their reviews of *Lee, Grant and Sherman* to the same
person—Thomas Robson Hay, Ph.D., author of *Hood's Tennessee
Campaign* (1929). Although a good and conscientious scholar, Hay
possessed a pronounced penchant for the pedantic, which took the
form in his reviews, all of which were essentially the same in substance, of criticizing Burne's book for its typographical and factual
errors, for inadequate documentation, and for failing to discuss the
"economic, social, and political condition of the Confederacy"—as
if that were relevant to a "Study in Leadership in the 1864–65 Campaign" that included Northern as well as Southern commanders.
Readers of Hay's reviews could not be blamed for concluding that
little was to be gained from perusing *Lee, Grant and Sherman.*

3. But the main reason, almost surely, why the book made so small
an impact on the historical community lay in its commentaries on
Sherman, Joseph Johnston, John Bell Hood, Phil Sheridan, and to
some extent Grant. They went counter, in greater or lesser degree, to
what then were the standard perceptions of these generals, perceptions
that continue to be widely held. According to them, Grant was the
greatest commander produced by the Civil War, with Sherman and
Sheridan being second and third among Union military leaders in
ability and accomplishment; among Confederates, Johnston was second only to Lee in skill following Stonewall Jackson's death; and
Hood was a total incompetent whose replacement of Johnston during the Atlanta Campaign led to utter disaster for the Confederacy.
Given the prevailing orthodoxy, which he shared, no wonder Hay took
Burne to task for his praise of Hood and merely reported his criticisms
of Sherman, Johnston, and Sheridan without commenting on their

validity. Obviously, he deemed this unnecessary, for obviously Burne was wrong. Likewise, he did not even mention Burne's assertion (page 202) that "Grant in his heart of hearts feared Lee." Why do so, since it could not possibly be right?

Yet, it is precisely in Burne's unorthodox judgments on the above generals that the value of his book is to be found. Not only did they make it original when published (his British publisher stated on the front flap of the dustjacket that Burne's "opinions are his own—in some cases very much his own") but they also anticipated a major shift, starting in the 1960s, in historical evaluations of military leadership during the Civil War that now has gained so many converts and promises to gain so many more that it might well be on the way to becoming the new orthodoxy.

What enabled Burne to be so prescient in spite of much of his research being, as Hay indicated, superficial and haphazard when judged by strict scholarly standards? Doubtless part of the answer lies in his being able to observe with his English eyes certain things that American historians failed to see. But the basic explanation was his reaction to the books that most influenced the writing of his own book.

For his accounts and analyses of Lee's operations in 1864–65 he relied on Freeman and rejected Fuller, who in comparing Grant and Lee contended that Grant was the superior general because, like Sherman and Sheridan, he "spiritually and morally belonged to the age of the Industrial Revolution" and so was a "modern" commander, whereas Lee, being the product of the "agricultural age of history," was "old-fashioned." To be blunt, these pompously pretentious phrases lack any substantive meaning. If they have one, it could be demolished merely by asking this question: If Lee, instead of Grant, had enjoyed a two-to-one numerical superiority, would he have failed to defeat Grant or would Grant have succeeded in defeating him? The question answers itself.

Regarding Sherman, Burne initially followed Liddell Hart, with his sole disagreement stemming from an error on his part (see endnote 29). But as he wrote further, he recognized what his compatriot had failed (or refused) to see, namely that Sherman's main, in fact sole, objective in the Atlanta Campaign was the geographical one of capturing Atlanta, not the strategical one of smashing the Confederate army; that Sherman based his operations on preconceived expectations about what the enemy would do that often proved unrealistic; and that Sherman, with his obsession for raiding, was incapable of waging an offensive battle with his full force and that, as a consequence, Hood's army survived to fight (and almost win) another day.

Burne achieved these analytical breakthroughs because he sought to understand Sherman as a general and did not, as did Liddell Hart, portray him as the embodiment of a pet theory about the secret of success in warfare (i.e., the "indirect approach"). For the same reason, Burne (unlike Liddell Hart) did not dismiss out of hand Sherman's contemporary critics, notably Henry V. Boynton and Henry Stone. They may have been, as Burne himself termed them, "disgruntled adherents of [General George H.] Thomas" (page 79), yet he seems to have checked into some of their strictures of Sherman and found them not without merit. Had Burne also come to realize how unreliable Sherman's *Memoirs* are, particularly in their characterization of Thomas as "slow," his account of the Atlanta Campaign and of subsequent operations in Georgia and Tennessee would have been more revolutionary—and more accurate—than it is. (See Albert Castel, "Prevaricating Through Georgia: Sherman's *Memoirs* as a Source on the Atlanta Campaign," *Civil War History* 40 [March 1994]: 48–71).

Having not at the outset written off Hood as a rash fool and therefore unworthy of serious consideration, Burne found that Hood's plans were excellent, sometimes even brilliant, in their conception, and that, although they failed in execution, under the conditions Hood faced he could not have done more or better than he tried to do, and that his defeats (other than that at Franklin) resulted from insufficient means and luck, not excessive blundering. After reading Burne's chapter titled "The Rebound," the same basic question that has been posed about Grant and Lee might be asked: Had Hood possessed strength superior to Sherman's, or even roughly equal numbers, would he necessarily have lost and Sherman inevitably won during their encounters around Atlanta? The answer, too, might be basically identical to the one given for Grant and Lee.

In sum, Burne's 1938–39 book offers much that historians writing thirty, forty, and fifty years afterward have found. As a consequence readers still bogged down in outdated platitudes about the Civil War will have, if they keep open minds, new historical vistas revealed to them. And readers who already are familiar with recent developments in Civil War scholarship will discover how a historical candle that flickered briefly and dimly sixty-some years ago before being snuffed out now glows with a prophetic light.

World War II began soon after the American publication of *Lee, Grant and Sherman,* and Burne returned to the Royal Army where he served as an artillery instructor. Even so, he found the time to write and publish in 1944 *The Art of War on Land,* and with the end of the war in 1945 he resumed his career as a journalist-historian, producing seven more books, three of which remain in print, before his death in 1959. With the reprinting of this book, that number becomes four.

Hay was correct in stating that *Lee, Grant and Sherman* contains numerous typos and factual errors—indeed, more of the latter than he realized, for his writings show that his own knowledge of the Atlanta Campaign and even of Hood's Tennessee Campaign, about which he had written a book, was inadequate and deficient by present standards. In both the British and American editions, an attempt was made to remedy the typos by inserting into the front of the book a slip bearing the unusual appellation of "Corrigenda" and listing the errata (but far from all of them). In this edition, to the extent that they have been discovered and it is practicable to do so, typos and misspellings have been corrected in the text. As for factual errors, and in some cases dubious or erroneous analyses, they have been remedied in the endnotes, except for those that are insignificant or involve matters concerning which there is no firm consensus among competent historians. In consulting the endnotes, the reader should bear in mind that what is important in the book are Burne's interpretations, not his expositions. The mistakes in the latter for the most part reflect his sources and a tendency, common to journalist-historians, to write with more verve than accuracy. To his credit, he did take the time and trouble, as well as go to the expense, of visiting the sites in America of the campaigns that he described.

A note on the maps for this edition: Northern troop movements are represented with the darker gray screen and Southern troop movements with the lighter gray screen.

The numbers for my editorial endnotes that begin on page 211 have been placed in the margins at the points deemed appropriate.

I speak on behalf of both the University Press of Kansas and myself in thanking Dr. Jonathan Wallis, Burne's grandnephew, and Joseph G. Rosa, an Englishman who writes, and writes well, about the American West, for their assistance in preparing this new edition of *Lee, Grant and Sherman*. A cousin of Burne describes him as having had an "enthusiasm for all things historical" and a "gift for friendship." Both Dr. Wallis and Mr. Rosa possess the same traits.

ALBERT CASTEL
Hillsdale, Michigan
February 27, 2000

INTRODUCTION

THE first value of the study of military operations by competent foreign soldiers is, of course, that with detachment they may combine the experience of their own army. In war as in science, the technique of every land advantageously may be tested by that of others. The manifest liability to error in such study may be lack of familiarity with the terrain, with the spirit of the belligerent peoples, with the personal elements that enter into the high command, and with, those subtle military values which every well-informed native may fail correctly to appraise. The first of these four difficulties in the correct presentation of a campaign may be overcome readily enough. Adequate research, particularly where uncensored newspapers are available for the period of a modern war, enables the military historian to recapture the spirit of the participants in a contest. It is in dealing with personalities that the foreign writer encounters a confusing factor. Particularly is this true of the American War between the States. On the Northern side, a small army, crippled by the resignation of many Southern officers, had rapidly to be expanded with volunteers to whose command inexperienced and sometimes incompetent politicans or community leaders were appointed. Not infrequently a brigade had at its head a military novice, thirsting for glory, while one of its regiments was under a professional soldier of long experience. Even armies occasionally were entrusted to "political generals" whose ignorance was excelled only by their arrogance and influence with the War Department or the President. Butler's attitude toward Grant—to cite the most notorious example—always must be taken into account in studying the operations of the Army of the Potomac from May to Christmas, 1864. The South had somewhat the same general problem. It was simplified by President Davis's willingness to shunt politicians to quiet sectors after Fort Donelson, and it was relieved in some quarters, from the onset of hostilities, by reason of the fact that Southern officers who resigned from the United States Army could be assigned to duty anywhere, without regard to past command or regimental duty.

On the other hand, personalities, in a different sense of the word, were aggravated by the conviction of the President that certain field commanders deserved support, regardless of public disfavor, and that other generals were not to be trusted. Even where this was not involved, the recruiting system depended for success on the attitude of the State governments. It never was practicable on either side, during the first half of the war, to disregard the adverse effect that might attend the removal from command of the favorite son of a populous State. Still again, in the South, officers of experience were so few, and casualties among them were so high, that men of moderate capacity or peculiarities of temperament had to be retained because no successors were in line who were not worse. Instances might be cited where delay was incurred in changing the order of march, or actually the order of battle, because this general was slow or that one was clumsy in his tactical dispositions. These, needless to say, are matters a foreign historian cannot be expected to take into account otherwise than after long and intimate study, yet they sometimes are the key to the understanding of a battle. The position of the three corps of the Army of North Virginia, for example, at the time of the order for the concentration on Gettysburg, probably influenced the course of the battle. In the opinion of the writer, Ewell's advanced position, which led him to approach Gettysburg from the north and consequently to form on the Confederate left, is attributable to General Lee's knowledge that Ewell was an excellent marcher.

Still more likely is a foreign writer to be misled by failure to weigh the difference in military values. It is natural to assume on the basis of European experience that transport, save in a demoralized retreat, is substantially as efficient on one side as on the other. It was not so in America. Rarely were the Confederate wagon-trains comparable to those of the Union armies. All logistics had to be based on the knowledge that if the Confederates were to outmarch the Federals, they had to leave behind them all wheeled vehicles except the ambulance and the ordnance trains. As the inimitable Dick Ewell put it, "the road to glory cannot be followed with much baggage." The result often was that the army slept hungry after having trod that road. Sometimes, victory could not be followed up because the wagons were far in the rear or did not suffice to transport enough food for the men in a devastated area. Similar differences existed in rations, in the supply of horses, in artillery ammunition, and in the guns themselves. In studying artillery action, it often is necessary to ascertain whether the engaged Confederate batteries were equipped with captured pieces. If they were not, they usually were outranged. Their percentage of "duds" would be twice that of the Federals. One high quality of Colonel Burne's book, which I have the privilege of introducing to the American public, is that it senses most of these values without laboring them. In this respect, if I may say so, it differs substantially from the work of one recent British critic of the Virginia campaign of 1864-65.

On Colonel Burne's detailed critique of Sherman's Georgia campaign, I am not qualified to speak. My study of it has never permitted me to feel that I understood enough about the personalities, the transport and the existing supplies to express an opinion. Basing judgment entirely on Hood's service in the Army of Northern Virginia, I have been much interested to see how highly Colonel Burne rates that officer. The belief of most Southern writers has been that Hood had no superior in combat at the head of a brigade or of a division, but that he did not possess the administrative qualities essential, under Confederate organization, to an army commander. General Lee's opinion, expressed at the time President Davis decided on the removal of General Johnston, was that Hood was "a good fighter, very industrious on the battlefield, careless off." He added: "I have had no opportunity of judging of his action when the whole responsibility rested upon him. I have a high opinion of his gallantry, earnestness and zeal." This was General Lee's tactful manner of saying that he did not know how strongly developed was Hood's strategical sense. Colonel Burne concludes that it was high. Hood was thirty-three in the year of the Atlanta campaign. Physically he had been superb and in action fiery but wholly the master of his nerves. Never, in the months prior to Gettysburg, had his endurance apparently been overtaxed. It is possible that his wound in that battle, followed in less than three months by the amputation of his leg, shook him more deeply than has been assumed. In the hard surgery of that period, a man rarely lost a limb without facing psychological readjustments. His condition during the last months of the war, as described by Mrs. Chestnut—staring in the fire, with "lurid spots" on his face, and perspiration on his forehead—may not have been altogether the result of Nashville.

Another central figure in Colonel Burne's narrative, Lieutenant-General Jubal A. Early, is not to be understood solely in terms of reports, casualty-lists, harvested crops and prolonged war. Personal elements of an unusual, even of a pathetic character were involved. "Old Jube," as his soldiers called him, had a tempestuous career prior to June, 1864, when Lee sent him to save Lynchburg and then to undertake a diversion in the Shenandoah Valley. At First Manassas, Early had arrived on the Federal flank precisely when and where he could do most to precipitate the Federal retreat; but at Williamsburg he had led a rash charge without proper reconnaissance, and at Malvern Hill he had lost his way. Sharpsburg had restored his reputation. If there were errors in his defence of Marye's Heights while Lee was engaged at Chancellorsville, the fault demonstrably was not his. After the death of Jackson compelled the reorganization of the Second Corps, Early for a time dominated the mind of Ewell. Whether he was correct in his contentions on the evening of July 1 at Gettysburg, military historians never will agree. The autumn of '63 was a dark period with him. He was as inept at Bristoe Station as A. P. Hill was precipitate. In the affair at the Rappahannock Bridge, he was powerless, but the loss of two brigades was charged against him. There followed an obscure clash with Ewell, the effects of which may be traced through the Wilderness and on to the Totopotomoy. When Lee placed Early in charge of the Second Corps, because he did not believe Ewell could stand further physical strain, there was much hard feeling. Whether it extended to any of the division commanders, the records do not show. Gordon, newly promoted, certainly had no reason to thank Early for delaying the attack on May 6, but Gordon was not a man to cherish grudges. Ramseur had recently been given a division. Rodes, though of a temperament wholly different from Early's, was a devoted veteran. Breckinridge was a Bayard and did not belong to the Second Corps. If any of the four shared Ewell's feeling when Early took command, they never showed it. In any case, after the easy success at Lynchburg and the first fine advance into Maryland, Early faced a task of great complexity. General Lee, tied to the Petersburg defences, could give him no more than temporary reinforcement. Furthermore, Lee strangely and consistently underestimated the strength of Sheridan. Early was left to attempt the impossible. It cannot be said that he made no mistakes. He did not coordinate the three arms of the service flawlessly, though it must always be remembered that his cavalry were torn by discord among the commanders. There undoubtedly was foundation, also, for General Lee's regretful criticism that Early fought too much by divisions, instead of employing his full strength. Possibly Early displayed upon occasion a certain lack of grasp of the terrain. His sense of direction was not of the best.

When these debits are written at the maximum, Early still has this notable credit balance, a personal credit: He took the forces at his disposal; he did his best to execute the broad strategic plan of his C-in-C, and he never added to Lee's difficulties by whines or by impossible demands for replacements that could not be sent him. This, I long have thought, was not so much the expression of Early's native independence as it was a display of consideration for the plight of his superior. Even among the numerous devoted lieutenants of Lee, only Jackson, it seems to me, would have been capable of such loyalty. Early's conduct was the more remarkable because he must have known that he was unpopular and that more men would rejoice over his failure than over his success. For these personal reasons, it is noteworthy that Colonel Burne concludes: "Taking it all in all, it is open to question whether Early's Valley campaign was not the most brilliant of the whole war, not excepting that of Stonewall Jackson." One need not agree with that conclusion to rejoice that Early at last is relieved of the discredit so unjustly cast upon him by some military writers.

Of Colonel Burne's critique of the campaign from the Rapidan to Petersburg, I shall not speak. I have had my day in court and I see no gain in discussing those points, chiefly affecting the operations on the North Anna, wherein Colonel Burne and I are not in agreement. Naturally I am pleased that his investigations confirm my oft-expressed conclusion that Lee was *not* surprised by Grant's crossing of the James in June, 1864, and that Lee's dispositions at that critical time strategically were sound. It may not be out of place to add that recent study of General Beauregard's earlier period of command in Virginia has given me a new appreciation of the difficulties General Lee encountered in trying to ascertain what force was in Beauregard's front on June 15–17.

As mankind faces the hideous possibility of another world war, with more destructive weapons indiscriminatingly employed, no student can flatter himself that the historical approach to Armageddon is the only one, or even the most important one. A vast revaluation of all the elements of national defence is under way. That does not imply mutation in the basic principles of strategy except as logistics are geared to motor vehicles and observation covers a wider field. The great masters of strategy still sit in council with the commander who has ears to hear. As Colonel Burne is an informed interpreter of the lessons some great modern soldiers have to teach, I am glad to present him to Americans.

DOUGLAS SOUTHALL FREEMAN.

EXPLANATORY NOTE

THE title of this book was suggested by the fact that three notable books, each written by a military expert, have recently been published in England on Lee, Grant, and Sherman. I refer to ROBERT E. LEE, THE SOLDIER, by General Sir Frederick Maurice, GRANT AND LEE, by General J. F. C. Fuller, and SHERMAN, by Captain Liddell Hart. Each general in turn is held up to our admiration, yet obviously all three cannot be equally admired, and it is the aim of this book to try and strike a balance between the rival protagonists.

To question the assessments of any of the above-mentioned eminent writers may appear temerarious, and I am aware that many of my own judgments run counter to generally held views. It may be thought that I am unduly critical of some of the leaders in the Civil War. If the quotation on the title page does not disarm these critics, at least I can claim to have entered on the examination of the problem completely unprejudiced (and, I am afraid, abysmally ignorant); and my opinions have been gradually built up from the study of contemporary evidence. In any case, it is one of the fascinations of the study of war that the assessments of no two persons are ever entirely identical.

I have cast my study in the form of an outline of events in the campaign of 1864–5, with a commentary at the end of each phase. Sections have been included on the little-studied but strictly relevant and illuminating campaigns of Generals Hood and Early. A Chronological Table is provided at the end for the use of readers whose knowledge of the general course of the war is sketchy. This Table is designed to convey to the eye a swift and proportionate picture of the whole vast war-theatre of the '64–'65 Campaign.

It is evident that in a book of this nature and scope it is only possible to touch lightly, if at all, on such questions as sea power, politics, economics, administration and supply. Nor must the reader expect to find mention of campaigns which had no direct bearing on the leadership of Lee, Grant or Sherman.

However much our modern biographers may vary in their assessments of persons, they are at one in considering the American Civil War a fruitful source of study, especially for those great countries where conscription is not in force, such as England and the United States of America. But the prospective student, in order to acquire a really passionate interest in this war, must visit the battlefields in person. Perhaps I may be forgiven for quoting from a letter received while this passage was being written, from an officer who had recently visited the battlefields of Virginia. "Before this visit I could never work up any enthusiasm for the Civil War, but once on the ground the dead bones of the past sprang to life with no difficulty, and now my imagination has been gripped by all the facets (if a facet can grip) of the struggle, human, political, military." It is perhaps significant that the French *École de Guerre* now studies this once neglected war.

The average reader hates footnotes, and I would gladly have completely dispensed with them. But some are unavoidable, if only because when a modern commentator is quoted it is only courtesy to give the reference. This I have done. Where the writings or sayings of contemporaries are concerned I have compromised by omitting them where I consider them already sufficiently well known, or easily found, to warrant it. I admit that this is a purely arbitrary selection, but I can think of no better method of keeping the references within limits. I agree with General Fuller, who writes in his *Grant and Lee*: "As my opinions on Grant and Lee run counter to many of those held by former writers I have considered it only just to marshal my evidence. . . ." In the same way I hope that those of my views which are not generally held can be traced to their sources where that is desired. It will be noticed, in this connection, that where I have sponsored an unusual view I have generally backed it by the opinion of someone better qualified than myself to judge.

A note regarding maps. I set great store by the adequate provision of maps in a military work, especially maps depicting the actual dispositions and movements of troops. Unfortunately it is very difficult in most cases to obtain sufficient data on which to construct such maps with any degree of reliability. Most historians seem content when depicting a battle to mark in the old trench lines left after a battle. This conveys as little idea of the course of the battle as a trench map of Flanders would convey of the movements of the troops at the battle of Ypres. An additional difficulty is that the Atlas accompanying the Official Records is at times misleading, and even self-contradictory. It consists of two big quarto volumes, badly put together, and containing maps and hasty field sketches made at the time. It gives no indication as to which are in error, even when, as sometimes happens, they contradict one another.   Only very occasionally do they mark the route taken by troops, and even this is not always accurate.   Who, for instance, can declare with certainty the course taken by Sherman's columns in the advance from Resaca to Cassville?   The Official Atlas gives three versions, and is serenely impartial about them!   General Schofield states in his book that a certain one of these is inaccurate, but he refrains from indicating in what respect!   The fact is, the country was badly surveyed before the war and the only accurate maps we possess were made after the war.   The movements shown on my sketch maps must therefore be regarded as only approximate, though I have done all I know to make them as accurate as possible. Every place mentioned in the text is either shown on one of the maps or its position is explained.

I have avoided the word FEDERAL, as I find that its similarity to CONFEDERATE creates confusion in the minds of some readers. Instead, I use the word UNION or NORTHERN throughout.

BIBLIOGRAPHICAL NOTE

ALL that can be attempted here is to give a few hints for the guidance of such students of the 1864-5 campaign as wish to pursue a course of further reading. Those seeking a fuller list are referred to the bibliographies contained in the following books:

For the campaign as a whole: THE CIVIL WAR AND RECONSTRUCTION, by J. G. Randall.

For Lee: R. E. LEE, by D. S. Freeman.

For Grant: THE RISE OF U. S. GRANT, by A. L. Conger.

For Sherman: SHERMAN, by Captain Liddell Hart.

Now for my hints. First, a word of warning. Eschew the autobiographies of the chief actors; they were generally written several years after the events they describe, with the memory growing dim, but before the publication of the Official Records, by which they could have checked their facts; they are usually of a self-exculpatory nature, which practically involves attacking other commanders. They must therefore be treated as suspect. By this I do not mean that they are valueless, but that they should be read *after*, and only after, all the facts have been ascertained from other sources. Even Grant, whose Memoirs are generally regarded as the least biased of all, is no exception to this rule. Colonel Conger describes his Memoirs as " old soldier campfire stories," and "not militarily instructive."

The primary source of first-hand contemporary evidence is contained in *The War of the Rebellion*, usually known as *Official Records*. But it is almost the last source that I would recommend the student to consult. It consists of 128 volumes, is scantily edited, and will prove almost unintelligible to anyone not already familiar with the facts and characters. For the most part it consists of an undigested mass of uncorrelated messages recorded day by day.

I would suggest rather that the student begins by running his eye over the *Photographic History of the War*, or failing this, over the engravings in *Battles and Leaders of the Civil War*, which are mostly taken from war photos. Next take a general history, Randall's (already mentioned), or *America's Tragedy*, by J. T. Adams. For the general military details consult *The Civil War in America*, by W. G. Shotwell, or *The Civil War in the United*

States, by W. B. Wood and J. E. Edmonds, or, for a short outline
with good, clear maps, *The American Civil War, 1864–1865*, by
Major E. W. Sheppard.   For the personalities of the chief actors
consult Freeman for Lee, Conger for Grant and Liddell Hart for
Sherman.   (It is curious that no American has written a satisfactory biography of Sherman: in fact, both Sherman and Grant
await their Freeman.)   The last-named book should be tempered
by the strictures on Sherman contained in General Schofield's
Forty-six Years in the Army, from which I have quoted freely.
Four main campaigns comprise the last twelve months of the war,
for each of which it is easy to recommend a standard history.
These are: *The Virginia Campaign*, by A. A. Humphreys; *The
Shenandoah Valley*, by G. E. Pond; *Atlanta*, by J. D. Cox; and
Hood's Tennessee Campaign, by T. R. Hay.   One might supplement the first by *The Campaign of '64–'65*, by C. F. Atkinson,
an admirable book which unfortunately stops short at Coldharbor.   The other books mentioned are all by Northern writers,
but they are utterly fair to the South, and give the facts in
adequate detail.

The best-informed and most penetrating criticisms and comments are contained in the *Papers of the Military Historical Society
of Massachusetts*.   These papers are generally written by junior
participants in the events described, and are therefore more dis-
passionate than the chapters in *Battles and Leaders* which are
frequently written by the chief actors themselves, which for
some reason (incomprehensible to me) is generally treated as a
primary source.   It should not be so treated.   Apart from the
Official Records the most reliable sources consist of the letters,
journals and autobiographies of junior officers who had no repu-
tations of their own to defend.   Notable among these are *Meade's
Headquarters*, by Colonel T. Lyman; *Campaigning with Grant*, by
General H. Porter; and *General Lee*, by Colonel W. H. Taylor.

After this the *Official Records* might profitably be consulted,
together with *Lee's Despatches*, edited by D. S. Freeman.   For
those who have unlimited time at their disposal *Southern Historical Society Papers* may be examined.   There are over 45
volumes of them and I doubt if they have ever been systematically
searched, unless it be by Dr. Freeman.   It is hard to procure
copies in this country.

Last of all we come to the autobiographies of the principal
generals.   All of them have published their side of the story with
the single exception of R. E. Lee.   What would we give to have
his own story!

ABBREVIATIONS USED IN THIS BOOK

Book	*Abbreviation*
Battles and Leaders in the Civil War	B. & L.
R. E. Lee, by D. S. Freeman	Freeman
Military Historical Society of Massachusetts	M.H.S.M.
Official Records	O.R.
Forty-six Years in the Army, by J. M. Schofield	Schofield
Southern Historical Society Papers	S.H.S.P.

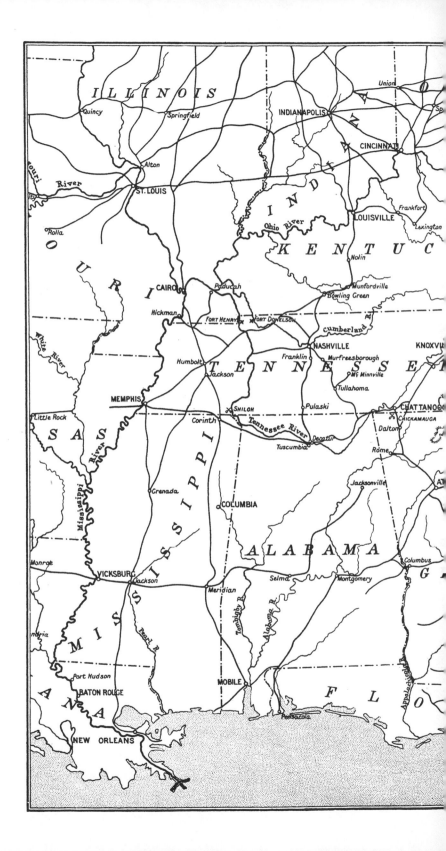

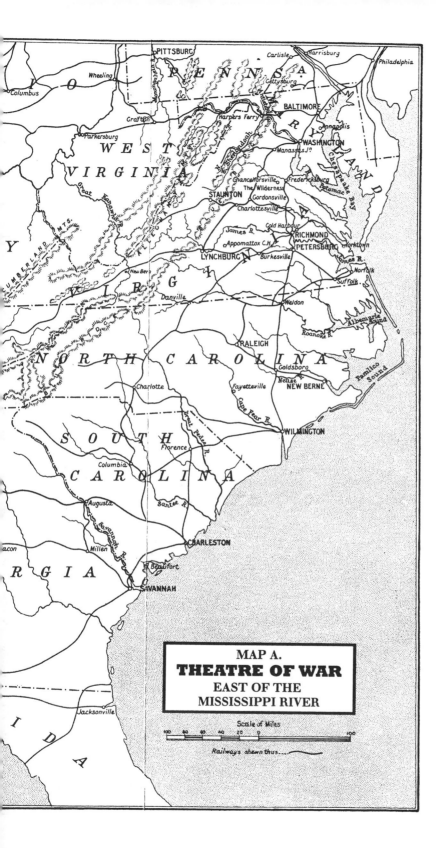

MAP A.
THEATRE OF WAR
EAST OF THE
MISSISSIPPI RIVER

Scale of Miles
100 80 60 40 20 0   100

Railways shewn thus....

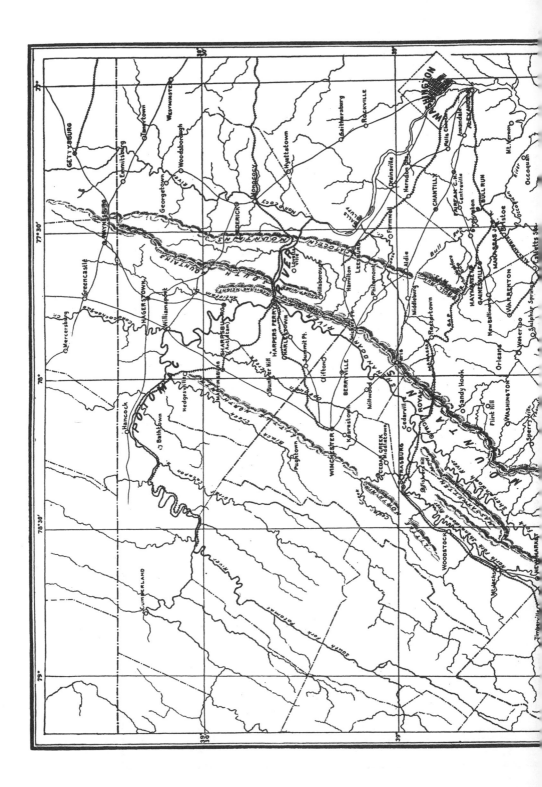

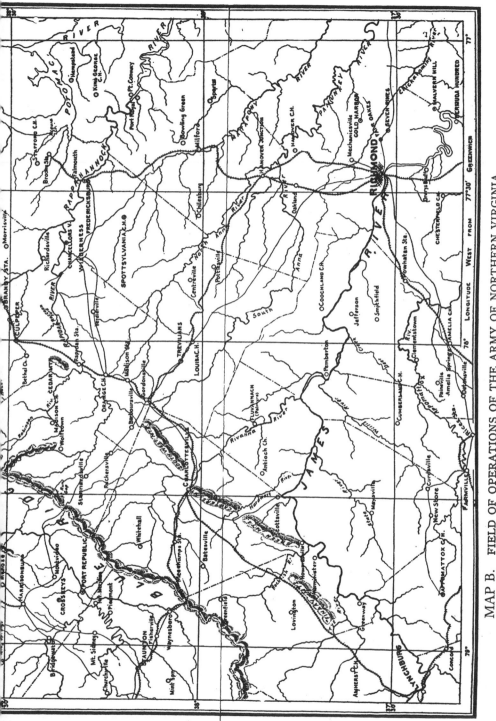

MAP B. FIELD OF OPERATIONS OF THE ARMY OF NORTHERN VIRGINIA

CHAPTER I

The First Three Years.

In the first quarter of 1861 eleven of the Southern states seceded from the Union. In April the Civil War broke out. The twenty-three Northern states contained a population of 22,000,000 while the eleven Southern states had only 9,000,000, including 3,500,000 slaves.

The North had enormous advantages at the outset. It was overwhelmingly superior in wealth, manufactures, finance and shipping. Owing to this last, it was enabled to establish a blockade of the Southern coast-line. The effect of this is well summed up by Colonel Henderson: " As the South was dependent for almost everything, except bread, meat, sugar, and tobacco, on other nations, the blockade was a most effective weapon against her. To starve her into submission did not seem difficult. She had no manufactories, except a few iron foundries; no tanneries; no wool or cloth; no powder factories, no gun factories; almost all the railway workshops were in the North; there was very little salt in her stores, and no tea or coffee. In fact, almost every single necessary of existence came from abroad, and had it not been that the arsenals within her territory were well supplied, and that her victories in Virginia provided her troops with equipment captured from the enemy, it is difficult to see how she could have carried on the war at all. As it was, the dearth of material resources always hampered her generals, as may be imagined when I state that they appear to have often depended for fresh supplies of ammunition on what they could take from the enemy."[1]

On the other hand the South had the advantage of fighting on interior lines; and they had the moral stimulus that a country fighting for its independence always possesses. The men of the South were also more inspired with the martial spirit than the Northerners, and being for the most part countrymen, took more quickly to the service of arms than their townsmen opponents. Also the disparity in population was not maintained in the numbers of trained men put into the field by each side. Until the last year of the war the strength of the Southern Army remained

[1] *The Science of War*, p. 249.

at a fairly steady proportion of 60 per cent. of the Union Army. As against this, the Confederacy required a long line of defensive posts and garrisons both on its land and sea frontiers, as it was on the defensive. On the other hand the Union, fighting in a hostile country, had large numbers of troops immobilised on its lines of communications, so that the proportion of numbers available for active operations maintained the same ratio of 5 to 3.

So much for what may be called the " raw material." When we come to summarise and compare the fighting machine built out of this material we are confronted with the difficulty that, just as was the case in the Great War, expansion, change and development went on all the time. The product at the end was very different from what it was at the outset. With this proviso, I will try to tabulate the main factors in general terms.

First, *the officers*. Though the regular army was at the disposal of the Union, many of the officers transferred their allegiance to the South, where they were generally placed in key positions and trained and commanded the volunteer formations of which the Southern Army was exclusively formed at first. But in the North the regular officers were generally retained with their own units. This had the double disadvantage of keeping their promotion slow and of depriving the new formations of expert help and leadership. Many of the generals in the new army were civilians and often their only qualification for the rank was political service. The Southern generals on the other hand were usually "West Pointers." The regular army only provided 13,000 for the war. The North also made the mistake of forming too many fresh units instead of keeping up to strength those already formed. All the benefits accruing from experience and *esprit de corps* were thus thrown away.

The bulk of the men on each side being civilians hastily thrown into uniform, discipline could not be expected to be of a high standard. The Northerner in particular was of an independent turn of mind. The consequence was that the Comte de Paris, who was an eye-witness on the side of the Union, wrote in 1862: " These troops are brave, but the bonds of subordination are weak in the extreme. It follows, then, that there is no certainty that what has been commanded will be exactly executed. The will of the individual plays far too large a part. The leader is obliged to turn round to see if he is being followed. Hence come hesitation and conditions unfavourable to daring enterprise."[2]

This tendency was not so marked on the side of the South,

[1] *Campagne du Potomac*, p. 144.

where the officers generally belonged to a class that was accustomed to command. Straggling was the besetting weakness of the Confederate Army. Even Stonewall Jackson could not cure it. The fact was, both armies were " National armies " in the same sense that the Boer armies were. But as the war progressed, discipline improved with experience, and by 1864 there was little to choose between regulars and volunteers—as was the case in the British army in the Great War in 1918. In the course of the war conscription was applied by both sides, but the vast majority of the troops remained volunteers right to the end. The Union recruited a few divisions of black troops in 1864; the Confederacy did not, but it used its black population in useful non-combatant work behind the line.

ARMAMENT EQUIPMENT, ETC.

Guns.—On both sides muzzle loaders, rifled and smooth bore.

Rifles.—Muzzle loaders. The Northern cavalry had breech-loading carbines.

Transport.—By rail and wagon. In both respects the North had much the most efficient supply service. It also had the use of seaborne transport.

Intelligence.—Owing to operating in their own country and to being accomplished and daring horsemen the Confederates possessed the best Intelligence service.

Shipping.—Apart from a few blockade runners, and privateersmen, the Union (after the disablement of the ironclad *Merrimac*) had a complete monopoly.

Clothing and Equipment.—The North had a great and increasing superiority in every department.

ARMS OF THE SERVICE.

Infantry.—Constituted in regiments (establishment about 1,000), brigades (three to four regiments), divisions (three to four brigades), and corps (three to four divisions), in both armies. The foot-soldier carried about 60 lb. in the Northern to 40 lb. in the Southern Army. The Southerner consequently generally marched the better. Tactics were much the same on each side.

Cavalry.—The South were better horsed, and mostly were natural horsemen, whereas the North were not a " horsey " people. Consequently the Southern cavalry established a marked superiority early in the war, and maintained it till 1864. They were armed with sabre and revolver, as well as carbine; but owing to the woody country the *arme blanche* was only once used on a large scale; usually both sides acted as mounted infantry, dismounting to fight.

They were organised in regiments (nominally 400 strong), brigades and divisions. There was no divisional cavalry.

Artillery.—The North was superior, both in weight of metal and training. But owing to the woody nature of the country the use of the guns was often circumscribed, particularly in 1864. The artillery was organised in batteries and battalions; and was, in the case of the North, only attached to divisions for special service.

THE HIGHER COMMAND.

Abraham Lincoln, the President of the Union, was an exceedingly gifted man. But neither he nor his War Secretary had any military training; yet he kept the military direction in his own hands till the last year of the war, much to the detriment of the Northern fortunes. General Hallech was his Chief of Staff in '64.

Jefferson Davis, President of the Confederacy, was an old army officer who had seen service in the Mexican war. He was also a man of strong character and ability: thus, though he also kept the control of strategy in his own hands almost up to the end, the results were on the whole fairly satisfactory. His chief difficulty was in overcoming the jealousy and parochialness of the different States. But the same difficulty would have confronted a purely military commander-in-chief. General Bragg was his Chief of Staff in '64.

TOPOGRAPHY.

The approximate size and shape of the Confederacy was that of all France, Germany as far east as Berlin, Switzerland, and Italy as far south as Florence. In this vast area every kind of country was naturally met with. The following description applies predominantly to Virginia, where the bulk of the fighting took place. Its features are: vast forests—in fact east of the Blue Ridge it might almost be described as one single immense forest with clearings in it—rivers and swamps. Roads are generally described as scarce; but in Virginia this is hardly true. The roads are of three classes: *turnpike roads*, metalled; *plank roads* (wooden corduroy) constructed in the 1850's (an unpropitious time, for the railways came along and ousted them a few years later) and country tracks, which were unmetalled. In wet weather the roads became very muddy, and sometimes quite impassable.

Railways were being rapidly developed, and in many places were still in an unfinished condition.

There were two outstanding features of the war theatre: *first*, the position of the rival capitals Washington and Richmond on the edge of their respective territories, and only 100 miles apart; *second*, the long line of the Mississippi, providing a waterway from north to south, and cutting off Texas from the remainder of the Confederacy. These two features conditioned the fighting in both eastern and western theatres throughout almost the whole war, as will presently be seen.

OUTLINE OF EVENTS, PREVIOUS TO 1864. (*See Map A.*)

Very early in the war the Northern Navy established a blockade of the Southern coast and maintained it throughout the war. By 1864 a number of Southern harbours had also been captured. The details do not affect this story.

On land the campaign resolved itself into two struggles—*In the east*, the Union tried to capture Richmond; *in the west*, to make itself master of the waterway of the Mississippi right down to the sea. In the east they were unsuccessful, largely owing to the superb generalship of Robert E. Lee, who defeated in turn the four Union generals that were sent against him, McClellan, Pope, Burnside and Hooker. Though eventually defeated by Meade at Gettysburg during an abortive invasion of Pennsylvania, he managed to retire into Virginia with an intact army and to continue to guard the approaches to Richmond.

In the west, after a great deal of spasmodic unco-ordinated fighting the Union was more successful. In July 1863, by the capture of Vicksburg, Grant opened up the whole waterway of the Mississippi, thus cutting off from the Confederacy the huge supplies of cattle in Texas.

By the spring of 1864, thanks to the gradual drying up of the Southern resources, to the pressure of the blockade and to the failure of the expected foreign intervention on the side of the South, the balance was slowly but surely swinging in favour of the North. The situation at this moment is well summed up by Professor Randall: " The Mississippi River was in Union hands; Tennessee, West Virginia, and Virginia north of the Rapidan were held by Federal forces; most of the coast fortresses along the Atlantic and the Gulf were in Northern control; Louisiana was largely in Union occupation. On the other hand the vast bulk of the Confederacy was still unshaken: Southern arms held the rich Shenandoah Valley; and two powerful armies —Lee's in Virginia and Johnston's in north-western Georgia— were ready to do battle against the Yankee invader."[3]

[3] *The Civil War and Reconstruction,* p. 540.

CHAPTER II

The Situation in April 1864.

IN February 1864 Lieut.-General Ulysses S. Grant had been appointed generalissimo of all the Union armies at the early age of 42.[1] He had been the most successful general in the west, his chief victories being Vicksburg and Chattanooga. Lincoln accorded him a free hand, writing, in a phrase that became famous, " The particulars of your plan I neither know nor seek to know. . . . I wish not to obtrude any constraints or restraints upon you." Being now in supreme command Grant was able to draw up a comprehensive plan for the whole vast area of hostilities. His general idea is best given in his own words: " I am determined to hammer continually against the armed force of the enemy and his resources until by mere attrition, if in no other way, there should be nothing left for him but submission." The plan he devised was as follows. The main blow would be struck by the Army of the Potomac (commanded by General Meade) against the Army of Northern Virginia (commanded by General R. E. Lee), while simultaneous subsidiary offensives would be launched in the other theatres: by Sherman in Georgia; by Sigel in the Shenandoah Valley in combination with Crook in West Virginia; by Butler from the mouth of the James River; and by Banks from New Orleans against Mobile. Such a combined operation had never previously been attempted by the Northern Armies, which contained no less than 17 separate District Commanders, each pulling his own way.

We will study the main offensive in detail. The Army of the Potomac consisted of three corps, II (Hancock), V (Warren), and VI (Sedgwick), with a Cavalry Corps under Sheridan. To work in conjunction with it, but under the orders of the C.-in-C., was the IX Corps (Burnside). Burnside had commanded the army at the disastrous battle of Fredericksburg, and both he and his Chief of Staff were senior to Meade,* which no doubt explained why Grant did not place him directly under the orders of Meade.

---

[1] The most vivid and detailed description of his appearance and character is given by his secretary, Badeau, in *Military History of Ulysses S. Grant*, ii, 20.

* Meade had served as a Divisional Commander in Burnside's army.

6

No less than 30 per cent. of the troops were foreign-born. The total strength of the army was 121,000. The II, V, and VI Corps were massed round Culpeper C.H. with outposts lining the Rapidan River. The IX Corps was guarding the railway from Culpeper to Alexandria. (See Sketch Map 1.)

The Army of Northern Virginia lined the southern bank of the Rapidan from the railway to Mine Run—a distance of 20 miles —with its infantry; Longstreet's (I) Corps being at and south of Gordonsville, Ewell's (II) Corps at Verdiersville and Hill's (III) Corps at Orange C.H. The Cavalry under J. E. B. Stuart continued the line of outposts to Fredericksburg, with its main body south of that town.

Thus Lee interposed with his army between Grant and Richmond. The Confederate Army with a strength of about 62,000 was half the size of the Northern, but it had been almost consistently victorious up to date, its *moral* was correspondingly higher, the power of Lee's name was " worth 40,000 bayonets," it had fewer recruits in its ranks and was altogether more homogeneous and national than its rival. The Northern Army was well clothed and equipped, being furnished with everything that money would buy, and possessed an enormous train of 4,000 wagons. The Southern Army was in rags and half starved.*

GRANT'S PLAN.

Grant was given as his objective, " Lee, with the capital of the Confederacy." But he interpreted his instructions as follows: " To get possession of Lee's army was the first great object. With the capture of his army Richmond would necessarily follow. It was better to fight him outside of his stronghold than in it." The difficulty was that so long as Lee remained behind his entrenchments Grant could not get at him to attack him advantageously. The problem therefore resolved itself into enticing Lee out of his entrenchments without allowing him to go right back into the Richmond defences. In other words, he must be manœuvred into the open somewhere short of Richmond and then attacked. Grant epitomised it in a phrase of his preliminary instructions to Meade which has since become famous: " Wherever Lee goes there you will go also."†

Now there were three possible ways of getting at the Army of Northern Virginia in the open.

* When Lee entertained some distinguished visitors to dinner the fare consisted of a dish of boiled cabbage, surmounted by a tiny morsel of bacon— which all the guests were too polite to take!
† This phrase had previously been used by Lincoln to Hooker in 1863.

1. Grant might feign a retirement himself, and entice Lee to cross the Rapidan.

2. He might threaten Lee's left flank and communications with his capital.

3. He might threaten Lee's right flank.

The first course does not seem to have been seriously considered. It had certain advantages, though no commentator has suggested that it should have been adopted. No doubt moral considerations ruled it out. The Army of the Potomac was all too accustomed to retire. It would never do to start the campaign in that manner. Points in favour of the second course were:

(a) The open country on the west flank would favour operations, and in particular Grant's superior artillery.

(b) It would cover his line of supplies—the Alexandria–Culpeper Railway.

(c) It would cut off the enemy's supplies from Staunton and the Shenandoah Valley.

(d) It would avoid the risk of Lee making a dash against Washington while the movement was in operation.

Disadvantages were that:

(a) The move would probably be spotted from Clark's Mountain, and surprise would thus be impossible.

(b) It would increase the distance between the Army of the Potomac and that of Butler on the James.

Points *against* the third course:

(a) It involved traversing the heavily wooded district of the Wilderness,* which was familiar to the enemy but not to Grant's own troops, and where his superior artillery would be wasted.

(b) It would uncover his line of supplies.

On the other hand:

(a) He might, by moving under cover, traverse the Wilderness and get into the comparatively open country beyond before having to give battle.

(b) Having command of the sea, he could shift his base to any of the inlets formed by the Rappahannock, York and James Rivers, as he moved round.

He could, of course, move his whole army round by sea, as McClellan had done in 1862. But, though by so doing he might

---

* The area south of the Rapidan, between Fredericksburg and the Mine Run, and ten miles to the South. The forest here had been cut down for fuel for smelting iron ore. The result was " a thick growth of small saplings, 15 to 30 feet high."

MAP 1

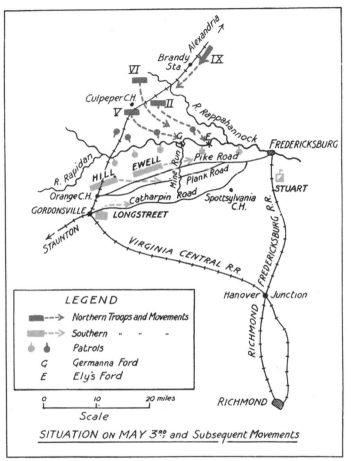

SITUATION ON MAY 3ʳᵈ; and Subsequent Movements

capture Richmond, it would offer no prospect of meeting Lee's army in the open, which, as I have said, was his supreme object. It would also give Lee the opportunity for another of his dashes into Maryland.

On April 25th General **Grant** announced his decision. He would move round Lee's right flank. Full of confidence in himself, he entered upon his first campaign in the east; and he was somewhat nettled to be told by Meade's Staff Officers: " You do not know Bobby Lee! "

How was the Army of Northern Virginia disposed to counter the coming move? A glance at Sketch Map 1 will show that it was NOT well disposed. Admittedly the cavalry were on the threatened flank, and might be counted upon to give warning and to impose delay: but if Lee wished to strike at Grant's exposed flank during his encircling movement his army was not well disposed; for the reserve—Longstreet's Corps—was behind the other flank. Apologists have explained this away by the assertion that Longstreet's Corps was not only the reserve for the Army of Northern Virginia but also a general reserve, which might be required to work towards the Valley. In any case Lee's left flank was his strategic flank. His right flank might be turned with comparative impunity, but if his left flank went his main line of supplies would be cut. Further, the railway junction of Gordonsville formed a convenient site for a reserve. By rapid marching, the Corps might reach the battlefield in time for the projected engagement. But Longstreet had not in the past been a rapid marcher when approaching a battlefield.

Lee was nevertheless quietly confident (if his letters to President Davis are good evidence). He expected Grant's attack, and the prospect did not worry him. Riding with General J. B. Gordon a few days later he outlined his course of action. He was almost convinced, he said, that " if we could keep the Confederate Army between General Grant and Richmond, checking him for a few months longer, as we had in the past two days, some crisis in public affairs or change in public opinion, at the North might induce the authorities at Washington to let the Southern States go."[2]

This significant statement by Lee should be borne in mind when reading the history of the ensuing campaign.

---

[2] *Reminiscences of the Civil War*, by J. B. Gordon, p. 268.

CHAPTER III

The Battle of the Wilderness.

ON the evening of May 3rd, 1864, General Grant's great operation opened. All his forces were put in motion, Sherman in the south, Butler in the east, Sigel in the west, whilst the Commander-in-Chief led the campaign against the Army of Northern Virginia in person.*

By 3 a.m. on May 4th Gregg's Cavalry Division had crossed the Rapidan at Ely's Ford, and Wilson's Division at Germanna Ford (Sketch Map 1). The Southern pickets were driven off, bridges were built, and the two divisions continued on their way, Gregg a short way beyond Chancellorsville and Wilson *via* Old Wilderness Tavern to Parker's Store (Sketch Map 2). Torbert's Cavalry Division was retained to the north of the river as escort to the Train—much to the disgust of the impatient Sheridan, the cavalry commander. A small cavalry patrol was sent along the Turnpike (or " Pike ") Road to Locust Grove. The Southern right flank appeared to rest behind the Mine Run.

The V Corps (Warren) crossed the river behind Wilson at 7 a.m., and halted for the night, closed up, at Old Wilderness Tavern. Warren however detached one division (Griffin) towards Locust Grove, as he was naturally nervous about his right flank. The VI Corps (Sedgwick) crossed behind the V Corps, and halted for the night three miles beyond the river. The II Corps (Hancock) crossed behind Gregg, and halted for the night at Chancellorsville.

The IX Corps, which was much scattered and had to do a forced march of thirty to forty miles, stopped a few miles short of the Rapidan. The Train crossed at Ely's and Culpeper Mine Fords.

On looking back on the first day's work Grant had every reason to be pleased with the course of events. His moves had been carefully planned and skilfully executed; everything had been carried out to the letter; and though the wording of Meade's operation order is open to criticism his intention had been

* Banks was engaged in fruitless operations on the Red River, and did not return in time to take part in the campaign. Thus 40,000 troops were wasted.

MAP 2

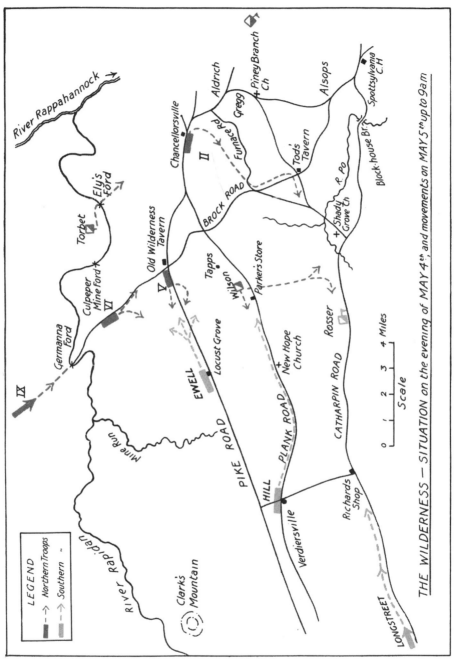

THE WILDERNESS — SITUATION on the evening of MAY 4th, and movements on MAY 5th up to 9 am

LEGEND

Northern Troops
Southern "

River Rappahannock

Ely's Ford

Torbet

Culpeper Mine Ford

VI

Germanna Ford

IX

River Rapidan

Clark's Mountain

Mine Run

PIKE ROAD

EWELL

Locust Grove

HILL

Verdiersville

PLANK ROAD

New Hope Church

CATHARPIN ROAD

Richards Shop

LONGSTREET

Rosser

Wilson

Tapps

Parker's Store

Old Wilderness Tavern

V

Chancellorsville

II

Furnace Rd

BROCK ROAD

Gregg

Aldrich

Piney Branch Ch

Tods Tavern

Alsops

Shady Grove Ch

R. Po

Block-house Br.

Spotsylvania C.H.

Scale

0 1 2 3 4 Miles

achieved, and that is the acid test of an order. The only cause for anxiety was that Lee, according to reports, instead of withdrawing on Richmond, appeared to have the intention of holding his ground, or even of advancing along the Plank Road.

Grant's orders for May 5th were simple. The movement was to be continued according to programme, in a south-easterly direction. Wilson was to guard the right flank, whilst Torbert was to join forces with Gregg, with a view to operating against the main body of the Southern cavalry which was believed to be coming up from the south of Fredericksburg. (The position of the Union forces in the early morning is shown on Sketch Map 2.)

THE SOUTH.

At 9 o'clock on the morning of May 4th the signal was flashed back from Clark's Mountain to Headquarters that the Union Army was moving to the right. The moment for decision had arrived. Lee did not hesitate. He at once recognised this movement as the genuine thing. His only miscalculation was that he assessed the enemy at 75,000 instead of 121,000. Even so, his own 62,000 would be outnumbered. He decided to attack. In Freeman's words (which cannot be bettered), " His plan was to catch Grant on the march, where his numerical superiority would mean least. Especially was he anxious to engage the new Union commander in the tangle of the Wilderness, where the fine Federal ordnance could not be employed. . . . For these reasons, and also because it would be difficult to bring up a sufficient force in time to dispute the crossing of the Rapidan, Lee determined to leave Grant alone till he was on the south side of the river. He then intended to attack him there as soon as Longstreet came up."[1]

Lee therefore ordered all three corps (less Anderson's Division of Hill's Corps, which was left temporarily to guard the railway) to move eastwards at once: Ewell (II Corps) along the Pike Road, Hill (III Corps) along the Plank Road, and Longstreet (I Corps) behind Hill. The last named however obtained permission to take the Catharpin Road. As Edmonds dryly puts it: " It was not Longstreet's habit to obey orders without demanding changes." About the same time Lee heard that Sigel was advancing in the Shenandoah Valley, and that Butler was moving on Bermuda Neck ten miles south-east of Richmond. But Lee recognised only two vital points in the whole far-flung battle line—Sherman's army and Grant's army. He therefore had no hesitation in working for a concentration at the decisive point, and asked for

[1] *Freeman*, iii, 273.

the return of Pickett's division of Longstreet's Corps, which was near Richmond.

The positions reached by the three corps at nightfall are shown on Sketch Map 2: Ewell at Locust Grove, Hill at Verdiersville, and Longstreet still eight miles short of Richard's Shop. He undertook, however, to reach that place by noon on the following day. On receipt of this assurance Lee, calculating that it would be feasible to attack with all three corps on the following day, issued the necessary orders.

COMMENTS ON MAY 4TH.

Grant's manœuvre was a masterly one. But if he had " known Bobby Lee " he would have taken more specific steps to protect his exposed right flank. The result of not doing so was that his position at nightfall was not in reality so favourable as it appeared to be. Grant did not suspect that Lee's army was bivouacking that night within five miles of his own. The blame may be attributed to the cavalry. Steele is severe in his criticism: " No poorer cavalry work was done in the Civil War than that done by the cavalry of Sheridan and Stuart."[2] The fact is, Sheridan, who had just been appointed to the command of the Cavalry Corps had only had 37 days experience with that arm: his reputation had been made as an infantryman. Nor were his brigadiers in much better position. Neither Torbert nor Wilson had ever commanded so much as a squadron: the former was an infantry man, the latter an engineer.

Lee's action in deliberately attacking a superior force was certainly a bold one; but it was only to be expected of a general who had won great victories by similar bold action in the past. There can be no doubt about the fact that he wished Grant to cross the Rapidan. At breakfast on the 4th he reported the fact to his officers, " smiling and joking, a sparkle in his eye."[3] This fact seems to justify Steele's criticism: " Grant violated the maxim of war, ' Never do what the enemy wishes you to.' "[4]

On the other hand Lee may justly be criticised for not moving Longstreet's Corps further to the right on May 3rd, when he had fairly clear indication of Grant's intention. To do so may be considered as taking a risk; but risks must be taken in war, if great results are to be obtained. As General Wolfe so well put it: " In war *something* must be left to chance."

[2] *American Campaigns*, p. 484.
[3] *Marse Robert*, by J. C. Young, p. 271.
[4] *American Campaigns*, p. 485.

MAY 5TH. (*Sketch Map* 2.)

The North.

Wilson, leaving 500 men on the Plank Road, continued south to the Catharpin Road. Torbet and Gregg, according to orders, assembled near Aldrich, and reconnoitred.

Of the infantry, the V Corps, leaving Griffin's Division still out on the Pike Road, started off towards Parker's Store, followed by the VI Corps. The II Corps, leaving one division with the Train, moved by a winding route towards Shady Grove.

(This is a good point for the student to map out the dispositions, and consider whether they were sound. . . .)

To continue the narrative. At 6 a.m. enemy were reported along the Pike Road. Griffin accordingly pushed a little further west and then entrenched—an obviously sound precaution. At 7.30 Meade, thinking that the force on the Pike Road could only be a division covering the retirement of the army, ordered Warren to suspend the move of the V Corps and attack the enemy. Grant approved of this action, in a letter ending: " If any opportunity presents itself for pitching into a portion of Lee's army do so without giving time for dispositions." Now it was Grant's wish to avoid a battle in the Wilderness. In approving of his subordinate's action he was therefore abandoning his own plan thus early in the campaign.

While Grant was penning his letter Wilson's detachment on the Plank Road was driven back by a superior force of infantry. This was a surprise. Could it mean that the enemy was no mere rearguard, but a force of at least two corps? At any rate the cavalry must be supported at once; so the II Corps was ordered to suspend its march on Shady Grove and make for Parker's Store, and Getty's Division of the VI Corps was ordered to the same place. Thus an entirely different complexion had suddenly been put upon the situation. It looked as if the bulk of the Army of the Potomac was to be involved in woodland fighting in the Wilderness after all.

Warren's attack took several hours to mount, owing to the woody country—much to Grant's annoyance. He had come from the West with a reputation for " drive," and he was impatient of the caution, if not timidity, shown by the Army of the Potomac against its redoubtable opponent. He would teach it not to be afraid of Bobby Lee! So Warren was bombarded with " gingering " notes. At noon the attack was launched by the V Corps and one division of the VI. It hit the leading

division of Ewell's Corps (Johnston).   After an initial success, the
attack was driven back, a young brigadier, Gordon by name,
whom we shall meet again, distinguishing himself in this repulse.
Ewell did not follow up this success as he had been told to
regulate his action by that of Hill.   Lee was himself with Hill,
and did not wish to bring on a general engagement till the arrival
of Longstreet.   But Longstreet was terribly slow; he was five
hours behind his time.

Meanwhile exciting things were happening on the Plank Road.
Wilson's troopers were hustled back by Hill's infantry almost to
the Brock Road.   But Getty came up in the nick of time, and
the front was stabilised.   In the early afternoon the II Corps
began to dribble up, and they in turn were ordered to attack Hill.
Four divisions, including Getty, took part in this attack; but
though fighting was fierce and prolonged, Hill's two divisions
were able to hold off their opponents.   Lee had taken up his
headquarters at Tapp's Farm, and during the battle he sent word
to Longstreet to leave the Catharpin Road and join Hill on the
Plank road.   This again illustrates his principle of concentrating
at the decisive point.   But Longstreet, instead of coming on,
halted for some hours at Richard's Shop.   Anderson's Division
was also on the way, but equally distant from the battlefield.
Lee had therefore to postpone his intention to attack till the
following day.

On the Catharpin Road there had been some cavalry activity.
Wilson had eventually been driven back by Rosser's cavalry to
Tod's Tavern, where Gregg came to his rescue.   Both Union
brigades spent the night there.

At night-fall, then, the V and II Corps were in line of battle;
the VI Corps was split into three, one division helping the II
Corps, one division in line on Warren's right, and one division
in reserve.   The IX Corps had three divisions south and one
north of the river.   The Train was near Chancellorsville.

COMMENTS ON MAY 5TH.

If things had gone according to plan on the first day they had
gone very differently on the second.   Instead of being clear of
the Wilderness, in the open country beyond, with the Southern
Army flying for its life, the Army of the Potomac was still in the
forest, committed to a battle that Grant had not desired but
which his adversary, contrary to expectation, had challenged.
Worse, the attack which Grant, changing his plan, had ordered
had been a complete failure; nowhere had it made any appreciable

impression on the enemy; and worst of all, Lee had only employed two of his corps. Where were Longstreet's three veteran divisions? This setback had no outward effect upon Grant who is described by a staff officer, Lyman, as "looking sleepy, stern and indifferent."[5] The strain on his mind was however shown by the fact that he smoked twenty strong big Havana cigars during the day.

Neither could Lee look upon the day's proceedings with complete satisfaction. It is true that his troops had fought with their old steadiness, and had held up superior forces of the enemy. But the battle had been entered upon too soon, and in a piecemeal fashion. Only five of his eight divisions were on the field; and there was a nasty gap in the forest between Ewell and Hill, which he had not succeeded in plugging up. The situation was thus not devoid of anxiety, and any surprise effect which might be gained from striking his opponent in the flank while on the march had now passed. He had shown his hand; but his usual heavy blow had not been delivered.

If Grant is to blame for not protecting his right flank on the 4th, still more is he blameworthy on the 5th. The result of not doing so was to bring on an unexpected battle, and to dislocate his plan. Assuming he was right to attack Ewell the question arises: Should he have waited till the VI Corps could join in the attack? To do so would obviously have made the attack more formidable, but it might have allowed the enemy to bring up reinforcements. This is a quandary that is almost invariably encountered by a general on the offensive. Yet there is little guidance to be obtained from military manuals on the subject. For the most part they discreetly ignore the problem. The answer seems to hinge on the respective *moral* of the two sides. If that of the attacker is uppermost, the immediate attack seems to be indicated. In this case the advantage of *moral* was held by the enemy.

One of the chief "frictions of war" is unfortunately that between the generals. The Army of Northern Virginia was fortunate in this respect, for it was commanded by a man who inspired universal confidence and respect. The Army of the Potomac, on the other hand, had a new commander, who was received with a certain suspicion. He was, according to Ropes, "grossly ignorant of the history of the Army of the Potomac, and somewhat contemptuous of it."[6] The system of command

[5] *Meade's Headquarters*, p. 191.
[6] *M.H.S.M.*, iv, 373.

was also to blame. Meade was supposed to be in command of the actual operations, but Grant located his headquarters alongside those of his subordinate, and was soon interfering in the execution of the battle. This probably upset Meade, who was described by one of his staff officers in a letter as " The Great Peppery." The pepper-pot was poured out unstintingly on the unfortunate Warren when Grant started girding at the slowness of the attack. This is what is now known by the expression " Passing the baby." Grant's Chief of Staff, Colonel Rawlins, wrote that Meade " seemed inspired with rage with everyone about him." Altogether it was not a very happy family that was engaged on the formidable mission of crushing Lee and his army.

Colonel Conger, the greatest living authority on Grant, lays the chief blame for this state of affairs on the commander. " He began the campaign of 1864 with a quite proper directive. . . . But when, during the first day of the Wilderness fight, he saw the battle going . . . he lost his balance and without justification began to hector and irritate Meade . . . and to divide with him the tactical control and responsibility for the battle."[7]

The situation was a delicate one for the high-strung Meade. Badeau describes him as "tall, restless, angular, with piercing eyes, aquiline nose, rapid gait and nervous manner—he looked every inch a soldier."[8] And, it may be added, he showed his soldierly qualities in the way that he accepted interference by Grant.

MAY 6TH. (*Sketch Map* 3.)

During the night Grant heard that Longstreet's Corps was approaching. He therefore decided to attack at dawn, before Longstreet could arrive. The II Corps and Getty's Division were to attack the front of Hill's Corps, while the IX Corps and Wadsworth's Division of the V Corps were to attack his left. This would be a formidable combination (if it *could* combine) and should concentrate nine divisions at the decisive point. But, amazing as it may sound, the IX Corps was retained under the direct command of Grant, instead of being placed under Meade, in spite of the fact that it was acting in the middle of Meade's line! The cavalry was to guard the left flank of the army and the Train. The V Corps was to be ready to attack if called upon.

The attack opened about 6 a.m. and Hill's Corps was pushed

---

[7] *The Military Education of Grant as a General*, p. 20.
[8] *Military History of U. S. Grant*, ii, 369.

back by superior numbers, and Lee's command post overwhelmed. If at this critical moment Burnside's IX Corps had come in on Hill's left flank as planned, the position for the Southerners would have been extremely serious.   But fortunately for them, Burnside's attack was timid and halting.   His troops were mostly recruits, and the fighting value of the Corps was consequently low.

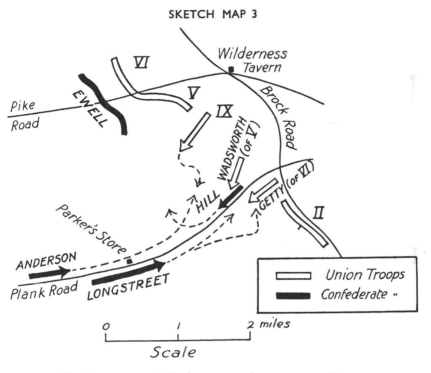

SKETCH MAP 3

May 6th 7 a.m., and Subsequent movements

In a dramatic scene Longstreet's Texans, coming up in the nick of time, rushed forward into the breach, and the position was saved.   The arrival of this corps evidently created a painful impression on the Union troops.   Grant had expected them on the Catharpin Road; he believed Pickett's Division to be present, and he had only one complete division (of the IX Corps) in hand.   He promised to send this division to help the II Corps " only in case of the last necessity."   This expression is hardly the language of a victorious general defeating an inferior force.

A projected attack by the V Corps was cancelled and the corps was used instead to provide reinforcements for the remainder of the line.   This was a strictly defensive measure.   Further to relieve the pressure Sheridan was ordered to attack Longstreet's right flank.

At 11 a.m. it was Lee's turn to attack.   A mixed force of the I Corps was sent round to the extreme right.   Then swinging round to its left it put in a completely surprise attack on the exposed left flank of the II Corps.   The whole I Corps pressed forward, Longstreet himself with them: but he was hit by a bullet fired by one his own flanking column, almost on the spot where exactly one year before Stonewall Jackson had fallen to a bullet fired by one of his own men.   Longstreet was carried off wounded, Anderson succeeded to the command of the I Corps and Mahone took his division.

The tardiness of the IX Corps was increased by the fact that, on the arrival of Longstreet, it was ordered to change direction to the left.   If it had been allowed to go straight on it would have either struck Longstreet's rear, or else the shaken troops of Hill's corps, which were just re-forming on Longstreet's left.   But such bold tactics were perhaps hardly to be looked for under the circumstances. (Sketch Map 3 shows the situation at the time of Longstreet's attack.)   Shortly afterwards Anderson's Division came up, in time to oppose the advance of the IX Corps.

During the remainder of the day a series of indecisive attacks were carried out by each side.   But both armies were busily entrenching, and the battle was gradually becoming " stabilised " in a manner very similar to the conclusion of a battle in the Great War.   Sheridan's attack on Longstreet's flank came to nothing; but in an engagement near Tod's Tavern he got the better of the opposing cavalry.   The battle was almost at an end; but Lee got in the last blow.   Moving across to the left wing he expressed the wish to deliver a blow at that point.   Both Ewell and Early demurred, but a 32-year-old brigadier, J. B. Gordon, eagerly asserted that it was possible, and he was deputed by Lee to carry it out.   The resulting attack exceeded all expectations.   It rolled up the left of the VI Corps, acquired 600 prisoners and created almost incredible alarm and commotion in the Northern ranks—an alarm that continued far into the night.

Thus ended in indecision the Battle of the Wilderness, a battle in which nearly 180,000 troops had been employed, and nearly 30,000 casualties suffered, 18,000 to the North and about 11,000 to the South.

COMMENTS ON THE BATTLE OF THE WILDERNESS.

The result of the battle was, at first sight, unpalatable to the Army of the Potomac. It had attacked in almost full strength, but had not gained a yard. It had suffered no less than 17,666 casualties, and had inflicted little more than half that total. Colonel Conger speaks of " the contrast between (Grant's) masterly plan and its sorry execution by so many of the subordinate leaders."[9] Other critics consider that Grant himself was largely to blame for hurrying the attacks unduly.

A good deal might be said as to the effects of wood fighting, but most of it must be obvious to the intelligent student. It is not surprising to find attacks unco-ordinated and delivered piecemeal, to see baseless alarms and rumours arising, and to note the quite disproportionate effect in relation to its weight of Gordon's twilight attack on the 6th. It is interesting to note that great use was made of the compass in directing advances through the woods.

The gap in the centre of the Confederate lines looks dangerous; but such dangers may pass unnoticed by the enemy in woodland fighting. In actual fact Burnside's IX Corps was directed straight into this gap; but so slow was his advance, due to the difficulty of the country and the inexperience of his troops, that he took over twelve hours to traverse three miles, and arrived too late to exploit the gap.

Artillery in this and the succeeding fight was very limited in its effect. Guns would be sited on roads and would fire point-blank down them: otherwise there was little artillery fire. On the other hand field fortification came into its own, for the first time in the Civil War. It generally took the form of timber breastworks, roughly and hastily covered with earth. At first the trenches were fairly straight in design, but, as we shall see, they soon developed into something like those to which we were familiar in the Great War.

In this respect the battle seemed to approach modern conditions; and it is of interest to enquire how far modern mechanised equipment would have modified tactics. As far as can be seen the modification would have been very slight. In such country, tanks and armoured cars would have been practically useless, machine guns would have had very limited fields of fire, while aeroplanes would have encountered obvious difficulties.

Longstreet's tardiness, combined with his insistence on marching

[9] *The Rise of U. S. Grant*, p. 347.

on the Catharpin instead of the Plank Road had blunted the effect of Lee's blow and probably deprived him of a resounding victory. Grant's chief meed to fame in this battle may be illustrated by a saying that became current in his army at the conclusion of the battle: " Lee no longer commands both these armies. We've got a general of our own." Lee also comes out of the battle well. Indeed Battine writes of him: " The march to the Wilderness and the tremendous battle that followed are among Lee's best performances."[10]

---

[10] *The Crisis of the Confederacy*, p. 369.

CHAPTER IV

Spottsylvania.

THE problem confronting General Grant on the evening of May 6th was a difficult one. He had attacked with nearly his whole force, had suffered very heavy casualties and had been held all along the line. Should he follow the examples of Burnside and of Hooker in somewhat similar situations, and retire on Fredericksburg? Should he stand his ground where he was, in the hopes that Lee would hammer in vain against it, wearing himself out in the effort? or should he persevere with the movement he had started upon, and continue to work round Lee's flank? The first course he dismissed—for a significant reason. Grant was no Hooker or Burnside; he was made of sterner stuff. The Northern Army was being led, or driven, by a man with an implacable will; he was not dismayed by his formidable opponent; there was nothing of the inferiority complex about him. There was to be no retreat. The second course was impracticable. Apart from the supply difficulty if he exhausted his trains, there was the danger that if he became passive Lee would take advantage of it, as he had done before, to slip past his refused right flank and make a dash for Washington. And Lee was quite capable of such a course. But the third course offered many attractions. In addition to getting his army into the comparatively open country, it would show conclusively that Lee had not succeeded in diverting him from his purpose. The original arguments in favour of this move still held good. In particular, the command of the sea now permitted him to move his base to Fredericksburg. There was only one new factor: he had shown his hand, and Lee might divine and anticipate his further move. However, as Wolfe so well said: "War is an option of difficulties; something must be left to chance." There was also just the chance that Lee would retire in the night.

If Grant thought this would happen, he did not know his man; the victor of Sharpsburg had not the slightest intention of retiring.

MAY 7TH.

Dawn disclosed the two armies entrenched and grimly watching one another. But scarce a shot was fired. Only on the southern

21

flank was there some cavalry activity. Lee had not retired, but Grant believed that he would do so that night, and he proceeded to draw up the plans for his next move. It was to be carried out that night, under cover of darkness. Spottsylvania was the objective. The routes of the corps are shown in Sketch Map 4. First, the V Corps was to sideslip to the left behind the II Corps, which was to cover its movement, and then follow in its tracks. The route was *via* Tod's Tavern and Alsops. The VI Corps was to march *via* Chancellorsville, also to Alsops. As for the IX Corps: though Meade's order directed the VI Corps to " follow closely " the V Corps, a sentence added, " It is understood that the IX Corps will follow the V Corps." Apart from the obvious contra- diction, this shows up in a glaring light the confusion that is liable to arise when an independent corps is added to a force without being placed under the orders of the force commander. Actually, the IX Corps followed the VI as far as Chancellorsville, and then inclined to the left. The wording of the orders for the cavalry was important: " General Sheridan will have a sufficient force on the approaches from the right to keep the Corps Commanders advised in time of the approach of the enemy." Yet Sheridan did not issue this important order to his cavalry till 5 a.m.! His order then was that Merritt (successor to Torbet) and Gregg should operate towards Shady Grove, and Wilson towards Spottsylvania.

THE SOUTH.

Early in the morning Ewell reported that the enemy had fallen back on his front. From this it could be inferred that the Union had abandoned their line of communications. That being so, they could not remain indefinitely in the Wilderness. Where were they making for: east to Fredericksburg, or south-east to Spottsylvania? Lee soon made up his mind as to the answer to this question. To Gordon he said: " Grant is not going to retreat; he will move his army to Spottsylvania." A few faint indications were enough for Lee, and in the afternoon he ordered Anderson's (Longstreet's) Corps to move that night to Spott- sylvania. Thus he was going to reduce his force in front of the enemy by over 25 per cent., although up to date he had no infor- mation that the hostile front was diminished. FitzLee's Cavalry Division was to cover his move, while Hampton's Cavalry Division watched the left flank at Corbin's Bridge.

The effect of the orders of the two commanders was thus likely to be a race on parallel roads between the V Corps and Anderson's Corps during the night for Spottsylvania. Which would win?

MAY 8TH.

At nightfall of the 7th, Grant's new operation was put in motion. General Meade accompanied the V Corps, and on arrival at Tod's Tavern about midnight, he found to his surprise that the Gregg's and Merritt's brigades, which should have been out protecting the march, were quietly sleeping! They had received no orders from Sheridan. Rousing the tired troopers, Meade sent Merritt towards Spottsylvania and Gregg towards Corbin's Bridge. Soon Merritt met with opposition from hostile cavalry, whom he slowly pushed back. But at daylight he was still three miles short of Spottsylvania, and called upon the infantry for help. Progress was then more rapid—till 9 a.m., when Warren found himself opposed by infantry. *Infantry!* Lee had evidently anticipated him!

Anderson's Corps had indeed won the race for Spottsylvania, but only by a narrow margin. Lee's orders had been that the corps was to withdraw out of the line after dark and rest before setting out. But Anderson, finding no suitable resting-place owing to the woods being on fire, decided to push straight on till he was within easy reach of Spottsylvania. On nearing that place he received calls for assistance from FitzLee, whose cavalry were opposing Warren's Corps (as we have seen) on the Tod's Tavern Road, and Wilson's cavalry to the east of Spottsylvania. The latter had approached by a circuitous route from the north-east. Anderson promptly sent one division against Warren and the other against Wilson. This resolute and timely action on the part of Anderson saved the situation for the South; for Wilson retired before his right division and though Warren attacked his left division the Union troops made no headway.

The II Corps did not move till dawn, and halted and entrenched at Tod's Tavern, relieving Gregg's Cavalry Division.

At daybreak, finding that the whole Union Army had departed, Lee ordered the remainder of his own army to follow Anderson. Hill was sick, and Early temporarily took his place and was succeeded in the command of his division by Gordon. At 2.30 p.m. Lee arrived on the field, followed two hours later by Ewell's corps. This was thrown in on Anderson's right, just as a further attack developed against it (Sketch Map 5).

The course of events at the Wilderness seemed to be repeating itself. Both battles opened with a surprise encounter, and in each case Grant, fancying he had only to do with a portion of Lee's army, decided to pin that part to its ground by attack whilst the remainder of his army continued its turning movement. The V and VI Corps were to make the attack that afternoon, and the II and IX Corps were to push forward on their way next morning. Meanwhile, in order to protect the Train, the IX Corps halted at Aldrich.

The attack by V and VI took place in the evening; but it was half-hearted and not very well conducted. The fact is, the troops

SKETCH MAP 4

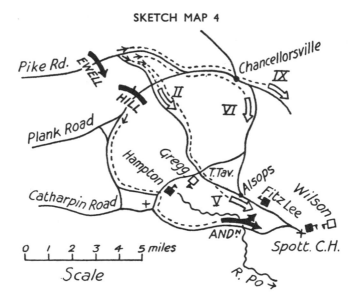

POSITION ON May 8th up to 7 a.m.

were not in a fit state, either physical or moral, to carry it out with any prospect of success. Meade suspected this, but the driving force of Grant prevailed. It is sometimes difficult to decide where driving force deteriorates into mere pigheadedness and refusal to face unpalatable facts.

Meantime, a personal quarrel had had a far-reaching sequel. Meade had bitterly reproached Sheridan for his delay in issuing orders to the cavalry, the result of which had been that Warren had lost the race to Spottsylvania. Sheridan replied hotly: "If I am allowed to cut loose from this army I can draw Stuart after me and whip him too!" Meade referred the matter to Grant,

MAP 5

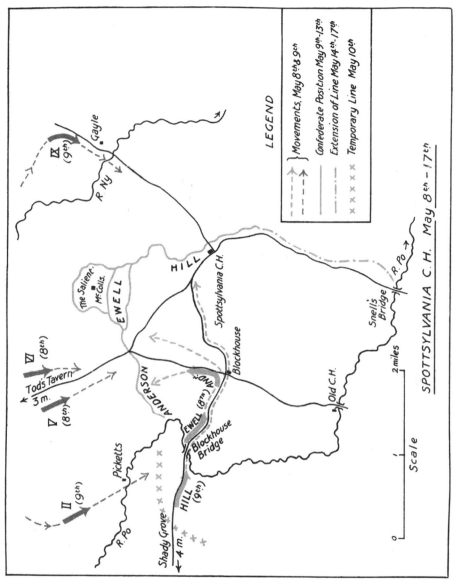

LEGEND

⎱ Movements, May 8th & 9th
⎰

———— Confederate Position May 9th-13th

—·—·— Extension of Line May 14th-17th

××××× Temporary Line May 10th

SPOTTSYLVANIA C.H. May 8th-17th

Scale

0   1   2 miles

Gayle

R. Ny

IX (9th)

The Salient.
McColls.

EWELL

HILL

Spottsylvania C.H.

Blockhouse

ANDERSON

Snell's Bridge

R. Po

Old C.H.

VI (8th)

Tod's Tavern
3 m.

V (8th)

EWELL (8th)

Blockhouse Bridge

Picketts

II (9th)

R. Po

Shady Grove
4 m.

HILL (9th)

who (probably in order to smooth things) decided to take Sheridan at his word. Thus originated Sheridan's famous raid, which started next morning.

At 7.30 p.m., Grant sent the following significant order to Burnside: "Dispose of your command so as to most easily and effectively guard the trains in your convoy, and at the same time be in readiness, on receipt of orders, to send two divisions to try and help to drive the enemy from Spottsylvania Court House, where he appears to have made a stand in very considerable force." Reading between the lines of this order, it is clear that Anderson's stout resistance, and the fatigued condition of the V Corps, had at last impressed itself upon Grant, and had caused him to abandon his morning plan to continue the turning movement. Indeed, he seems to have reverted to his idea of joining Butler, for he wrote to Halleck on this day: "My efforts will be to form a junction with General Butler as early as possible."

Hill's Corps, which had been the last to march, came into contact with the II Corps near Tod's Tavern, and went into bivouac. That night the situation was not without anxiety for the Confederates. Lee had, it is true, succeeded in blocking the road to Richmond against Grant's army. But disturbing news came in from the other theatres. Butler had landed at Bermuda Neck and had cut the railway between Richmond and Petersburg. His cavalry would delay the approach of a force under Beauregard coming up from the south. Cavalry were also threatening the railway from Richmond to Lynchburg. Sigel was expected to advance at any moment. Meanwhile the Army of the Potomac, though its immediate purpose had been foiled, was fighting with an intensity that was new to it. It evidently now possessed a master. Lee could not afford to take the risks against Grant that he had employed with such dazzling success against his predecessors.

COMMENTS ON THE MOVE TO SPOTTSYLVANIA.

Nowhere does Grant's essential greatness show up more than in his decision not to retreat after the Battle of the Wilderness (as his predecessors undoubtedly would have done) but to continue the plan he had mapped out for himself. Henderson considers this decision to be the turning-point of the campaign. But if the conception is above criticism the same does not apply to its execution. It has been said that Lee only won the race for Spottsylvania by "a fluke." Even if this were so—and it is true to the extent that Lee's luck was in at that moment—Grant could still have won the race had he sent off the II Corps in the lead instead of the V Corps.   His reason for not doing so was one of precaution —to cover the movement of the remainder.   But great results cannot be achieved by half-measures.   A further half-measure was to halt the II Corps after it had only marched a few miles, at Tod's Tavern.   Had it continued its march on to the battlefield, Anderson might have been crushed by the immensely superior forces thus thrown against him, before Ewell could arrive.   But by halting as he did, Hancock allowed Ewell to march right across his front and to arrive on the battlefield at the critical moment.

The absurdity of the system of command on the Union side is shown up by the fact that Grant gives direct orders to the IX Corps and only *suggests* orders to the Army of the Potomac, though both were engaged in the same complicated manœuvre. If Meade had not fallen in with the " suggestion " chaos would have resulted.

There was a certain slowness of execution on the part of the Northern troops.   Meade himself described them as being " exceedingly hesitating "—no doubt the result of the rude reception they had received in their attack in the Wilderness.

Lee's perspicacity—genius is not the right word—in guessing correctly Grant's objective has been universally praised, and his action in countering it could hardly be improved upon except for the somewhat vague wording of his instructions to Anderson. Freeman asserts that: " A close study of Lee's logistics on May 7th–8th will show them to have been flawless."[1]

Lee's use of his cavalry was also excellent; it was pushed ahead to seize and hold the vital spot until the infantry arrived.

MAY 9TH.

This was a day of rest and reorganisation for the North. Sedgwick had been killed and the command of the VI Corps devolved on Wright, his place being taken by Russell.   Robinson's Division of the V Corps had suffered so severely that it was broken up.   Grant took advantage of the respite to prepare his plans for a great attack on the following day.   But a trivial error had curious and far-reaching results—as so often happens in war. In preparation for the attack on the 10th, the IX Corps had been ordered to march to a spot shown on the map as " Gate."   Not recognising Gate when it reached the spot (it was in reality merely the gate of a field) it marched two miles further to Gayle, which it supposed to be its destination (Gate being presumably a

[1] *Freeman*, iii, 431.

misprint for Gayle) and reported the enemy at that spot.   Grant, supposing that the enemy were thus at "Gate " two miles further north, naturally came to the conclusion that the Confederates were advancing north. He therefore altered his plan in favour of one which, though clumsily and vaguely worded, was (according to Atkinson's interpretation)[2] an effort to catch Lee between the " anvil " of Burnside and the " hammer " of Meade.   But there was confusion owing to orders for. Burnside not going through Meade, who consequently did not fully grasp the plan.   Perhaps it was fortunate for the Union that the plan never got as far as being put in operation.   Preparatory to it, the II Corps was moved south from Tod's Tavern, across the River Po, and then eastwards towards Spottsylvania.   But its progress was slow, and at nightfall it had not reached Block House Bridge.   The cause of this slow progress was that Lee, on hearing of the approach of the II Corps had switched two divisions of Hill's Corps across from his right flank (where it had gone into the line on the right of Ewell) to his left, in the nick of time.

Lee, as well as Grant, had profited by the short respite.   Up at 3 a.m., he rode round his lines.   He was an engineer by profession, and he made good use of his technical knowledge.   The line he traced out had the flanks so sharply refused that it assumed the form of a pronounced salient.   On Ewell representing the advantage of including some commanding ground in front of the centre of this salient, Lee allowed this centre to be still further advanced till it took the curious shape shown in Sketch Map 5. It was however strongly entrenched and provided with guns. The weakness of the position lay in the fact that the ground in front was thickly wooded, and a hostile approach would be screened from view till the last moment.

MAY 10TH.

The stiff resistance of Hill's Divisions soon showed Grant that he had wrongly appreciated the situation.   The Confederates were evidently not advancing by their right, as he had supposed. Quietly but promptly he recast his whole plan.   The II Corps was to withdraw, and with the V and VI Corps was to attack the hostile centre at 5 p.m.   This long delay before the attack could be launched was chiefly due to the difficulty of manœuvring through the thick undergrowth of the woods.   Warren considered that too much time was being allowed, and at his request the attack was put forward to 4.30 p.m.   But when it was launched

[2] *Grant's Campaigns*, by C. F. Atkinson.

it was only partial and disconnected, and, as a result, failed disastrously. Two hours later the VI Corps carried out its part of the programme with greater success. It penetrated the hostile trenches and captured 1,000 prisoners. But owing to the lack of success elsewhere, it was recalled at nightfall. On the other flank the IX Corps attacked at 5 p.m., but very feebly, and Hill's Corps held its ground without difficulty. A satisfactory day for the South, except that Lee learnt that on the 9th Sheridan had slipped round his left flank, had cut the central railroad towards Gordonsville, and had destroyed enormous stores of food. The question was, could Lee now take advantage of Sheridan's absence to attack Grant? Lee regretfully decided that he could not.

The first phase of the battle of Spottsylvania was over. Lee had successfully blocked Grant's road, and, as at the Wilderness, Grant had then turned fiercely upon his opponent, but without attaining any appreciable result. Would history still further repeat itself—in other words, would Grant make another side-slip to his left, in the hope of edging Lee back into open country? The answer is given in Grant's despatch to Lincoln of the following morning.

MAY 11TH

The morning was again spent quietly by the Union troops. But Grant had evidently been pondering over the problem pretty deeply, as a result of which he penned a despatch to Lincoln which contained a passage afterwards to become famous: " I am now sending back all my wagons for a fresh supply of provisions and ammunition, and propose to fight it out on this line if it takes all summer." This was an expression of immense significance. It meant, in essence, that Grant was about to abandon his original plan of manœuvring Lee back to Richmond, in favour of a mere " hammer and tongs " operation. This was bound to involve heavy casualties to both sides; but Grant had come to see that, since his own resources were practically inexhaustible, both in men and material, whereas those of the South were strictly limited, he would stand to gain if losses were approximately equal, or even if his were up to 50 per cent. greater. Thus for the first time creeps in the doctrine of " attrition "—to become so familiar to us in the Great War.

" I am satisfied that the enemy are very shaky," wrote Grant to Halleck this day, and fortified in this belief, the Federal commander laid his plans for another great attack on the morrow.

This time the II Corps was to assault the Salient, while the IX Corps assaulted its eastern face.

But Lee was completely in the dark as to this fundamental change of plan. His cavalry had reported signs of rearward movement that betokened a repetition of the enemy's sideslip from the Wilderness still further to their left. Lee did not on this occasion go so far as to anticipate this move with one of his own corps—the evidence was not strong enough to warrant it—but he ordered all steps to be taken for a prompt countermove, and in particular he had the majority of the guns removed from the Salient as the tracks were narrow and difficult, and the operation would therefore be a long and slow one.

Thus Grant had every prospect, though he knew it not, of springing a big surprise on his opponent when he launched his attack next morning.

MAY 12TH.   THE BATTLE OF THE BLOODY ANGLE.
    (*Sketch Map* 6.)

During the night the II Corps had passed behind the V and VI Corps in order to take up its position opposite the tip of the Salient.   The V and VI Corps were to be ready to exploit the situation.

At 4.35 a.m. all four divisions of the II Corps were launched to the attack.   The advance was by compass.   It fell upon Johnson's Division of Ewell's Corps with complete surprise, and with corresponding success.   The bulk of the division, including the famous Stonewall Brigade, was captured and 20 guns taken.*

An hour later Gordon's Division, as ordered by Lee, counter-attacked and partially restored the situation, but the absence of guns was a tremendous handicap to the Confederates.†   The artillery of the II Corps was employing overhead fire into the middle of the Salient with deadly effect.   At 6.30 the two divisions of the VI Corps came up to the assistance of the II Corps, though there were already as many troops in the tip of the Salient (henceforth known as " The Bloody Angle ") as it could well hold—if, not too many.

Grant remained in his camp, awaiting news.   Soon it became apparent that the attack of the IX Corps was hanging fire, and to

* I have been privileged to hear from the mouth of one of the survivors of Johnson's Division the story of that affair. My informant and the unit he was with was completely surrounded before they were aware what was happening.

† Several guns returned to the Salient, but were captured before they could fire a round.   This explains the apparently puzzling fact that though Lee had withdrawn the guns several of them were captured.

a complaint that connection had been lost between it and the
II Corps he wrote: " Push the enemy with all your might. That
is the way to connect."   Admirable instruction!

Lee, on the other hand, was with difficulty restrained from
flinging himself into the midst of the fray.   " As he rode majesti-
cally in front of my line of battle," writes Gordon, " with un-

SKETCH MAP 6

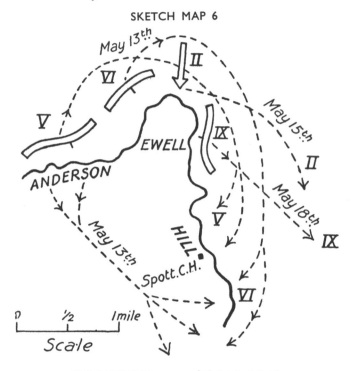

POSITION ON MAY 12th,
and Subsequent moves

covered head, and mounted on Old Traveller, Lee looked a
very God of War."[3]   His blood was up; but " General Lee
to the rear! " was echoed down the line, and reluctantly he
turned back.   Yet though so close up to the firing line, he had
not lost control of the battle as a whole.   Keenly conscious of the
value of interior lines, he again switched a portion of Hill's Corps
across the Salient, to the help of Ewell.

The struggle for The Bloody Angle went on for over 16 hours.
The fighting was of an intensity and desperation that had never

[3] *Reminiscences of the Civil War*, p. 278.

previously in the Civil War been seen, nor was it to be surpassed, or even equalled, throughout the remainder of the war. A single extract from the account of one of the actors will suffice to depict the nature of the homeric contest: " Nothing but the piled-up logs and breastworks separated the combatants. Our men would reach over the logs and fire into the faces of the enemy, would stab over with their bayonets; many were shot and stabbed through the crevices and holes between the logs. Men mounted the works and with muskets rapidly handed to them, kept up a continuous fire until they were shot down, when others would take their places and continue the deadly work." But it was all of no avail; after the first half-hour the line, though it swayed, did not break. In vain was the V Corps thrown in; in vain were two divisions of the VI Corps brought up in support; in vain did Grant and Meade storm and fume; no further impression could be made on the hostile position. Meanwhile, the Confederates were fever- ishly constructing a new line across the base of the Salient. By nightfall it was finished and Lee's battered divisions fell back within its protection. The fighting had been sanguinary beyond all knowledge. The Union casualties amounted to nearly 7,000. Those of the South are not exactly known, but including prisoners they probably exceeded those of the North.

Though Grant could hardly look upon the issue of the day with satisfaction still less could Lee. Never before had he lost so many prisoners, nor guns; and he attributed the disaster directly to his own action in withdrawing the guns from the Salient. To fill the cup of his mortification he heard that the irreplaceable " Jeb " Stuart, who had been sent out with his cavalry to head off Sheridan's raid before it reached Richmond, had been killed in an encounter 7 miles north of that city. The final blow came that night. Sheridan had succeeded in cutting off his connection with Richmond, and Federal cavalry had cut the railway to the south of Petersburg which was relied on for the transportation of grain. No supplies for either men or horses were arriving. " All this load of death, disaster, and threatened hunger was put on Lee's shoulders that dreadful 12th of May; yet he bore it with so stout a heart that even those who knew him best did not realise that in its agonizing demands upon him the day of The Bloody Angle was second only to the final day at Gettysburg. He did not admit the imminence of ruin or lament the things he could not control. Unafraid, with faith in God, he faced the doubtful morrow.[4]"

[4] *Freeman*, iii, 328.

MAY 13TH–17TH.

For the following four days it poured with rain. Operations were practically impossible. The North utilised the respite to reorganise their troops, recuperate, and to strengthen and extend their entrenchments till they formed one continuous line. Mott's Division of the II Corps which had suffered heavily was amalgamated withBirney's. Grant's intentions for the future are shown in these words: " We must get by the right flank of the enemy for their [sic] next fight." In preparation for this, he switched the V and then the VI Corps round behind the IX Corps and brought them up on its left (Sketch Map 6). He ordered them to attack on the night of the 13th–14th. But the " friction " of war determined otherwise. The darkness, the rain and the difficult unfamiliar woodland terrain made the V Corps hopelessly late, and the attack came to nothing. Lee had been too quick. Again profiting by his interior lines he switched Anderson's Corps across from left to right to counter the hostile attack. There was some blundering on the part of one of the brigadiers, but Lee refused to make a scapegoat of him, and his reasons go far to meet the objection levelled against him that he was too lenient to blundering subordinates: " General Wright is not a soldier; he is a lawyer. I cannot do many things that I could do with a trained army. . . . If you humiliated General Wright the people of Georgia would not understand. Besides, whom would you put in his place? You'll have to do what I do. When a man makes a mistake I call him to my tent, talk to him, and use the authority of my position to make him do the right thing the next time."

Next day Gordon was promoted Major-General for good work on the 12th. Anderson's Corps extended the line as far as the River Po. During this lull 12,000 reinforcements joined the Northerners, but as none reached the Southerners, the superiority of the former proportionately increased.

The situation was an extremely anxious one for the South, and President Davis urged Beauregard, who was now in position with 25,000 men opposite Butler's army of 37,000 to attack it. Davis also suggested that Lee should call troops from the Valley to his assistance, as he had so successfully done in 1862. But Lee, though depressed at not being able to fathom Grant's new plan, largely owing to the death of Stuart, was averse from this step, till Sigel had been defeated. This fortunately happened on the

7 15th at Newmarket, and Breckinridge, with 2,500 men, was at

once ordered to come in.   More good news on the 16th; Beauregard attacked Butler and neatly hemmed him in in the great loop between the James and Appomattox Rivers, known as the Bermuda Neck.

MAY 18TH.

On the 18th Grant launched a great attack against the base of the Salient with parts of three corps.   This involved a good deal of reshuffling, the details of which are of no particular interest, except that his position on exterior lines rendered the movements slow and difficult.   Suffice it to say that the attack was a complete failure.

MAY 19TH.

The II Corps had abandoned the tip of the Salient on the 15th, and gone into reserve behind the centre.   Absence of opposition on this northern flank led Lee to wonder whether a fresh turning movement might not be under way.   To clear up the point, Ewell was ordered to attack on the 19th.   This attack came as a complete surprise to the Union Army and considerable alarm and confusion in the trains was caused.   At an earlier period of the war it might have led to general panic.   But Grant's troops had been tried in the furnace and were now tempered steel. After the initial setback they recovered, and Ewell's men lost heavily in their withdrawal.   Lee's object had been merely of a reconnoitring nature, though he had not yet abandoned hope of attacking Grant.   On the 18th he had written to Davis: " My object has been to engage (the enemy) when in motion and under circumstances that will not cause us to suffer under this disadvantage (inferior artillery). . . . I shall continue to strike him whenever any opportunity presents itself."   Considering that Grant's intentions were almost precisely the same the chances of a fight in the open would appear to be considerable.

Sheridan's great raid had now almost come to an end.   After the defeat of Stuart's cavalry there had been no further actions. After frightening the inhabitants of Richmond, Sheridan had passed on to the south-east of it and rested for three days on the James River.   Thence he had returned by the east to the main army.   Apart from the death of Stuart (a lucky fluke for Sheridan) nothing of permanent value had been accomplished; and the army had been deprived of the services of its cavalry during an operation that might have proved decisive.

The last shot had been fired in this great battle, the last blow delivered, and that blow (as at the Wilderness) was struck by General Lee.

COMMENTS ON SPOTTSYLVANIA.

Grant's decision to break off the battle met with general approval. Meade wrote at the time to his wife: " Even Grant thought it useless to knock our heads against a stone wall." Grant's difficulties had been great, and were due to two main causes: the wooded nature of the country, and the interior lines held by Lee. As to the first, it was found impossible to locate the exact position of the enemy short of making a reconnaissance in force. Cavalry proved useless for the task. As for the second, Lee was able to march Hill's Corps backwards and forwards across the Salient at his will. No less than four times was this done, and always with good results.

Though we are not concerned with local tactics, those of the battle of The Bloody Angle were of such outstanding interest that brief allusion must be made to some of them. The success of the attack was undoubtedly due to surprise. The commander of the Stonewall Division was captured before he had become fully aware what was happening. Thereafter the mistake made by the attackers was that they threw too many troops into the middle of the Salient. It is generally maintained that the reserve should have been kept further back. On the other hand, Grant had been criticised only two days before for not sending the reserves in sooner. The way of the commander is a hard one! Nothing can be more difficult than to know just when to throw in the reserves. All that can be said on the point is that the commander should take adequate steps in advance to ensure his getting timely and correct information of the situation at the front. This also is easier said than done. To depend upon troops who are busy fighting for their lives to do so is to rely on a broken reed.

The " traverse " appears in open warfare for almost the first time in military history in this battle. The cause was obvious. Owing to the sharp salient in the Confederate line, the Northerners were able to enfilade it, and even to take it in reverse. The troops therefore threw up traverses without orders from anyone, in sheer self-defence. A section of one of these trenches has recently been restored, and shows a traverse in the breastwork, an almost exact counterpart of many of the trenches constructed 8 in the Great War. Later on, at Coldharbor, there was not the same need for traverses, and to this day the trace of long sections of the front line can be seen, completely devoid of traverses.

CHAPTER V

North Anna.

MAY 20TH.

By the 19th Grant realised that it was no use going on attacking the Confederates in their entrenchments. He must by some means get them on the move again. The way to do this was fairly obvious—a threat to Lee's communications with Richmond. Ewell's attack had prevented the new move being started that day, but now orders were issued for the II Corps to advance down the railroad that night towards Bowling Green and Milford. Grant's instructions read: " If the enemy make a general move to meet this, they will be followed by the other three corps, . . . and attacked if possible before time is given to entrench."

This order was later developed into an instruction to the V Corps to be ready to follow Hancock or to follow the enemy if he turned upon Hancock. On this Atkinson argues that it was to be another attempt at " hammer and anvil " tactics—Warren would be the hammer and Hancock the anvil. Another way of expressing it would be to say that Hancock was to be the decoy, and the other three corps the guns. The orders published in Official Records, Vol. 36, hardly bear out Atkinson's theory. In fact, I can find no allusion to it, but rather a defensive attitude. There is much about cautions, precautions, and much nervousness as to the possibility of Lee attacking, in the absence of the II Corps. Details of the proposed move do not seem to have been worked out; only 30 minutes before the V Corps was due to move Humphreys wrote to Warren asking what road he proposed to take!

Meanwhile Lee got an inkling that Grant was contemplating another sideslip; he even made the shrewd and correct guess that Grant would shift his base to Port Royal on the Rappahannock 20 miles south-east of Fredericksburg. In order to counter this move, should it materialise, he ordered Ewell's Corps to move south on to the line of the River Po by dawn of the 21st.

MAY 21ST. (*Sketch Map* 7.)

In accordance with its orders, the II Corps made a night march and reached Guiney's Station by dawn. At about 10.30 a.m. the

V Corps moved off for Guiney's, while the VI and IX Corps received orders to follow that night.

Ewell was now in his new position along the Po. Lee had obtained definite information that Grant had started his move, and the question arose, where should he move his own army to? As long as Grant kept to the east of the Mattapony, as he appeared to be doing, Lee could not get at him. Also, if he followed the Union Army down the Mattapony he would be drawn towards the east and might end in endangering his own left flank—his strategic flank because it connected him with the hinterland. About 20 miles to the south ran the North Anna in an east–west direction. If he could hold this line it would protect the important junction of the two railways—Hanover Junction. At noon Lee decided to adopt this course and issued his orders. Ewell was to move forward at once for Mud Tavern (due west of Guiney's Station), and the other corps were to follow, provided that the enemy had actually decamped. Anderson behind Ewell, and Hill (now back with his corps) further to the west. These orders were duly carried out, and the march was continued throughout the night. The curious spectacle was thus presented of both armies moving by parallel roads only a few miles apart throughout the night.

The IX Corps tried to cross the Po at Stannard's Mill and use the Telegraph Road. But Lee blocked the crossing and forced Burnside to follow the V Corps round by Guiney's Station.

MAY 22nd.

The position at dawn is shown on Sketch Map 7. It will be seen that Ewell had outmarched Hancock and was bound to reach the North Anna first. Hancock, after driving off a small detachment from Pickett's Division, had halted at Milford. Why?* It certainly looks as if Grant had temporarily lost his grip upon events. His orders had given out an uncertain sound, and "if the trumpet give out an uncertain sound who shall prepare himself for battle?" In any case, it was quite clear that a "hammer and anvil" affair was now out of the question, for Lee refused to lay himself upon the anvil, and the anvil made no motion to approach Lee. No doubt Grant felt handicapped by the scarcity of cavalry, Sheridan not having yet returned from his raid. In addition, his maps were inadequate and faulty.

To make things still better for the South, Pickett's Division

* The reason given by Badeau is: "Until the other corps could be brought within supporting distance." *Military History of U. S. Grant*, ii, 223.

of the I Corps had been sent back from Richmond and was on the
North Anna, together with Hoke's Brigade from Beauregard's
army. Further, Breckenridge was just arriving from the Valley.
All this meant a welcome reinforcement of 8,500 men to the Army
of Northern Virginia.

During the day Grant moved his base to Port Royal, as Lee
had prophesied. By night-fall Lee had all his army behind the

SKETCH MAP 7

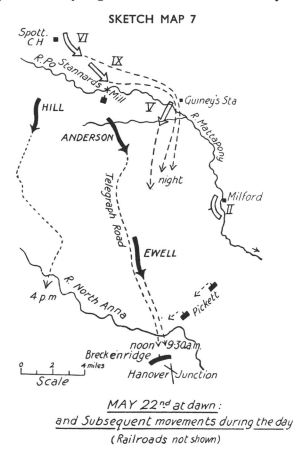

MAY 22ⁿᵈ at dawn :
and Subsequent movements during the day
(Railroads not shown)

North Anna, while Grant's army was strung out from Milford
to the north-west.

MAY 23RD. (Sketch Map 8.)

The country in which the protagonists now found themselves
was more open than the country that they had been operating
in for 18 days. On the other hand maps of the district were

meagre and bad. The North Anna at that period of the year was generally fordable almost anywhere, so it formed but a feeble obstacle. Further, the north bank commanded the south bank, except in the centre of the position. Nevertheless, it would seem that Lee hoped to hold the line of the river. If this was so, he was soon to be disappointed. Warren's V Corps managed to ford the river on the west flank at Jericho Mills, and though Hill, who was on the left, flung a division against the intruders near Noel's Station, it was badly handled, and fell back again. Lee was much annoyed at this setback, which seems clear evidence that his plan had been to hold the river line. This view is confirmed in a passage in his dispatch to the President on May 25th: " We have been obliged to withdraw from the banks of the N. Anna."[1] On the eastern flank in the evening the II Corps managed to cross the river by the North Anna Bridge. But the centre was not attacked, and maintained its position. Lee now decided on a rather remarkable realignment. Though he had said, after The Bloody Angle, that there were to be no more salients he now proceeded deliberately to create another one. That is to say, to draw back both wings, leaving his centre still on the river. The new line that he selected and entrenched is marked on Sketch Map 8. It is to be observed, however, that his new salient was not so vulnerable as that at Spottsylvania, for its eastern flank was protected by the river and by a swamp. The new position also gave him the considerable advantage of interior lines. Lee cannot fail to have appreciated the advantage interior lines confer, for he had made such striking use of them only a few days before. His new line formed what has been termed " an inverted V." All commentators make much of the fact that Lee's new line had the effect of dividing the Army of the North, owing to the course of the river. If Grant should wish to reinforce one wing from the other he would have to cross the river twice. This would certainly be a handicap, but seeing that the river was fordable the disadvantage was not in actual fact very great.* A much greater handicap was the fact that he would be operating on exterior lines.

Lee's view of the situation and his intentions as regards the future are given in a significant passage of his despatch to Jefferson Davis written this day: " Whatever route (Grant) pursues I am in a position to move against him, and shall endeavour to

[1] *Lee's Dispatches*, p. 200.

* Lyman states in a letter that the river was " in most places over one's head." But this is in contradiction to the other accounts.

engage him while in motion.   I shall be near enough Richmond,
I think, to combine the operations of this army with that under
General Beauregard, and shall be as ready to reinforce him if
occasion requires as to receive his assistance."[2]   It is clear from
this that Lee had every intention of exploiting his strategical
as well as his tactical interior lines to the full.

SKETCH MAP 8

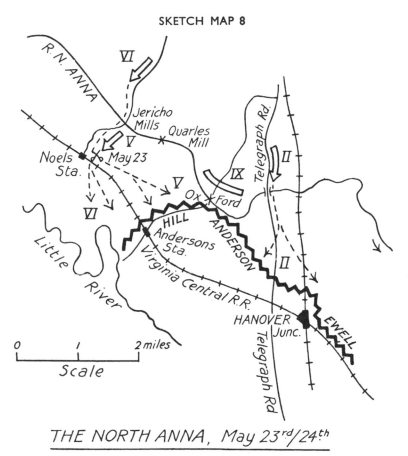

THE NORTH ANNA, May 23ʳᵈ/24ᵗʰ

MAY 24TH.

Lee had now drawn back both his wings, and Grant jumped to
the conclusion that his opponent was retiring.   The progress
Grant made on both flanks confirmed this belief.   The consequence was that in the afternoon he issued orders for a " continu-
ance of the pursuit."   This order was as much at variance with

    [2] *Lee's Dispatches*, p. 168.

the facts as the order to the British troops to " continue the pursuit " on September 13th, 1914, when the enemy were not, and had no intention of, retiring. However, Grant discovered his mistake that evening, as his troops gradually came up against the newly entrenched line.

The VI Corps had now come up on the right of the V; and the IX Corps (which was now at long last placed under Meade's orders) held the centre of the line, on the north bank of the river.

It is generally considered that Lee now had a good opportunity to attack one or other of Grant's flanks, owing to his interior lines. No doubt this was so, but unfortunately Lee fell sick, and though he refused to give up the command he was not in a fit state to initiate a great blow against his adversary. That he realised the desirability of so doing was evident from his reiterated remark, " We must strike them a blow! " But before he could do so Grant had moved again.

Comments on the North Anna.

Just as Grant could have won the race to Spottsylvania, so he could have won that to the North Anna. The II Corps had a twelve-hour start of Ewell and could easily have reached Hanover Junction several hours before him, even though Hoke and Pickett were converging on the spot. Again, if Stannard's Mill had been occupied by the II Corps the V and IX Corps could have marched straight down the Telegraph Road. If Sheridan's cavalry had not been sent off on his almost useless raid it could have delayed the advance of Pickett, or alternatively have delayed Ewell. The remainder of the army could have outmarched Hill and Anderson. But, it may be argued, Hanover Junction was not Grant's objective: he hoped to engage Lee in the open to the north of that place. That is so—or may be so—but the steps by which he attempted to bring it off—the " hammer and anvil " trap—though ingenious, were too rigid in conception. If the fly will kindly walk into the parlour all well and good, but the prudent spider will at least face the possibility of the other alternative. War is " an option of difficulties," the enemy possesses free will, the power to choose; and the plan made should envisage the possibility of him selecting the course that we do not want him to take. In this case Grant should have said, " Suppose my little trap does not come off? Suppose Lee retreats straight to the North Anna? What then? Hancock should therefore have received definite orders to push right on to the North Anna if he was not attacked by Lee by a certain time. The impression is inescapable that

Grant lost his usual tight grip over things during the advance to the North Anna. On the other hand, seldom did Lee display greater brilliance than in his swift move to the North Anna. Not only did he win the race, but he won it by over 12 hours.

He never showed his gift of eye for ground more notably than in his selection of the line at the North Anna, with its two refused flanks, and its centre firmly affixed on the river. Henderson probably had this episode prominently in his mind when he wrote: " His eye for ground had much to do with his successful resistance to Grant's overwhelming numbers."[3] And Swinton's verdict is: " The game of war seldom presents a more effectual checkmate than was given here by Lee."[4]

---

[3] *Science of War*, p. 333.
[4] *Campaigns of the Army of the Potomac*, p. 470.

CHAPTER VI

Coldharbor.

MAY 25TH–27TH. (*Sketch Map* 9.)

As a result of a careful reconnaissance of the Confederate position, Grant decided that an attack held out no prospect of success. He therefore resolved to sideslip once more. Sheridan had now rejoined with the cavalry corps, which would simplify the protection of his exposed flank during the forthcoming march. The withdrawal was made in two stages. On the night of the 25th–26th the right wing—V and VI Corps—was withdrawn, and sent off in the direction of Hanover C.H. On the following night the remainder of the army followed suit. The move was a difficult and delicate one, especially in view of the absence of good maps, and the staff work was of a high order. At dawn on the 27th Lee discovered that the enemy had disappeared, and promptly ordered his army to fall back. Ewell was sent off towards Ashland, followed by Anderson: Hill brought up the rear, moving that evening.

Grant's fourth " sideslip " was in full swing throughout that day. In the morning his cavalry crossed the Pamunkey at Hanover Town (8 miles south-east of Hanover Court House), driving some Southern cavalry before them. The bulk of the Northern Army spent the night strung out along the road some way to the north of Hanover Town. Withdrawal of the troops from the face of the enemy—always a delicate matter—had been successfully carried out, but it was a lengthy and trying job. This move restored the Gordonsville Railway to Southern control, to Lee's great relief. He was now getting into country already familiar to him. The position he was making for was the low watershed between the Chickahominy and the Totopotomoy Creek. After Ashland his route diverged slightly from the railway. The army did not halt till it was close to Atlee's Station. A glance at the Sketch Map 9 will show that Lee was again marching along the chord of a circle, whilst Grant was marching along its arc. Lee was therefore likely to win the race again.

MAP 9

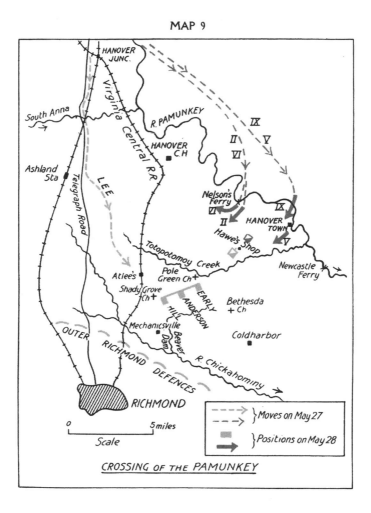

CROSSING OF THE PAMUNKEY

MAY 28TH.

Sheridan, now back from his raid, drove the Southern cavalry from Hawe's Shop (three miles south-west of Hanover Town) and ascertained that Ewell and Anderson were four miles to the west of him.   Meanwhile the infantry were crossing the Pamunkey River, V and IX Corps at Hanover Town, VI and II to the west of it.   Thereafter they spread out in a line in order from right to left, VI, II, IX, V, with their left resting on the Totopotomoy Creek.   This same day Grant called to his aid the XVIII Corps (General Smith) from Butler's army.   It was to come by sea, disembarking at White House, on the Pamunkey, which Grant made his new base, twenty-two miles in an air line southeast of Hanover Town.

Lee drew up his army on his pre-selected spot.   For the moment he kept each corps concentrated: Ewell near Pole Green Church, Hill near Shady Grove Church, and Anderson between the two.   Lee had a good reason for this " waiting position." Grant had not yet shown his hand.   Assuming that Richmond was his ultimate objective, he might approach from Hawe's Shop by cutting west to the Telegraph Road, which lay west of and parallel with the Virginia Central Railway; or he might make off south and then west by Mechanicsville.   From his position on the watershed, Lee was centrally situated to counter either move, when it developed.

Later in the day Lee heard as the result of a cavalry engagement that at least two corps were to the east of him, near Hawe's Shop. It thus seemed unlikely that Grant could intend to come down the Telegraph Road in any strength.   Accordingly, he wheeled his army into line facing north-north-east, parallel to and behind the Totopotomoy.   Here he entrenched in the usual manner. Lee had not yet recovered from his indisposition, and to make matters worse Ewell had to leave the field sick, his place being taken by Early.   On the credit side we must note the arrival of South Carolinian Cavalry, under their redoubtable commander Butler.   The very next day these splendid troops were to give a good account of themselves.

MAY 29TH.

The Union Army moved slowly forward in line, feeling—somewhat gingerly—for their opponents.   The result of this reconnaissance in force was that Grant became satisfied that he had the whole Army of Northern Virginia in his front.   But until the arrival of the XVIII Corps he did not propose to attack.

The only event of note on the side of the South was a meeting between Lee, President Davis and General Beauregard. Lee had been trying for some time to establish closer co-operation between the two armies, or failing that, to obtain some reinforcement from Beauregard's force. But the latter made difficulties, and Davis would not drive him against his will. The conference therefore came to nought. Beauregard showed undue nervousness for his position. Although, after the departure of the XVIII Corps his 12,000 men were only detaining a force of 13,000 under Butler, he wrote that he "considered it unwise to send reinforcements to the Army of North Virginia, as the War Department was already pressing me to do." Fortunately the War Department prevailed.

MAY 30TH.

The Northern Army continued its deployment and cautious reconnaissance, pushing forward 2½ miles west of Hawe's Shop, the V and IX Corps crossing to the south side of the Totopotomoy. The bulk of the cavalry was on the left flank, but it was kept close in hand, lest Lee should suspect another sideslip and fall back on Richmond. Grant's object was, presumably, to engage him well outside the Richmond defences. These defences were now only a few miles distant. Lee had, however, already come to the conclusion that another sideslip was imminent. At 11 a.m. he wrote to Anderson: " After fortifying this line they will probably make another move by their left flank over towards the Chickahominy." He accordingly decided to attack such of the enemy as had crossed the Totopotomoy without more ado. There was no time to stage an attack by the whole army, but Early's Corps was ordered to withdraw out of the line and attack the enemy near Bethesda Church. Anderson extended his line to fill up the gap thus made, and Early moved off. His attack struck the enemy by surprise, and at first it was successful; but not for long.

Meanwhile Smith's XVIII Corps was disembarking at White House, and Lee was promptly informed of it. This news was serious, and Lee took the unusual course of applying direct to Beauregard for reinforcements, instead of doing so through the President. After some demur, Beauregard gave way, and dispatched Hoke's Division. As it was able to move direct by road, whereas the XVIII Corps had to go round by sea, there was a chance that it would arrive first on the battlefield, thus illustrating in a very clear manner the advantage of interior lines.

Comments.

What was Grant's real motive in crossing the Pamunkey? Critics are not agreed. Fuller asserts that his intention was to " move against Lee's left and cut him off from Richmond."[1] Livermore does not go quite so far as this: " His motive was to move around the flank of the enemy and strike them where there were no breastworks."[2] Ropes, on the other hand, says: " Grant does not seem to have had a very definite idea of accomplishing anything by this move." And, still more caustically, " Grant's only idea seems to have been, on having crossed the Pamunkey, to find out as soon as he could where Lee's entrenchments were, and then to assault them."[3] Judging by the cold record of fact, Ropes would appear to be right! But Meade had yet another idea, as shown in a letter on May 29th: " I am in hopes that we will continue to manœuvre till we compell Lee to retreat into the defences of Richmond." A still further possible explanation is that Grant did not really expect to accomplish very much by the move, but that it would bring him closer to Butler and the James. This idea seems to have been never very far absent from his mind. It is also possible that Grant was under the weather on the vital 29th–30th, and lost his usual drive. He had suffered from a sick headache a few days before, and perhaps had not completely recovered. On the other hand, Marlborough was a chronic sufferer from headaches but they did not seem to effect his operations.

Whatever may be the explanation of the apparent hesitancy in the operations of the Northern Army at this date, the fact remains that Grant had spent three days groping for Lee's flank in the area north of the Totopotomoy, while all the time Lee's army was to the south of it. It is also a curious fact that events had taken a somewhat similar course three times running. On every occasion the Army of the Potomac had started off boldly and well; on every occasion hesitancy or half-measures had supervened, allowing the Army of Northern Virginia to catch up, as it were. If Grant really wished to strike Lee's flank on the south of the Pamunkey before he had time to entrench he must have been aware by now that his only chance of so doing was to push in boldly, even blindly, not allowing Lee time to prepare a new position. Time was on the side of the Confederates—and it remained there.

Lee's forecast in his letter to Anderson of Grant's move by his

---

[1] *The Generalship of U. S. Grant*, p. 271.
[2] *M.H.S.M.* iv, 442.
[3] *Ibid.*, p. 395.

left had been fulfilled precisely—as striking an example as exists in this campaign of Lee's almost uncanny insight into his opponent's intentions and moves.

MAY 31ST.

Early's surprise attack on the 30th convinced Grant that Lee was beginning to manœuvre round his own left. Now the XVIII Corps, having disembarked, was approaching from that flank. The question thus arose, should it be flung straight against Lee's turning movement (an operation for which it was ideally placed) or should it join the army first? Grant seems to have favoured the second procedure for he ordered it to Newcastle Ferry, due east of Bethesda Church, whereas if he had favoured the first course he would presumably have directed it on to Coldharbor, three miles to the south. There are however some slight indications that he had in mind to attempt once more the " hammer and anvil " tactics, for in his orders to Smith he wrote: " The movement of the enemy on our left . . . would indicate the possibility of a design on his part to get between you and the Army of the Potomac. This will be so closely watched that *nothing could suit me better than such a move.*" Clearly his meaning is that in that case he would turn the remainder of his army on to attacking the Confederates and so get them between two fires. The XVIII Corps arrived at Newcastle Ferry without opposition by 3 p.m. But it was very tired, and weak in numbers. It was in fact somewhat of an uncertain quantity. It bivouacked for the night five miles east of Bethesda Church.

Grant had received a report that Hoke's Division from Beauregard's army was in the neighbourhood of Coldharbor. If this were correct, Smith would require help. Applying a manœuvre that he had practised at Spottsylvania, Grant now switched his VI Corps round from his right to his left flank. Marching all night and making a large detour, Wright approached Coldharbor on the following morning. (Sketch Map 10.)

Just as Grant heard of the approach of Hoke, so Lee heard of the approach of Smith, and took similar action. That is to say he ordered Anderson's Corps to move across to the right. The resemblance ends here. Lee's action was not defensive: Anderson was, on arrival, to attack in conjunction with Hoke, who was to come under his orders for the operation. Hoke's Division (not to be confused with his old brigade which joined Lee on the North Anna) was marching from Richmond, and reached New Coldharbor in the evening of the 31st. Lee would have liked to

MAP 10

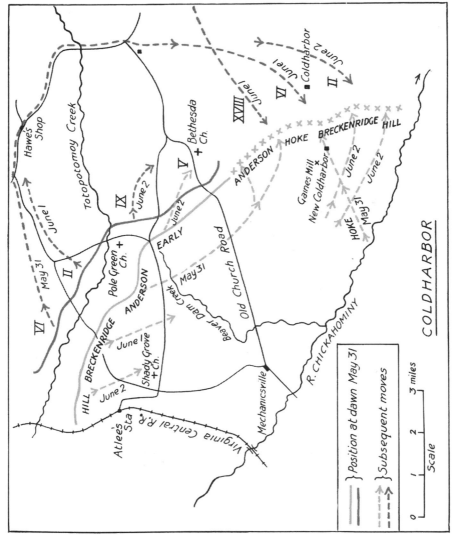

COLDHARBOR

Atlee's Sta.

Virginia Central R.R.

Mechanicsville

R. CHICKAHOMINY

Old Church Road

Beaver Dam Creek

Shady Grove + Ch.
June 2

BRECKENRIDGE
HILL
ANDERSON

Pole Green + Ch.

EARLY

May 31

June 2

June 2

IX

Totopotomoy Creek

Bethesda + Ch.

V

II

May 31

June 1

VI

Hawe's Shop

ANDERSON   HOKE

BRECKENRIDGE HILL

Gaines Mill ×
New Coldharbor ×

HOKE
May 31

June 2

June 2

XVIII
June 1

VI

II

Coldharbor
June 1

June 2

Position at dawn May 31

Subsequent moves

Scale

0   1   2   3 miles

control this attack in person, but he was still a sick man, and he did not feel equal to it. Anderson was therefore left to his own devices. His corps arrived to the north-west of Coldharbor in the night, and with Hoke on his right, opposite Coldharbor, he arranged to attack at dawn.

JUNE 1ST.

Anderson's attack duly took place at dawn; but it was no more successful than Early's had been on the previous day. The failure was all the more unpalatable because his opponents were cavalry (dismounted). Hoke had failed to co-operate. Wright was marching to the sound of the guns, and during the morning his VI Corps arrived on the battlefield, shortly followed by the XVIII. Grant, having defeated Anderson's attack, now took up the offensive in his turn. The VI Corps which had been brought round for the merely defensive role of supporting the XVIII Corps was now ordered, with it, to attack. This attack took place at 6 p.m, and was slightly more successful than that of the Confederates in the morning. A small salient was captured, and a number of prisoners taken.

Lee's counter to this was to order Breckinridge's Division round from its position between Hill and Early. This order was in fact given before the evening attack, but the troops could not be expected to arrive till next day. Lee also tried once more to entice Beauregard's army towards the decisive point. Trading on that officer's well-known ambition, he promised him that if he came he could have the command of the right wing of the army.

JUNE 2ND.

For nearly a fortnight the two armies had been manœuvring, without ever really getting to grips. This suited Lee's purpose for the time being, but it did not suit Grant's. The latter's declared intention was to destroy Lee's army before it could get within the Richmond defences. It was now within a few miles of those defences, and was far from having been destroyed. It was no longer possible to attempt another outflanking movement. Already Lee's right was within a mile of the Chickahominy, with the Richmond defences behind this forbidding looking stream. It was therefore a case of a frontal attack, or nothing. Further, it was a case of " now or never "; for delay would enable Lee to entrench and strengthen his position, in the way that he so well knew how. To transfer the Army of the Potomac to the James

River at this stage would have a harmful moral effect both upon that army and also upon the public.

Grant therefore determined to make one supreme effort to destroy the Army of Northern Virginia without more delay. His plan was a simple one—to throw an overwhelming force against Lee's extreme right flank before it had time to organise an effective position. Three corps were to form the hammer with which the blow would be delivered. On the right the XVIII Corps, in the centre the VI Corps, on the left the II Corps, which was pulled out of the line on the evening of June the 1st and marched all night to its appointed place on the left. The two remaining Corps, the V and IX, were to deliver subsidiary attacks, within the discretion of their commanders. Originally Grant intended to deliver this attack on the morning of the 2nd; but the " friction " of war was never more in evidence; the II Corps received conflicting orders and arrived late in its allotted position. No one was quite happy about the impending attack; indeed, Smith wrote bluntly that " an attack would be simply preposterous." The attack was therefore postponed till the afternoon, and again till the following morning.

Lee took good advantage of this respite, as may be imagined. He was gradually recovering from his indisposition; he seemed to " sense the battle from afar," and it reacted favourably upon his physical system. He mounted his horse and rode forward to Gaine's Mill, the scene of his first victory in the Peninsula. He had hoped to attack with Breckinridge's Division in the morning, but the same friction of war that had delayed the opposing II Corps infected Breckinridge also; he lost his way and did not get into the line on the right of Hoke till late in the morning. Meanwhile Lee had heard that the enemy was disappearing from in front of Hill. Concluding that this presaged an attack by Grant's left wing, Lee ordered Hill across to his own extreme right. This march was carried out expeditiously, in spite of the great heat, and by evening Hill's right extended to within half a mile of the Chickahominy. All danger of his right flank being turned had now vanished. But Lee was not content with this. Arguing that if Grant was intending to attack by his left he was probably weakening his old centre, he ordered Early to mount an attack in the direction of Bethesda Church, if he found a favourable opening. The ardent Early could be expected to find such an opening, and promptly he launched an attack. This attack had at first considerable success, driving the enemy back almost to Bethesda Church. But short of this place the enemy had run up some new defences, behind which they now took refuge.

The battle then died down, and both sides prepared themselves for what everyone realised would be a stern contest on the morrow.

JUNE 3RD. THE BATTLE OF COLDHARBOR.

How am I to describe this amazingly one-sided battle? Fortunately a long description is unnecessary. Grant had ordered an attack along the whole line, but the spear-head of the attack was at the southern end of the line, and was undertaken by the II, VI, and XVIII Corps. The last named was fairly new to this type of fighting; the other corps were veterans. Perhaps they had had *too* much experience: at any rate they laboured under no delusions as to what was in front of them; and many occupied the previous afternoon sewing their names into their clothing—a home-made form of Identity Disc. The *elan* that had distinguished their earlier attacks was therefore lacking among the serried ranks that at 4.30 a.m. moved forward to the attack. The result was the same practically all along the line. The attackers were met by a sheet of flame, and were mown down, almost as wholesale as if they had been caught in a machine-gun barrage. The attack was repeated time and again, but always with the same result. A portion of trench was reached here and there, which led Grant to issue a significant order to the effect that when a local attack did succeed in penetrating the line " push it vigorously, and if necessary pile in troops at the successful point from wherever they can be taken." This was the forerunner of what are now known as " soft spot tactics."

At the height of the battle Lee was visited by some Government officials. " General," asked one of them. " If he breaks your line what reserve have you? " Quick came the reply: " Not a regiment; and that has been my condition ever since fighting commenced on the Rappahannock. If I shorten my lines to provide a reserve he will turn me: if I weaken my lines to provide a reserve he will break them." This epitomises in a nutshell Lee's fundamental difficulty throughout the campaign.

At 1.30 p.m. Grant addressed Meade as follows: " The opinion of Corps Commanders not being sanguine of success in case an assault is ordered, you may direct a suspension of further advance for the present." This was a euphemistic way of recognising that the attack had come to a hopeless and complete standstill. More than 7.000 of his men lay dead or wounded, while the loss of the Confederates did not exceed 1,500. One staff officer described it as " perhaps the easiest victory ever granted to the Confederate arms by the folly of the Federal Commanders."

COMMENTS ON COLDHARBOR.

The critics, being of course wise after the event, have almost unanimously condemned Grant for attacking at Coldharbor. But I am of opinion that he was justified. It was a question of " Now or Never." If Grant's true aim throughout had been to defeat Lee before he could get inside the Richmond defences, he must take the bit between the teeth and attack at once. The longer he looked at it the more unpalatable the task would become —as Massèna found at Torres Vedras. If ever a risk was justifiable it was now. A more valid criticism is that he ought, realising the desperate nature of the task, to have taken more careful steps to ensure perfect preparation and co-ordination of the attack. Here again is shown up the vicious system of command. Meade, not Grant, was in charge of the actual arrangements, and Meade had not his heart in the business to the same extent as the Commander-in-Chief. Result, disaster.

If the bold course had been taken of directing the XVIII Corps against Lee's extreme right via Coldharbor, instead of bringing it into the centre of the line, striking results might have been obtained.* To attempt to join forces on the actual battlefield is widely conceded to be one of the most difficult feats of generalship. Napoleon used to declaim against it; yet his downfall at Waterloo is directly attributable to such an operation!

The use of oblique and even enfilade fire was largely responsible for the Confederate victory. It requires a fairly high standard of discipline to get troops to fire at any enemy except the one directly in front of them, which is a tribute to the fire discipline of the Southern Army. The heavy losses of the Germans at Le Cateau was largely due to this same cause.

REVIEW OF THE CAMPAIGN OF THE WILDERNESS.

General Grant's problem was a difficult one. It was, to get the Army of Northern Virginia out of its prepared position, and to defeat it in the open before it could withdraw inside the Richmond defences. To achieve this object there were three possible courses open to him. The first was to fall back himself, entice Lee across the Rapidan and then fall upon him in the open. This course was not seriously considered: considerations of moral were too strong. The second course was to get round Lee's rear and then force him to attack. This course was impossible of fulfilment owing to Lee's grasp of the situation and to

* Badeau asserts that Smith was intended to march via Coldharbor. But in any case his ultimate objective was in the centre.

his speed in movement. The third course was to get Lee on the move by threatening his flank and then to attack him in the open. To this course Grant bent all his powers. To accomplish it he made a series of five flank movements, all of which failed in their object, mainly for the following reasons:

No. 1. *The Wilderness.* This was spoilt by Lee himself taking the offensive.

No. 2. *Spottsylvania.* Spoilt because the II Corps was not moved off in the lead.

No. 3. *North Anna.* Spoilt because of the immobility of the II Corps at Milford.

No. 4. *The Pamunkey.* Spoilt because of Grant's own hesitation and slowness on May 28th and 29th.

No. 5. *Coldharbor.* Spoilt because Grant delayed in order to bring up the XVIII Corps by a circuitous route.

We will now review the relative moral effects of the campaign on the two participants. Opinions are agreed on this point. The North was cast down; the South was buoyed up with fresh hope. General Meade's comment was: " I think Grant has had his eyes opened and is willing to admit now that Virginia and Lee's army is not Tennessee and Bragg's army."[4] And the common talk in the Union ranks was: " It is no use who is given us. We can't whip Bobby Lee." On the other hand, Swinton bears witness to the fact that, ' the moral of Lee's army was never higher than after the battle of Coldharbor."[5] And, on the other side of the picture he writes: " So gloomy was the military outlook, and to such a degree by consequence had the moral spring of the public mind become relaxed, that there was at this time great danger of the collapse of the war."[6] One is forcefully reminded of the result of the prolonged Passchendaele offensive in the Great War The moral effect of operations on the general public as well as on the troops, is of paramount importance.

Next we come to the question as to how far Grant's new " attrition " policy had succeeded. The total Union losses came to over 60,000, including sick. Those of the Confederacy are not exactly known, but they are generally agreed to have been only slightly more than one-third of that figure. The striking disparity in the casualties could not be disguised from the civil population, and it played a big part in the lowering of the Northern moral.

---

[4] *Life and Letters of G. G. Meade,* ii, 201.
[5] *Campaigns of the Army of the Potomac,* p. 492.
[6] *Ibid.,* p. 495.

If attrition was to be continued indefinitely in the proportion of three Northerners to one Southerner there was a good chance that the North would " crack " before the South.

A word now regarding the rival commanders. In spite of many disappointments Grant had achieved a greater measure of success than his predecessors. For the first time in the war Lee was permanently reduced to the defensive. This degree of success was chiefly due to Grant's most striking and most laudable characteristic: his *tenacity of purpose*. The danger inherent in such tenacity is, however, that the line that divides it from sheer pigheadedness is a narrow one. When does the one merge, chrysalis like, into the other? This is one of the major problems confronting a commander. Where, for instance, if at all, did the one merge into the other in the Great War at Verdun and at Passchendaele?

II

Lee has received almost universal praise for his conduct of the campaign. Outnumbered by nearly two to one, he never made a major mistake. I consider him, however, distinctly open to criticism on two counts. First, for not bringing Longstreet's corps over from the left to the centre before the Wilderness. I cannot advance a satisfactory reason for this omission. Second, for not attacking Grant's right wing on the North Anna, on May 24th. The reason commonly given for this failure is Lee's indisposition on this day. There may be an element of truth in this; but a more probable reason (one that I have never known to be put forward) is that Lee (as stated in his confidential despatch to Davis) believed this wing to be retiring to the north bank of the river on the 24th, so that the opportunity to attack it under advantageous circumstances would be gone. In any case, the blow could only have been a partial one; Grant would only have been temporarily crippled. Lee's movements to counter those of his opponent were masterly in the extreme, though a cold analysis of the actual steps taken shows nothing spectacular, and students who expect from their heroes scintillating blows, such as that of Wellington at Salamanca or of Lee himself at Chancellorsville, will have to be disappointed! Lee's achievement was none the less a remarkable one, and it is well summed up by one of his subordinates, General J. B. Gordon: " Lee's native and untutored genius enabled him to place himself in Grant's position, and to reason out his antagonist's mental processes, to trace with accuracy the lines of his marches, and to mark on the map the points of future conflict."[7]

[7] *Reminiscences of the Civil War*, p. 297.

CHAPTER VII

The Crossing of the James.

AFTER the battle of Coldharbor both sides settled down to trench warfare for a few days, interspersed by some local offensives on the part of the Confederates.

On June 7th Sheridan started out on his second raid. His orders were to break up the railways to the north and west, and to effect a junction with Hunter (Sigel's successor in the Valley) at Charlottesville. He succeeded in his first objective, but the bulk of the Southern cavalry, under Wade Hampton—J. E. B. Stuart's successor—followed him and managed to get between him and his second objective. The only practical effect of the raid was that it deprived Lee of his " eyes " at a time when, as will be seen, he had most need of them.

Hunter's advance up the Valley was becoming threatening—he had already reached Staunton with 15,000 men—so Lee felt compelled to return Breckinridge with his 2,000 men to Lynchburg, which brought the total there to 9,000. Sherman, with a superior force, was also pushing J. E. Johnston's army back towards Atlanta.

The situation round Richmond thus became as follows:—

NORTH

Grant	.	.	110,000
Butler	.	.	10,000
Total		.	120,000

SOUTH

Lee	.	.	45,000
In Richmond		.	7,500
Beauregard	.	.	8,000
Total		.	60,500

Lee's intentions are indicated in a remarkable and significant statement of his to Early about this time: " We must destroy this army of Grant's before he gets to the James River. If he gets there it will become a siege, and then it will be a mere question of time." Freeman's comment on this is: " Clearly and unshadowed, he saw Appomattox from Petersburg."

On June 9th Petersburg was attacked by a force despatched by Butler for the purpose. Beauregard sent help to the very scratch garrison, and repulsed the attack. On June 11th Hunter, advancing victoriously, reached Lexington, at the southern end of the Valley. Lee thereupon took the bold step of detaching Early's Corps from his already weak army, and sent it to the relief of the Valley. Early's orders were to dispose of Hunter's force and then dash north and demonstrate against Washington.

Meanwhile General Grant was maturing his plans for his next step. Before the commencement of the campaign he had indicated that if he failed to defeat Lee in the open field before Richmond he might cross the James and attack from the south side, in co-operation with Butler. He had also had pontoons prepared for the crossing. The attempt to destroy Lee's army having manifestly failed, Grant now decided to put the second part of his plan into operation. Richmond, not Lee, was henceforth to be the objective, and Sheridan's raid was in the nature of a curtain-raiser to the main performance. If a city is to be reduced the first essential is obviously to cut off its means of supply. Sheridan's raid would, it was hoped, cut off the line of supply by the railway to the Valley. The main objective is given authoritatively in Humphrey's words: " To destroy the lines of supply to the Confederate depot, Richmond, on the south side of the James as close to the city as practicable after those on the north side had been rendered useless. The capture of Petersburg would leave but one railroad in the hands of the Confederates, though with that and its connections, they would still retain access to a large region of supply. Following the possession of Petersburg would be the turning of Beauregard's entrenchments in front of Butler and an advance towards Richmond. Finally, but not immediately, the remaining railroad would be severed, or, in anticipation of it, Richmond would be abandoned, and the Army of Northern Virginia would retreat towards Damville or Lynchburg."[1] (See Map B.)

The spot selected by Grant for the crossing was Wilcox Landing —Windmill Point, twenty miles in an air line south-east of Richmond. The move started on June 13th. II and V Corps went by a fairly direct route, leading past the battlefield of Malvern Hill; VI and IX Corps made a detour further to the east, while the XVIII Corps returned, as it had come, by water from White House on the York River. The move was effectually covered and screened from view by cavalry that had been retained for the

[1] *The Virginia Campaign of '64 and '65*, p. 198.

purpose. The wooded nature of the country rendered this a fairly simple matter. On June 14th the whole army, less the XVIII Corps which landed on Bermuda Neck, concentrated at Wilcox Landing. By midnight an immense pontoon bridge, 2,000 feet long, constructed in eight hours, was finished. Forty-eight hours later the army was across.

Early on the 13th Southern patrols discovered that the hostile trenches had been abandoned during the night. Lee promptly ordered a pursuit, and his whole army moved to the south-east of Richmond. So far all was simple. But the enemy's cavalry patrols prevented his own depleted cavalry from locating Grant's main army. Was he going to cross the James?

Lee guessed that he was; and as usual Lee guessed right. In a letter to the President on the 14th he wrote: " I think the enemy must be preparing to move south of the James River."[2] And still more positively to Bragg: " I think it probable that he will cross the James."[3] Lee therefore ordered Hoke's Division to Drewry's Bluff, ready to go on to Beauregard's aid if required. He obviously could not in this case take the bold action he had taken in the Wilderness when he foresaw the enemy's intention, because conditions were different. In the previous case he had room to manœuvre without endangering the capital—in fact his action tended to safeguard it—but in this case he could not afford to cross the river in anticipation of Grant's crossing, for it would uncover the city that he was expressly enjoined to protect. Lee was always punctilious about regarding the directions he received from the political head of the State.

JUNE 15TH.

Grant occupied the whole day crossing the James, while the XVIII Corps advanced against Petersburg. But the advance was so cautious and the reconnaissance by the Corps Commander on arrival opposite the works so deliberate that the attack was not delivered till 7 p.m. By that time Beauregard had scraped together a scratch collection which managed to hold up the attack before it had got very far. Grant had intended that Hancock's II Corps should assist in the attack; for this purpose it had been ferried across the river in advance of the remainder of the army. But owing to shocking staff work all along the line it did not arrive on the scene of operations till late that evening. The

[2] *Lee's Dispatches*, p. 70.
[3] *Ibid*. All further references in this chapter, unless stated to the contrary, are from *O.R.*, vol. 40, part ii.

IX Corps also was delayed by the Wagon Train starting to cross the bridge in front of it. Thus was a great opportunity lost to capture Petersburg.

Meanwhile what was Lee doing? We have seen how he had already correctly prognosticated Grant's crossing; he therefore started planning to move his army nearer Drewry's Bluff, still covering Richmond, when he received a message from Beauregard which led him to suppose that the crossing was merely the XVIII Corps, rejoining Butler. Cavalry activity on the north bank also contributed to this view. But early next morning, the 15th, he ordered Hoke to push right on from Drewry's Bluff to the help of Beauregard. At 11 a.m. an A.D.C. arrived from Beauregard, asking for help. But, according to Lee, he admitted that " the general was of opinion that if he had his original force he would be able to hold his present lines in front of General Butler and at Petersburg." Now Lee had already returned him all the " original force " that he had under his command, namely Hoke's Division. All that remained was Ransom's Brigade, which was in Richmond, under the President's direct control. Lee therefore asked Davis to send Ransom to Beauregard's army. This Davis did.

In the afternoon and again in the evening Beauregard wired to Lee *via* Richmond that he would require another division, and that he would have to abandon Bermuda Neck; but Lee had not received these wires by 2 a.m. on the 16th when he received the following further wire from Beauregard: " I have abandoned my lines of Bermuda Neck to concentrate all my force here. Skirmishers and pickets will leave there at daylight. Cannot these lines be occupied by your troops? The safety of our communications requires it. 5,000 or 6,000 men may do." On receipt of this message, Lee ordered Pickett's Division of Anderson's Corps to march *via* the Bluff to the help of Beauregard, and told Anderson to accompany it in person. So far, no reasonable person can aver that Lee had not done all that prudence required to meet the situation, as he knew it. Unfortunately for him he did not know it correctly.

JUNE 16TH.

Owing to the withdrawal of Beauregard's troops the X Corps was able to push back the pickets on Bermuda Neck and to cut the railway between Petersburg and Richmond. (Sketch Map 11.)

Meanwhile Grant's main front was being steadily reinforced.

By 9 a.m. the IX Corps was up on the left of the II, and the V was approaching on its left. But it was not completely in line till nearly midnight. Unco-ordinated fighting went on all day, and at 6 p.m. an organised attack by the II Corps assisted by portions of its neighbours was launched against the Confederate position. It succeeded all along the line and the enemy had to fall back upon a temporary line further to the rear. Counter-attacks during the night were unsuccessful. The system of command was nebulous on this day. Grant went on ahead of Meade, and passed the latter at noon, near City Point, coming from the front, to which Meade was only then on his way!

Hoke's Division had arrived at Petersburg in time to meet the attack of the II Corps. Pickett's Division was also on the way, and crossed the river at Drewry's Bluff between 8 and 9 a.m. This left only 18,000 of Lee's army on the northern bank.

At 9.40 a.m. Lee crossed at the same spot and set up his head-quarters nearby. At the same time he received a request for help from Beauregard. But the latter had as yet given no indication whether Grant's army had crossed the James, or whether it was only Butler's troops returning. Until he received some assurance on this point Lee did not feel justified in denuding the northern bank any further. By so doing he might fall into a trap set for him by Grant, who might suddenly spring upon Richmond from the north bank. The defence of the capital was his primary task. Lee therefore contented himself with replying: " I do not know the position of Grant's army . . . " a plain hint that Beauregard should procure this information. However at 1 p.m. Anderson reported that the troops on Bermuda Neck had been driven back and the railway cut. Lee on this ordered up the remainder of Anderson's Corps. Field's Division was to cross at once and Kershaw's was to wait for orders at the Bluff. Only Hill's Corps was now left on the northern bank; and Grant's whole army might be there, too. It was as painful and delicate a situation as any Lee had encountered in the whole course of the war. By 3 p.m. the situation was improving, for Anderson was now driving the enemy back on Bermuda Neck, and a more reassuring message arrived from Beauregard containing the welcome sentence: " We may have force sufficient to hold Petersburg." Throughout the day Lee was enquiring as to the presence of Grant's army on the southern bank, but without eliciting any reply on the point from Beauregard. At last, late at night, came more precise information from Beauregard, timed 7 p.m.: " There has been some fighting to-day without result. Have selected a new line of defences around the city, which will be occupied to-morrow, and hope to make it stronger than the first. . . . No satisfactory information yet received of Grant's crossing James River—Hancock's and Smith's Corps are however in our front." The natural inference from this message was that Hancock's Corps might only be a reinforcement to Butler: Lee seems to have put this interpretation upon it at any rate.

That day Lee was placed by Davis in supreme command of

SKETCH MAP II

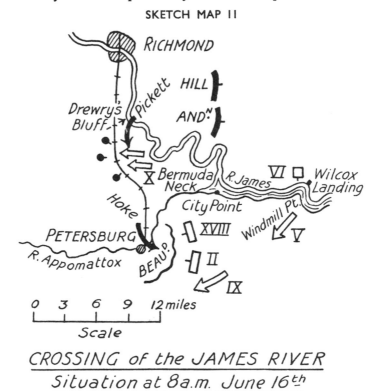

CROSSING of the JAMES RIVER
Situation at 8a.m. June 16th

all operations in Virginia and North Carolina—a unification of command that only a great emergency could apparently bring
13 about. (History repeated itself in the Great War.)

Grant was full of confidence on the 16th. He smoked but few cigars, and that evening he was observed to smile.

JUNE 17TH.

Owing to the strong resistance put up by Beauregard on the 15th and 16th, Grant appears to have had ideas of forcing a decision on Bermuda Neck, for he sent the XVIII Corps back there, and also the bulk of the VI. No attack was however made by these troops. On the main front several attacks were made by the IX Corps and some partial attacks by the II Corps. Very little success was achieved. The battle seemed to be turning gradually in favour of the Confederacy. A considerable success was attained by Pickett's Division on the Neck, and the old Confederate lines were regained. A curious message was however received by Lee from Beauregard, timed 9 a.m., which merits quotation in full. " Enemy has two corps in my front, with advantage of position. Impossible to recover with my means part of lines lost. Present lines entirely too long for my available forces. I will be compelled to adopt shorter lines. Could I not be sufficiently reinforced to take the offensive thus get rid of the enemy here? Nothing positive yet known of Grant's movements." It is probable that the final sentence was the one that stuck most firmly in Lee's mind. Grant's main army might not have crossed after all, and Beauregard was evidently maintaining his position, and his request for reinforcements was no longer in order to maintain his position but to take the offensive and drive the enemy right away. But Lee certainly could not spare the troops for such an object while the whereabouts of Grant's main army were still a mystery. In order to clear up this point he ordered his cavalry at 3.30 p.m. to " push after the enemy and endeavour to ascertain what has become of General's Grant's army."

At 4.30 p.m. however a message arrived from Beauregard, stating that still more of Grant's troops had crossed. The chances that Grant's main force might still be on the northern bank were now getting distinctly faint, and Lee felt justified in ordering his one remaining corps to the Bluff, and Kershaw from the Bluff to the Neck. Later in the evening the long-awaited message at last reached Lee that (according to prisoners) Grant's whole army was across the river. This was followed by another message from Beauregard stating that he would have to retire to shorter lines in the night and hinting that, if he did not receive reinforcements, he might have to abandon the town. On this, Lee ordered Kershaw and Field to push on to Petersburg, and Hill to cross the river at the Bluff.

During that evening and night Beauregard sent three staff officers in succession to demand a personal interview with Lee and to impress on him the desperate nature of his position. There is a certain amount of doubt as to what exactly happened at these interviews, though it is asserted that to the first of these staff officers Colonel Taylor said: "The corps you speak of as being in front of Petersburg . . . are reported by our scouts as being still in our front." What is quite certain is that at 3.30 a.m. on the 18th Lee, being now satisfied that Grant's whole army had crossed, ordered Hill's Corps to proceed right to Petersburg and shortly afterwards proceeded there himself.

JUNE 18TH.

Meade ordered a general assault of the lines for dawn. But the Confederates had quit and taken up their new lines. The Union troops accordingly spent the morning working up to the new position, which they attacked in the afternoon. But there was no sting in the attack: "the men went in without spirit," says Lyman, an eyewitness[4]; the troops were worn out, and there had been no time for artillery preparation. It is not surprising therefore that the attack was held up everywhere in front of the position. In vain did Meade, "the Peppery One," storm at his Corps Commanders. To one of them he wrote in flaming words: "I am greatly astonished at your dispatch. What additional orders to attack do you require? My orders have been explicit, and are now repeated, that you each immediately assault the enemy, with all your force, and if there is any further delay the responsibility and its consequences will rest with you." Anderson's troops had arrived in the nick of time, Kershaw at 7.30 a.m. and Field at 9.30. The battle of Petersburg was over. Petersburg was saved for the Confederacy, but it had been, in the Duke of Wellington's expressive phrase, "A damned nice thing."

COMMENTS.

No reasonable person reading this account of the crossing of the James for the first time—every statement in which can be substantiated from the records—would suppose that Lee has almost universally been charged by the critics with having been "surprised" by Grant, and with criminal inactivity while Beauregard was fighting for his life a few miles away.*

4 *Meade's Headquarters*, p. 170.
 * To give but a couple of examples: Badeau describes Lee as being "completely deceived," *U. S. Grant*, ii, 367.
 Even that eminent critic, General Fuller, writes: "Beauregard was attacked on the 15th, 16th and 17th, and sent message after message asking for support; Lee however did nothing till the 17th," *Grant and Lee*, p. 227. It is hard to understand how he could have penned such a passage after the publication (in 1915) of Lee's Confidential Dispatches.

The incontestable facts are: 1, that Lee expected Grant to adopt the course that he did adopt; 2, that it was only the failure of Beauregard to ascertain by what troops he was opposed that induced Lee to delay in moving his own army across the James; 3, that, in any case, he sent one division to the support of Beauregard before ever the latter asked for help; and 4, that he sent or caused to be sent, three divisions and one brigade by the evening of the 16th, although he still had no news of Grant's position.

On the face of it, it would be hard to say what more Lee would have been justified in doing, on the facts as known to him at the time (not to the critics with all the facts at their disposal) unless it be that he might have moved his army nearer to Richmond on the 15th. Even had he done so, the result of the battle would have been much the same, though the final line taken up might have been rather further from the town. " The proof of the pudding is in the eating "; the Confederate's pudding in this battle eats better than that of the Union! Freeman sums up the matter in the terse sentence: " Lee was not out-generalled nor taken by surprise."[5]

There are four main causes that led to Lee's mystification and apparent hesitation:

1. Lack of precise information from Beauregard.

2. Bad and misleading work by his own cavalry. Such information as they did give him seemed to indicate that only a portion of Grant's army had crossed the James so late as the evening of the 17th.

3. Grant's ability to disguise his movement, up to a point, by the fact that the XVIII Corps was in any case returning to Butler's command simultaneously with the move of Grant's own army. It is doubtful whether Grant foresaw the advantage this would give him in concealing his own movement. But in point of fact it played a considerable part.

4. The fact that Beauregard had frequently cried: " Wolf, Wolf! " during the preceding weeks no doubt tended to discount the urgency of his situation in Lee's mind on this occasion.

Turning now to the part played by the Northern Commander: All critics are agreed that the execution of his move across the James River was masterly, and this in spite of the fact that he had certain natural advantages, such as the wooded nature of the country, the paucity of the Southern Cavalry, the wretched state

---

[5] *Op. cit.*, iii, 445. See also Maurice's excellent comments in *Robert E. Lee the Soldier*, pp. 251–7.

of the intelligence service on the Confederate Petersburg front. Steele, to quote but a single tribute, describes it as " among the very finest achievements of strategy to be found in our civil war."[6] But if the work of Grant was praiseworthy up to the crossing of the river, it was lamentable after that.   He seems to have thought that " all was over except the shouting."   Freeman asserts that " the actions of June 15–17 were as much mismanaged as any that Grant ever fought in Virginia."[7]   No doubt his subordinates were largely to blame.   But the fact remains that for three days he had the best opportunity open to him throughout the campaign of winning a great victory.   In this connection it is of interest to consider the comparative strengths ranged in battle during those critical days.   Commentators frequently give the respective numbers on the south side of the James from day to day.   But a fairer figure is that of the troops actually engaged, for Grant's bridge was 19 miles from the Petersburg battle-line, a day's march, and troops at that distance could not affect the immediate decision.   I have therefore tried to compile such a table, but it must only be accepted as very approximate.

NUMBERS PRESENT ON THE BATTLEFIELD

Date	North	South
June 14	16,000	11,000
June 15—noon . .	36,000	19,000
7 p.m. . .	60,000	20,000
June 16—10 a.m. . .	76,000	27,000
June 17—dawn . .	96,000	31,000
evening . .	112,000	31,000
June 18—10 a.m. . .	112,000	50,000

From the above it will appear that the odds against the Confederates gradually rose from $1\frac{1}{2}$ to 1, to 4 to 1, and when the whole of Lee's army arrived the odds only sank to what they had been on the 16th, namely $2\frac{1}{2}$ to 1.   These odds sufficed to hold a defensive position equally on the 16th and 18th.   They also show that Grant's most favourable moment was on June 17th when the odds in his favour were over three to one.   On this, Ropes comments: " Grant does not seem to have been equal to the occasion on the 17th."   Such odds, however, for an attack on a defensive position, carried out by tired troops, are not excessive.   Roman's

[6] *American Campaigns*, p. 529.
[7] *Freeman*, iii, 444, note.

description of " fearful, almost incredible odds " is an abuse of language.

It should be noted that Beauregard had an open right flank throughout the battle. No attempt was made to turn this flank. It is however possible that the Union Troops were too tired to march round it.

This brings us to a consideration of the moral and physical state of Grant's army. Evidence on this point is unequivocal. The testimony of Meade himself will suffice. He attributed the failure to " the moral condition of the Army" and on the 21st he writes: " The army is exhausted and absolutely requires rest to prevent its morale being impaired."[8] This can be traced directly to the hammer blows delivered against it by General Lee's army.

A word is necessary on the conduct of the defence of Petersburg by Beauregard. It has received universal and unstinted praise. Roman speaks of " a feat of war almost without precedent."[9] Freeman writes that Beauregard handled his troops " with great skill and boldness,"[10] and Fuller considers " him probably the ablest of the Confederate generals " even including Lee.[11] I have searched the records to obtain particulars of this brilliant defence by Beauregard. The search has been somewhat barren. Beauregard took over the command of the battle in person on the 16th, setting up his headquarters in Petersburg. Thereafter he made the allocation of the various reinforcing units to the defence. He also traced out, with his chief engineer officer, the line to which he withdrew the troops during the night of the 17th. This line met with the approval of Lee on the following day. Beyond that I have not been able to ascertain how Beauregard influenced the battle. Therefore I am unable to appraise the correctness of the verdict so unanimously passed on him by the commentators. Unanimity in such cases is sometimes more imposing in appearance than in reality, namely when the commentators follow and copy one another. It may not be so in this case, but Freeman significantly remarks: " The excellence of Beauregard's battle grew as the story was told."[12] He attributes this growth largely to Colonel Roman, the author of Beauregard's biography. Roman describes the night retirement on the 17th as " one of the boldest manœuvres attempted during the war."[13] But he himself admits

[8] *Life and Letters of G. G. Meade*, p. 206.
[9] *Military Operations of General Beauregard*, ii, 227.
[10] *Freeman*, iii, 443.
[11] *Grant and Lee*, p. 193.
[12] *Freeman*, iii, 443.
[13] *The Military Operations of General Beauregard*, p. 233.

that before it was started " firing had almost entirely ceased." Night withdrawals, if the enemy is passive, are safer than daylight ones. The prosaic fact is that a general conducting a defensive war in an entrenched position can have very little direct influence on the fight. Lee had little at Coldharbor, and it does not seem likely that Beauregard had much more at Petersburg. The intensity of the attack on the 17th seems to have been exaggerated. One of Beauregard's staff officers in his report described the great battle of the 17th in the following mild sentence: " Skirmishing was very active in the morning, which in the evening increased to a battle." We have already seen that Meade attributed the defeat, not to the action of the opposing general, but to the moral condition of his own army (to which should in justification be added the mistakes of some of his subordinates). On the whole, then, the claim that Beauregard's defence of Petersburg was " a feat of war almost without precedent " must be set down as hyperbole.

CHAPTER VIII

General Comments on the Wilderness Campaign.

THUS ended a period of fighting the like of which had never previously been seen in the Civil War, nor was ever to be seen again. In this tremendous six weeks' campaign Grant had, by sheer will power, fought his way from the Rapidan to Petersburg. A new intensity of purpose in the leader, and a new ardour in the led, foreign to the old Army of the Potomac, had become evident. " In some subtle fashion General Grant infused into his well-seasoned troops a confidence they had never previously possessed."[1] Lee no longer commanded both armies. On the contrary, the Army of Northern Virginia had at last been placed permanently on the defensive.

But at what a cost had all this been achieved! Grant's casualties amounted to the tremendous total for those days of 64,000, nearly three times those of his opponents. Such losses could not fail to have a demoralising effect upon the troops. According to the historian Rhodes: " The morale of the troops was distinctly lower even than on the day after Coldharbor."[2] The effect upon the " home front " was no less profound: the national will for war was impaired, and a strong move for peace with those terrible Rebels began to make itself felt. The full import of the casualty figures has been disguised by some of Grant's apologists by the simple but ingenious method of giving them in the form of a percentage of the strength of each side. Livermore started this fashion, and he has been followed by the adherents of the Army of the Potomac. But such a method of computation is meaningless. An extreme example will illustrate my point. Suppose that an army of 10,000 defeats one of 100,000 and inflicts 5,000 casualties, and only loses 1,000 itself. It would be considered to have done pretty well. It would be no answer for its opponents to point out that it had suffered 10 per cent of casualties whilst they had only lost 5 per cent.

This method could only possess any validity if it were the fact that while the reinforcements available for the South were strictly limited those for the North were illimitable. Such was far from

[1] *Freeman,* iii, 447.
[2] *History of the Civil War,* p. 323.

being the case. The North was experiencing increasing difficulty in obtaining decent recruits. There had been serious anti-recruiting riots in New York and other towns. The quality of the drafts obtained was rapidly deteriorating; already no less than 30 per cent of the Army of the Potomac consisted of foreign-born troops; and the riff-raff who were forced into the service deserted in large numbers.

In spite of the immense casualty roll, the peace party could point to the fact that Grant was now further from Richmond than he had been at Coldharbor, and he was still opposed by Lee's intact army. Not only that, but Lee had dared to divest himself of one-third of his own army, and to send it away, with astonishing audacity, right to the Shenandoah Valley. To all outward appearances the situation was most unfavourable for the Union, and Ropes goes so far as to write: " The campaign must be pronounced a failure."[3]   Lee had good reason to be satisfied with himself. " His generalship had never been finer, if, indeed, it had ever been quite so good," is Freeman's final verdict.[4]

The frustration of his hopes was felt acutely by Grant, and it is not surprising to read that " The bitterness of disappointment drove him for a while to drink."[5]   It must be recognised that he had had many difficulties to contend with.   Coming to the East as a comparatively unknown character, he was confronted with the tremendous power of Lee's name.   Added to this, the Confederacy had the advantage of interior lines, both strategical and tactical. And it made good use of them.   Strategically, troops were transferred backwards and forwards between the Valley and the Army of Northern Virginia, and between it and Beauregard's army, as we have seen.   Tactically, at Spottsylvania, the North Anna and, to a lesser extent, at Coldharbor, Lee was able to transfer troops from one flank to the other quicker than Grant. The latter must be given full credit for the way in which his many exterior movements were carried out, but the best staff work in the world would not suffice to offset the advantage possessed by a nimble opponent such as Lee.

On the other hand, Grant had certain advantages over Lee. He was not, like his opponent, sick on 11 out of the 44 days of the campaign. Again, he had command of the sea, which enabled him to change his base no fewer than three times in the course of the campaign, thus shortening his communications and

[3] *M.H.S.M.* iv, 403.
[4] *Op. cit.,* iii, 447.
[5] *History of the Civil War*, p. 325

ensuring that his line of supply lay always perpendicular to his front. Regarding this matter of supply, the student may wonder at the apparent absence of difficulty with which corps were frequently transferred from one flank to another without any impairment of the supply service. The explanation is simple: during such movements the troops subsisted on rations carried on the person, or gathered in the country through which they passed. The trains only operated when the army halted.

The political factor enters into, and is apt to complicate, all military strategy. In this instance the Confederacy was more fortunate than the Union. The defence of both capitals was, of course, urged and enforced by political considerations. Apart from this, purely military considerations were paramount in the South. But the political game was played much more keenly in the North. Many of the commanders were " political generals." The virtual commander-in-chief, Lincoln, was primarily a politician himself. The Presidential election was approaching, and the course of the war was bound to be influenced by the success or defeat of Abraham Lincoln. Lee realised this, and it supplied the key to his strategy in 1864. Lee was content to stand on the defensive, trusting that the heavy casualties he could inflict on the Army of the Potomac would make the Northern public war-weary, and thus bring about the defeat of Lincoln, the incarnation of the war spirit. Political considerations forced on Grant the strategical objective of the Rebel capital. Agreeing with Clausewitz that the true objective is the enemy's main army, Grant tried to evade the mere siege of Richmond by arguing ingeniously that if he could defeat Lee's army the capital would automatically fall. It was only after a month's fierce fighting that he adopted directly the strategy required of him, and, giving Lee's army the slip, aimed a direct blow at Richmond itself. It has been averred that Grant's policy throughout was to " pin " Lee's army. It is difficult to see how he expected, or intended, to do this, either by attacking it in the first instance—" Where Lee goes there you will go "—or by slipping past it and attacking the capital. In truth, it is mighty hard to " pin " an army that does not wish to be pinned. Even Kluck could not pin Smith-Dorrien at Le Cateau; and try how we might, when did we ever succeed in pinning the Turkish army in Mesopotamia except by completely surrounding it? Lee's army remained at Richmond just so long as it suited it to. When it eventually decided that it would be a good time to quit, it quitted. But this is anticipating.

As to the system of command, though neither was ideal, the

Army of Northern Virginia had a distinct advantage. Its three corps received their orders direct from Lee, while the Army of the Potomac suffered from two disadvantages. First, the IX Corps was at the outset independent of it, although taking part in the same tactical operations. We have seen what muddles arose from this vicious system of command; and it is surprising that worse things did not befall it. Second, even after it was incorporated in Meade's army there remained the awkwardness, to put it no higher, that the strategical and tactical commands were vested in two different persons, living practically side by side. Grant asserted that he left all the details to Meade, but in actual fact he frequently interfered with the details. On the other hand Meade's staff tended to feel that they did all the work and that Grant received all the credit. Frequent passages in Meade's letters point to this, and Lyman wrote home that " Meade does all the work, so much so that Grant's staff really do nothing, with the exception of two or three engineer officers."

English students of the war should bear in mind the different type of discipline in vogue in both armies from what is generally met with in Europe. American writers tend to take this for granted, so that Henderson was justified in stressing it in *The Science of War*, where he pointed out, with prophetic perspicacity, that in a future world war we might find ourselves with a similar citizen army, and with a very similar system of discipline. " Our men will not all be regulars. They will come straight from civil life, and to civil life they will return. The habits and prejudices of civil life will have to be considered in their discipline and instruction."[6] Broadly speaking the American soldier of either army was accustomed to think for himself. In woodland fighting, in particular, this is essential if rapid progress is to be made. Unfortunately it carries with it the corollary that occasions may arise when the soldier will do *too much* thinking, in the sense that he will think differently from his commander, and may act accordingly. There was at least a suspicion of this at Coldharbor, and afterwards at Petersburg. It is the old dilemma—how to encourage intelligence without endangering dependability and obedience.

How far would modern weapons of war have modified the result? We have seen that in the Wilderness the modification would have been but slight. The same applies, though less markedly, in the remainder of the campaign. Nowhere was the country really open. Apart from the vast woodlands it was intersected with

[6] *Op. cit.*, p. 310.

rivers, swamps and creeks, which would have neutralised the effect of tanks, and, to a lesser degree, of armoured cars. Air work would also have been at a disadvantage, with one striking exception. The crossing of the James River by Grant's whole army could scarcely have gone undetected nor unimpeded for three days.

Mechanical transport would have been incommoded by the narrow, soft woodland tracks, where in the case of breakdowns it would seldom be possible either to reverse or to get a breakdown gang to work without great delay. Modern artillery would not be able to utilise its increased power and range to any great extent, and accurate survey work for the artillery would prove exceedingly difficult. Night marches—such a feature of modern war—were also a feature of this campaign; and it is noteworthy that an attack on top of a night march nearly always failed.

In short, we are led to the rather surprising conclusion that if another war were fought in Virginia the conditions and methods would not be so very different to what obtained in 1864.

The respective merits of the two great commanders in this campaign may be fittingly summed up in the words of General Sir James Edmonds in his introduction to the 1938 edition of *The Civil War in the United States*, by Wood and Edmonds. He concludes that Lee's conduct of the campaign " has never been surpassed as a masterpiece of defensive tactics." And he considers that Grant proved himself " a strategist of the highest order."

CHAPTER IX

Introducing the Atlanta Campaign.

To get this campaign into its proper setting we must go back to the autumn of 1863. On November 25th Grant defeated Bragg at the Battle of Chattanooga, and drove him back to Dalton, twenty-five miles to the south-east. Grant's army had consisted of the Army of the Cumberland under General Thomas, and the Army of the Tennessee under General Sherman. Meanwhile, General Burnside, with the Army of the Ohio, was successfully

14 opposing General Longstreet to the east of Knoxville. That winter various changes were made in both armies. Schofield succeeded Burnside, and J. E. Johnston succeeded Bragg, who became President Davis's Chief of Staff. Meanwhile Sherman had departed with his army for Vicksburg, whence in February he carried out a raid on Meridian.

This brings us to March 4th, 1864, on which day Grant, having been summoned to Washington to receive the appointment of Commander-in-Chief, wrote a valedictory letter to his successor, William T. Sherman. On March 10th the latter replied to it in a somewhat remarkable letter for a subordinate to write to his commander. ". . . I believe you are as brave, patriotic and just as the great prototype Washington: as unselfish, kind-hearted and honest as a man should be, but the chief characteristic is the simple faith in success you have always manifested, which I can liken to nothing else than the faith a Christian has in a Savior. . . . For God's sake and your country's sake come out of Washington. . . . I now exhort you to come out West. Here lies the seat of the coming empire, and from the west when our task is done we will make short work of Charleston and Richmond and the impoverished coast of the Atlantic."[1]

A short description must now be given of this remarkable man, the most colourful and dominating personality in the Union Army. The best pen-portrait I know is that of Badeau in his *Military History of U. S. Grant*. Badeau knew Sherman personally. "(He) was tall, angular, and spare, as if his superabundant energy had consumed his flesh: sandy haired, sharp featured;

[1] *O.R.* XXXII, iii, 49.

his nose prominent, his lips thin, his grey eyes flashing fire as fast as lightning on a summer's night; his whole face mobile as an actor's and revealing every shade of thought or emotion that flitted across his active mind; his manner pronounced, his speech quick, decided, loud.   His words were distinct, his ideas clear, rapid, coming indeed almost too fast for utterance; but in dramatic brilliant form, while an eager gesticulation illustrated and enforced his thought, simultaneously with speech itself. Boiling over with ideas, crammed full of feeling, discussing every subject and pronouncing on all, provoking criticism, and contradiction and admiration, by turns; . . . starting new notions constantly in his own brain, and following them up, no matter how far or whither they led; witty, eloquent, sarcastic, logical; every attribute of person or temper or intellect indicate genius . . . every peculiarity fascinated or commanded the attention."[2]   To this brilliant portraiture we may add a passage from a less sympathetic witness, Colonel Henry Stone: "Quick-eyed, ingenious, nervously active in mind and body, sleeplessly alert on every occasion, with a clear idea of what he wanted and an unyielding determination to have it, he made himself and everybody around him uncomfortable till his demands were gratified; and when that was done some other enterprise was undertaken, with the same tireless and exacting spirit."[3]

Sherman was at this time 44 years of age; a West Pointer; he had served in the Mexican War, and afterwards retired into civil life; served as a brigadier at Bull Run, and after that became Grant's right-hand man in the West.   His opponent, J. (" Joe ") E. Johnston, will not require so elaborate a description. The following is taken from Cox's *Atlanta*: " His military experience and knowledge were large, his mind eminently systematic, his judgment sound, his courage imperturbable. He was not sanguine in temperament, and therefore was liable to lack in audacity. Inclined by nature to a Fabian policy, it was settled conviction with him that in the existing conditions of the Confederacy such a policy should be imposed on the most audacious, unless a great blunder on the other side should reveal an opportunity for a decisive advantage."[4]   His age was 56.   He had commanded round Richmond till wounded at the Battle of Seven Pines, May 31st, 1862, but had incurred President Davis's displeasure for retreating from Fort Monroe.   He had afterwards commanded in the West.

15

2 *Op. cit.* ii, 19.
3 *M.H.S.M.* iv, 348.
4 *Op. cit.* 27.

Grant's grand plan for the '64 campaign consisted, as we have seen, of a main attack against Lee's army and Richmond, together with various subsidiary offensives, of which that of Sherman was to be the most important. On April 4th, Grant sent Sherman his orders. The operative passage reads: " You I propose to move against Johnston's army, to break it up, and to get into the interior of the enemy's country as far as you can, inflicting all the damage you can against their war resources." Sherman showed that he comprehended these instructions, for he replied: " I am to knock Jos. Johnston, and do as much damage to the resources of the enemy as possible." Later in his letter he adds: " Johnston is at all times to be kept so busy that he cannot in any event send any part of his command against you or Banks." It should be noted in passing, that in Grant's letter there is no mention of the word Atlanta, and that Sherman makes it quite clear that he is aware that his primary objective

16 is the opposing army. At the same time Atlanta was bound to bulk large in the forthcoming campaign. It was an important railway junction. In fact, it owed its very existence to the railway as much as does Crewe. Since the fall of Chickamauga, its importance as a railway junction was halved, but it possessed

17 large steel foundries, etc., and so would prove a valuable prize.

On April 17th, Grant visited Sherman and discussed the plan with him; and on his return he wrote to him again: " If the enemy on your front show signs of joining Lee, follow him up to the full extent of your ability. I will prevent the concentration of

18 Lee upon your front if it is in the power of this army to do it."

Meanwhile the Confederates were also plan-making—or trying to. On March 7th, General J. B. Hood, one of Johnston's Corps Commanders, with whom we shall have a good deal to do, wrote to President Davis, of whom he was a personal friend. He expresses the wish to " move to the rear of the enemy. We should march to the front as soon as possible, so as not to allow the enemy to concentrate and advance upon us. . . . He is at present weak and we are strong. . . . Your friend and obedient servant, J. B. Hood." This was quite after the style of Stonewall Jackson, under whom Hood had served; upon the latter Jackson's mantle was generally considered to have fallen.

A letter from Bragg to Johnston probably crossed this, instructing the latter to "draw him out, and then if practicable force him to action in the open field." On the 13th, Johnston writes to Longstreet: " We ought to let the enemy advance if he will, that we may fight him as far as possible from his base and near to ours." This passage shows a radically different viewpoint from that of Bragg, who had no wish to give up more territory than was necessary. On the same day Hood writes a letter (marked " Private ") to Bragg: " I have done all in my power to induce General Johnston to accept the proposition you made to move forward. Hardee (another Corps Commander) has written to the President."

Thus the Confederate leaders were at sixes and sevens, in unhappy contrast to their opponents. Indeed, Johnston's defensive attitude had created such alarm at Richmond that he sent his A.A.G. thither in order to explain that he " had no intention of expressing a disinclination to begin offensive operations. . . . On the contrary, he was anxious to advance being fully satisfied of the expediency and necessity." While his A.A.G. was taking this disclaimer to Richmond, Johnston was writing the previously quoted letter to Longstreet. Could prevarication go farther?

But whatever his real strategic views may have been, Johnston was rapidly knocking his new command into shape. Snow quotes the *Mobile Advertiser* in April as saying: "In ninety days he has so transformed this army that I can find no word to express the extent of the transformation but the word regeneration."[5]

While one general was quickening his army the opposing general was equipping his. The railway was commandeered, and vast quantities of stores were accumulated along it. In this work Sherman shone. He turned his command into probably the best equipped and supplied army in the Union. General McPherson had succeeded him in the command of the Army of the Tennessee, and by the end of April had brought his army back to the region of Chattanooga. The Army of the Ohio was also approaching, Longstreet having gone back to rejoin Lee in Virginia. In accordance with Grant's orders, the campaign opened on May 4th.

The armies and their approximate strengths can best be given in tabular form—with the warning that numbers on each side were constantly changing as reinforcements were continually coming up, and (in the case of the Union Army) detachments were being continually made.

UNION ARMY (General W. T. Sherman)
Army of the Cumberland (General Thomas)
IV Corps (Howard)
XIV Corps (Palmer)   60,000
XX Corps (Hooker)

5 *Southern Generals*, by W. P. Snow, p. 281.

Army of the Tennessee (General McPherson)
XV Corps (Logan)   }   25,000
XVI Corps (Dodge) }

Army of the Ohio (General Schofield)
XXIII Corps   14,000

Cavalry Divisions of Stoneman, Garrard,
McCook, Kilpatrick   10,000
—————
Total .   .   .   110,000

N.B.—XVII Corps (Blair), 9,000 strong, joined McPherson on June 8th.

The effect upon the operations of the disparity in size of Sherman's three armies will be dealt with later.

CONFEDERATE ARMY (General J. E. Johnston)
Hood's Corps   24,000
Hardee's Corps   24,000
Polk's Corps   20,000

May 13th onwards—
Wheeler's Cavalry Corps   8,000
Jackson's Cavalry Division (with Polk)   .   .   4,000 ·
—————
Total   .   .   .   80,000

CHAPTER X

Sherman *versus* Johnston.—Resaca and Cassville.

THE situation on May 5th when the campaign opened is shown on sketch-map 12. Sherman's primary task was "to knock Jos. Johnston"; his second was to penetrate into the enemy's country as far as possible. At first sight these tasks seem mutually contradictory. The first is a military, the second a geographical objective. To achieve the second it would be to Sherman's advantage to drive the enemy back. This might be achieved by threatening the railway in his rear, on which Johnston (like Sherman himself) was entirely dependant. But this would militate against the achievement of the first objective—the destruction of the opposing army; for the farther Sherman penetrated south the weaker he would become in relation to his opponent. Both commanders appreciated this, as their writings show. It is clear that the soundest way to carry out both his tasks would be to DESTROY JOHNSTON'S ARMY BEFORE IT RETIRED, AFTER WHICH HE COULD PENETRATE THE ENEMY'S COUNTRY AT HIS LEISURE. Before giving the plan that Sherman decided upon we must describe the position occupied by his opponent. Just west of Dalton runs a long rocky ridge, north to south. Two gaps—Buzzard's Roost Gap and Dug Gap—and the railway pass through this ridge. Johnston held a position on the ridge covering these gaps. This position has been described as impregnable to direct assault. It had, however, the great disadvantage that it was not square to the front; indeed, the centre portion ran parallel to the vital railway, with the right flank refused across the line. The left flank was thus the strategic flank, and would require careful watching. Ten miles south of Dug Gap the ridge was cut by another gap—Snake Creek Gap—seven miles long, and emerging opposite Resaca. Johnston gave orders for this gap to be watched. His army then consisted of about 60,000, but Polk's Corps was on its way and was expected to join in a few days. It only remains to add that the army had quite recovered its morale, which had been shaken by the events of the past autumn, and awaited the oncoming foe with confidence in its chief and in itself.

21

We can now get back to Sherman's plan. Shortly stated, it was to be a holding attack in front by the Armies of the Cumberland and Ohio, while the Army of the Tennessee threatened the hostile left flank. (Hereinafter these three armies will normally be designated by the names of their commanders—as also the Southern Corps by the names of their commanders.) Sherman's first idea was that McPherson should direct his attack against Rome (35 miles in rear of Dalton), approaching from the West. But for various reasons he modified this bold plan. It is a well-known fact that to effect a junction of armies from divergent directions on the actual battlefield is one of the most difficult operations of war—and sometimes one of the most risky. But it must be admitted that it would not involve as great risk against Johnston as against some of the other Confederate leaders. Be this as it may, McPherson was eventually ordered to march through the Snake Creek Gap and strike the railway about Resaca. In view of the controversy that has raged ever since on the part played by McPherson in the ensuing battle it is of importance to ascertain exactly what his orders were. Unfortunately, the matter is complicated by the facts that his orders for the operation are missing, and that he died before making a full report. There need, however, be no mystery about it if we carefully collate all the references made AT THE TIME by Sherman. I stress these words because, writing after the event, and after McPherson's death, Sherman gave a version of these orders which cannot be substantiated. He says: "I ordered General McPherson to move rapidly . . . via Snake Creek Gap, directly on Resaca, or the railroad at any point below Dalton, and to make a bold attack. After breaking the railroad well, he was ordered to fall back to a strong defensive position near Snake Creek Gap, and stand ready to fall upon the enemy's flank, when he retreated, as I judged he would." It is the words, " make a bold attack " in the first sentence to which objection must be made. Some historians implicitly accept this statement, by accepting as final and unaltered instructions Sherman's letter to McPherson of May 5th. This letter contains the phrase: " I want you to move to . . . Snake Creek Gap, secure it, and make a bold attack on the enemy's flank, or his railroad, at any point between Tilton (six miles north of Resaca) and Resaca." But from what he wrote ON THE DAY OF THE BATTLE it is clear that Sherman had made a small but essential alteration to his instructions. I refer to his despatch of this day to Halleck. In this despatch there is no mention of " a bold attack on the enemy's flank or his railroad," but simply "After breaking the road good, his orders are to retire to the mouth of Snake Creek Gap and be ready to move on Johnston's flank, in case he retreats south." Sherman repeated this statement in a despatch on the following day. So there can be no doubt about it. Sherman evidently visualised the situation as follows: Snake Creek Gap and Resaca would either be very lightly held or not at all. At all events McPherson would encounter no difficulty in breaking the railway. That, and that alone was to be McPherson's first and clear-cut task. This would dislodge Johnston by the threat of starvation. Sherman wrote to General Webster at Nashville: "General McPherson will there break the (rail)road *and leave Johnston out of rations.*"[1] McPherson was then to fall back into his spider's lair at Snake Creek Gap, and wait for the inevitable effect of his action—the retreat of Johnston. As soon as that began Thomas and Schofield would convert their demonstration into a vigorous attack upon Johnston's retreating army, while McPherson would spring out of his lair and attack Johnston's flank "boldly" as it went streaming past him.* Johnston would, he calculated, lose half his army and all his artillery and wagons. A pretty picture.

We will now proceed from plan to execution. On the north the operations of Schofield and Thomas developed successfully, and the Confederate picquets were pushed back into their main line. McPherson was equally successful in carrying out the first part of his task. Snake Creek Gap was unoccupied, and by noon on May 9th he was within two miles of the railway, with 23,000 men in or through the Gap. But unexpected resistance then developed. McPherson had very few cavalry, and his leading infantry were held up. The ground was difficult, the tracks all running the wrong way, and by nightfall only a handful of men had reached the railway and had not succeeded in damaging it. He accordingly resolved to fall back for the night to the Gap, and reported his· action in the following terms: ". . . After skirmishing till dark and finding I could not succeed in cutting the railroad before dark or getting to it, I decided to withdraw . . . for the following reasons: First, between this point and Resaca there are half a dozen good roads, leading north towards Dalton

---

[1] *Sherman's Historical Raid*, by H. V. Boynton.

* This is confirmed by Schofield, who, being one of Sherman's Army Commanders, should know. "His plan clearly appears to have been to make the main attack in front at the moment Johnston should be compelled to let go from his stronghold by reason of McPherson's operations in his rear, while McPherson . . . should strike Johnston in flank during the confusion of retreat."

down which a column of the enemy could march, making our advanced position a very exposed one. Second, Dodge's men are all out of provisions . . ." He adds that if he could have had a division of good cavalry he could have broken the railroad.

Resaca was, in fact, strongly held by a force of 4,000 men, and more were approaching. Johnston had no fear for it. He held the interior lines. Marching down the railway he could reinforce it in a few hours. Indeed, in the evening he did send three divisions to its help. They arrived next morning, but finding that McPherson had retreated they returned to Tilton. On the 11th, Polk's corps began to arrive at Resaca. On the evening of the 9th, Sherman was full of confidence in the success of his plan. To quote Lloyd Lewis: " 'I've got Joe Johnston dead!' roared Sherman, beating the supper table till the dishes rattled."[2]

Sherman was furious when he heard at 10 a.m. on the 10th of McPherson's failure; but he contented himself with replying to him: " I regret beyond measure you did not break the railroad, . . . but I suppose it was impossible." No mention, here, of failure to " make a bold attack." During that day Sherman meditated and corresponded on his next move. By the evening his mind was made up; he would pass his main body through Snake Creek Gap and attack Resaca. This operation he proposed for two days ahead, and explained his deliberation to Halleck: " Certain that Johnston can make no detachments, I will be in no hurry." He was also anxious to await the arrival of Stoneman's Cavalry Division before moving.

Without any undue haste, therefore, arrangements were put in train, and by dawn on the 13th Sherman's whole army, less one corps left in the old position to amuse Johnston, was debouching from Snake Creek Gap. That day was spent in cautiously feeling their way forward, pushing back the Southern picquets; and when in the evening they came in sight of Resaca they found Johnston's whole army drawn up in a strong position in front of the town! Just as Lee had so often won the race against Grant, so Johnston now for the first time won the race against Sherman. He had arrived there that morning. Round One: Joe Johnston wins!

COMMENTS.

The McPherson affair has given rise to much controversy and dispute as to the relative blame to be cast upon Sherman and his lieutenant. But I hope the way I have set out the facts

---

[2] *Sherman*, by Lloyd Lewis, p. 357.

makes it unnecessary for me to follow them in detail. More important for our purposes is to elucidate the lessons to be learnt. There appear to be two main ones. The first is the danger of picturing with too great precision and certainty the course of future events. The picture that Sherman (and probably McPherson also) had formed in his mind was faulty in two vital respects: it presumed that McPherson would experience next to no difficulty or delay in reaching the railway; and it assumed that his cutting of it would induce Johnston to retreat across his flank. All arrangements were made on this assumption; McPherson left his trains in rear of the Gap, for he assumed that he would be back from his railway raid by nightfall; he would then have ample time to replenish stores while Johnston was getting under way. If he had not formed such a fixed picture of what would happen he would have provided for the possibility of delay in cutting the railway and ensured that food should be available for his troops wherever they found themselves at nightfall.

The second lesson is that a force attacking on exterior lines must not allow the enemy time to manœuvre. Either both portions of Sherman's army should have attacked almost simultaneously or a portion at least of Thomas's Army should have been within a few hours' supporting distance of McPherson, instead of being a day's march distant.

Sherman suggested in his Memoirs that McPherson " could have placed his whole force astride the railroad above Resaca. . . . Had he done so I am certain that . . . we should have captured half his army and all his artillery and wagons." But his orders to McPherson never suggested such an operation. He goes on: " McPherson seems to have been a little timid,"* but stultifies his whole case against him by adding (quite truthfully), " Still, he was perfectly justified by his orders."

Some American critics (disgruntled adherents of Thomas) are unduly hard on Sherman. They criticise him for not sending the Army of the Cumberland (as proposed by Thomas) instead of that of the Tennessee against Resaca. But, apart from the complication that would have been involved in crossing two armies over each other, the result would not have been different, *always assuming that Sherman's orders remained the same.* If 23 Thomas had succeeded in damaging the railway and had then withdrawn to Snake Creek Gap the course of the battle would have remained the same; Johnston would have retired to Resaca at

---

* It is significant that Sherman altered the word " timid " to " nervous" in his second edition (but it remained " timid " in the English edition).

his leisure. A sounder criticism would be to arraign Sherman's orders to McPherson. Instead of cutting the railway and running away again, he should have been directed to do the very thing that Sherman afterwards regretted that he did not do, namely, " placed his whole force astride the railway." This criticism is endorsed by General Schofield, who proclaimed himself a friend and admirer of Sherman—though a candid friend. His conclusion, with which, I think, every unprejudiced student is bound to agree is: " Impartial history must, I believe, hold Sherman himself mainly responsible for the failure."[3] His own solution is: " Thomas's position . . . was virtually as unassailable as Johnston's. . . . At least one half of Sherman's infantry should have been sent through Snake Creek Gap to strike the enemy's rear." Two or three brigades could invest Resaca and the remainder take up a position astride the railway.[4]

Both Steele and Stone are severe on Sherman for his dilatory movements after the 9th. Steele goes so far as to say: " Sherman apparently had an opportunity to destroy Johnston's army at Resaca, but neglected to take advantage of it " first by slowness on the 13th, and later: " If Sherman had shown boldness and attacked Johnston with the whole strength and vigour of his army on the 14th, or even on the 15th, he must have captured a large part of Johnston's army before it could have gotten across the river. But instead of trying to destroy Johnston's army, Sherman simply manœuvred it out of its position."[5] The latter part of this criticism at any rate is sound. Stone calculates that by the evening of the 11th, 70,000 troops could have been concentrated in Snake Creek Gap, ready to seal Johnston's fate next day. But this is probably an optimistic calculation and does not allow for the " friction " of war, which, incidentally, was very much in evidence on the 12th and 13th. Stone sums it up: " Thus ended in failure, dissatisfaction and humiliation the first of Sherman's great flank movements." Nevertheless, Sherman must be given credit for one thing that has generally escaped notice. When he did eventually propose to switch almost his entire force to Snake Creek Gap, and asked Schofield for his opinion, the latter expressed the fear that Johnston would make a dash for Chattanooga. To which Sherman replied: " Chattanooga cannot be taken by Johnston with us on his heels. I'll risk that."[6] This showed on Sherman's part a refreshing

[3] *Schofield*, p. 126.
[4] *Ibid.*, p. 124.
[5] *American Campaigns*, p. 550.
[6] O.R. XXXVIII, iv, 123.

combination of shrewdness and of willingness (at the outset of the campaign) to take risks that are the hall mark of the great commander.

Johnston's conduct of the operations had been flawless—if we except the failure to hold Snake Creek Gap, about which there is some dispute: Johnston's Chief of Staff, General Mackall, told Colonel Stone that it was due to "flagrant disobedience of orders." Johnston, fully aware of the advantage which interior lines conferred upon him, timed his departure till the last possible moment; it could scarcely have been better timed or better carried out; and his despatch of Hood to strike McPherson's left flank   24 was excellently devised.

FROM RESACA TO ALLATOONA. (*Sketch Map* 12.)

The battle of Resaca took place on May 14th and 15th. On the first day Hood attacked the Union left and McPherson attacked the Confederate left, both attacks achieving only partial success. But on the second day one of McPherson's divisions on the extreme right crossed the Oostanaula River and threatened Johnston's rear. During that night, therefore, the Southern Army resumed its retreat, and for five days retreated almost uninterruptedly. Johnston had intended to stand at Adairsville, but changed his mind; and again at Cassville, with the same result. The story of this last change of plan is a curious one, and has never been set out in detail outside the Official Records. As it contains a good example of the *imponderabilia* of warfare it is worth relating.

The Southerners had retreated from Adairsville by two diverging roads: Hardee took the Kingston road which ran due south, while the other two corps (Polk's had now all arrived) took the Cassville road running south-east. Sherman sent one division to capture Rome on his right flank, while the remainder pursued in four columns on a fairly wide front. It has been asserted—and repeated—that Sherman purposely assumed a wide front in order to tempt Johnston to battle, so that at the moment when Johnston struck, Sherman by his wider front would be able to envelop his opponent's attacking flanks. The facts will not sustain this theory. Nowhere does Sherman state that such was his intention, and his orders and messages at the time indicate clearly that his object in assuming this wide front was merely to utilise as many roads as possible. In the case of an army of over 100,000 men, marching on unmetalled roads, that is a natural course to take. It indeed seems likely from the reports sent in by his column commanders that a wider front was taken up than Sherman anticipated. It must be remembered that maps were bad, and communications, when the whole army was on the move, were precarious. For forty-eight hours, from May 17th to 19th, Schofield received no direct orders from Sherman, and his messages to his chief grew almost despairing in tone. McPherson, on the other wing, also exclaims distractedly that he " did not know what to do." The fact is, that so far from wanting a wide dispersion of his columns, Sherman wished to keep them as closely united as possible. While yet at Calhoun, he formed the opinion—almost assumption—that Johnston would advance upon Kingston; and he ordered his left-flank column, that of Schofield, to converge on that town. The other columns were to do the same. On the 18th, being confirmed in his opinion that the whole Confederate Army had retreated on Kingston, he ordered all his columns to concentrate on that town on the 19th. Writing to Halleck he said: "I now have four columns directed on Kingston with orders to be within four miles by night." These four columns were, from right to left, McPherson, Thomas's IV and XIV Corps, Hooker's XX Corps, and Schofield's XXIII Corps. Sherman's plan was clear and simple: if Johnston stood at Kingston he would overwhelm him with a tremendous concentration: if Johnston retreated, he would follow him up and attack as soon as he got within striking distance. Those were the two possibilities. Sherman does not seem to have considered a third—but Johnston, as we have seen, was disobliging enough to take a third.

MAY 19TH.

This day deserves a section to itself, for the events on it were about the most curious and remarkable of the whole campaign. Sketch map 13 illustrates Sherman's plan for the day, founded on the assumption that the Southern Army was concentrated at Kingston. But in reality it was concentrated in the position at Cassville (marked dotted in the sketch map). If, therefore, Sherman's orders were carried out in accordance with his wishes Johnston would be provided with a splendid opportunity to strike his opponent's left wing as it passed across his front. But was Johnston prepared to take the offensive? Yes, he was! On the evening of the 18th his somewhat outspoken Corps Commanders had pressed on him the opportunity that now presented to strike the enemy in detail. It is very likely that Johnston

MAP 12

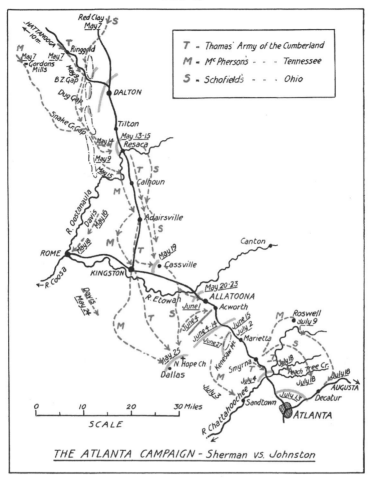

THE ATLANTA CAMPAIGN - Sherman vs. Johnston

needed no urging, and that Hardee's diversion to Kingston and then back to the main army at Cassville was intended to mislead and disperse the enemy, though I can find no direct contemporary evidence on the point. Anyway, Johnston on the morning of the 19th issued a grandiloquent order, including the phrase: " You will now turn and march to meet the advancing columns." The battle ground was to be just north of Cassville. Hardee was drawing in from Kingston on the left, Polk was in position

SKETCH MAP 13

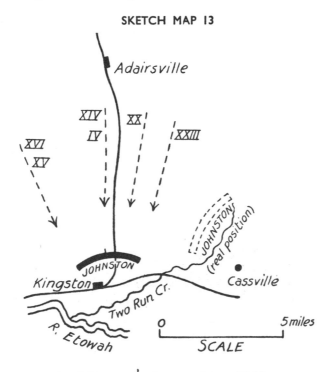

SHERMAN'S PLAN May 19th

in the centre, and Hood on the right was now ordered to throw his right shoulder forward, and come up in line with Polk, preparatory to a general advance to the attack. No actual orders for attack were issued, perhaps because, up to noon, no considerable bodies of the enemy had been located. But it was generally supposed that about half the Union Army was advancing on Cassville and the other half on Kingston. Actually, as we have seen, it was not Sherman's intention that *any* of his army should advance on Cassville.

Leaving the curtain down for the moment on the Northern columns, we will follow the peculiar turn of events in Hood's Corps, as it started to move forward.   The movement had only just commenced when General Mackall was sent with a message to Hood, and found him, to his surprise, starting to draw back his line again.   Hood explained that the enemy had been reported advancing on his right rear on the Canton Road and that he was throwing back his flank to face them.   When this report reached Johnston he expressed his incredulity, as that area had been reported free of the enemy.   According to his A.D.C., Lieutenant Mackall (son of the Chief of Staff), Johnston then called for a map and having studied it, exclaimed: " If that's so, General Hood will have to fall back at once."   The attack was called off, and, not content with that, Johnston withdrew his whole line to a position on a line of heights behind the town of Cassville. This line was occupied that afternoon, and Johnston informed the Mayor of Cassville that he was ready to accept battle on the following day.   But later that evening the Northerners who had followed up his withdrawal brought some guns up and started shelling the new line from a spot whence they could enfilade it. This was pointed out by Johnston's artillery commander, and also by Polk and Hood, who were holding a conference with Johnston. They told him they would prefer to attack next day rather than hold that position.   After a long silence the Commander-in-Chief, not wishing to defend a position in which two of his Corps Commanders had no faith, and presumably not wishing either to attack, incontinently gave orders for a further retirement. The retreat was carried out that night in haste and confusion. To the troops who had just been bolstered up by the welcome announcement that the retirement was at an end, this further retreat made a painful impression and their morale was for a time impaired. We must now return to the Union side in order to discover how the Confederate stroke had been foiled.   Was it due to some action on the part of the Army Commander; or of some quick-witted subordinate; or was it merely " the fortune of war?"   It was " the fortune of war," as shall now be related.

Sherman's intentions were not carried out, partly because he had inadequate maps, partly because his couriers got lost, partly because his column commanders got lost, and finally because a small unit in the XX Corps got lost! But—and this is the amazing part—the very fact of these setbacks proved the downfall of Johnston's plans, as the following narrative will show.

The two right columns took approximately the road intended,

but the other two veered to their left, leaving Adairsville on their right hand and bearing down from the north on Cassville, Hooker leading and Schofield following in his tracks.*

Thus, instead of Johnston striking the Union left column in flank, as should have happened if Sherman's orders had been carried out, he found himself confronted by two Corps, who, when he retired followed him up and shelled his new position that same evening, as we have related.

But what about the flanking force that caused Hood to suspend his forward movement, and ultimately to result in the attack being abandoned? Johnston afterwards bluntly stated that the report was " manifestly untrue." But Hood gave circumstantial details, including the fact that five men fell wounded almost alongside him. Johnston's A.D.C., Lieutenant Mackall, gives the apparent reason two days later in his excellent diary: "Learned about the failure at Cassville from ——; mistake about name of road 'Canton,' " i.e. the flanking force was wrongly reported to be on the Canton road. But that was not the end of the matter, for, in 1874, General Carson, who was in the Union Army, stated that there *was* such a force on the Canton road, and that it belonged to Butterfield's Division of the XX Corps. Strange to relate, neither Butterfield, nor anyone else, as far as I have been able to ascertain, ever gave any explanation of its presence on this road. The strong probability therefore is that it had lost its way, and in its efforts to rejoin its companions had unwittingly been instrumental in foiling the best opportunity Johnston ever had presented to him of defeating his redoubtable opponent!   25

What lesson are we to learn from this extraordinary episode? Surely this, that in war " the best plans gang agley," and that all ranks must be led to expect the unexpected, so that when the unexpected does supervene it will not throw us off our balance, as Hood appears to have been on this occasion. Look at it how we will, it is incontestable that Hood " blotted his copybook "— to use a slang but expressive phrase. But it must never be forgotten that he was a cripple, and handicapped in finding out things for himself. And Johnston? Was he not guilty of infirmity of purpose, both that afternoon, and again that evening

---

* I purposely leave the exact route vague, for the good reason that no man alive, either then or since, seems to be certain of it! The maps were atrocious, and Schofield, who is more precise in his account than anyone, remarks that the map (in the Official Records Atlas) is inaccurate, but does not say in what respect! To add to the difficulty the O.R. Atlas maps are themselves sometimes contradictory.

when he found himself at variance with two of his Corps Commanders? At the moment when Hood was advancing to the attack the situation was, as near as I can estimate it, as shown in sketch map 14. From this it will be seen that he had an excellent opportunity of delivering a heavy blow against Sherman's two leading Corps. Even when reinforced by the XIV and XXIII Corps he would still be in superiority, and McPherson could not hope to reach the battlefield that day, for he was halted at Woodland, seven miles north-west of Kingston till 1 p.m. or later. And right up till the evening Sherman shows no glimmerings of perception of the fact that the whole Confederate Army was concentrated at Cassville.

Johnston crossed the Etowah and took up a position astride the Allatoona Pass, where he rested his troops for the next three days. Sherman also rested his army for three days at Kingston whilst he repaired the railway and got up supplies.

COMMENTS.

Sherman in this stage of his advance exposes himself to many criticisms.

1. It has been urged that he should have advanced straight on Cassville from Resaca, thus cutting the corner made by the railway at Kingston. If Johnston took the roundabout Kingston road, Sherman would thus either overtake him or turn his flank. There seems no answer to this criticism. His reason for taking the Kingston road is one that leads on to the second criticism.

2. Sherman was again wedded to a preconceived idea—that Johnston would concentrate on Kingston. It must have been present in his mind on the 17th, when he ordered Schofield, his easternmost army, to march on that town. The result shows the danger of becoming wedded to an idea as to " the probable course of the enemy." It never does to " go bail on it."

3. Though it appears on the surface at times as if Sherman was intentionally adopting the march formation of " parallel lines " that cannot have been really his intention. His intention clearly was to draw in all his columns at the point where he expected his enemy to make a stand. He did this at Adairsville, and again at Kingston. Between whiles he allowed his columns to sag outwards in the search for roads—merely as a convenience for more rapid and comfortable marching. He would have done better to adopt deliberately the formation of parallel lines. The theory underlying this formation (as preached, but not practised,

by the Germans) is that all the columns march straight to their front till the enemy is encountered by some of the columns; the remainder, continuing straight to their front, thus automatically turn the flank of the hostile position. In this case his four columns, covering a front of about twelve miles, would have included both Kingston and Cassville; the left columns would have been held up at Cassville (as they were), while the other two, *without checking their march*, would have turned Johnston's

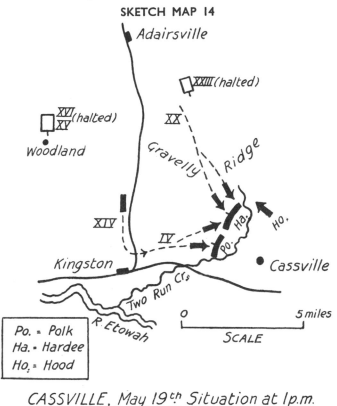

SKETCH MAP 14

CASSVILLE, May 19ᵗʰ Situation at 1p.m.

flank, and if he did not retreat, close in on his flank and rear. In any case, when the moment of contact came, his columns were for all practical purposes reduced to two. The reason for this brings us to our fourth criticism.

4. Owing to the unequal size of his armies Sherman found it difficult to control them.* The Army of the Cumberland was

* For some time Sherman was completely out of touch with Schofield, and was reduced to asking Hooker to pass on orders to him.

too big, the Army of the Ohio was too small. By detaching Hooker from Thomas's line of march on the 18th–19th, Sherman in effect divided his army into three groups of two corps each, a very sensible division—if a commander has been detailed for the new group of the XX and XXIII Corps. But there lay the difficulty. Apart from local territorial jealousies, Hooker was senior to Schofield, but he was only a Corps Commander, while Schofield was nominally an Army Commander. Washington had not laid it down definitely which should rank in such a case; consequently trouble of this sort was to recur more than once. The result of there being no commander to these Corps was that they both got on to the same road, and Schofield complained that he was blocked by Hooker.

5. Sherman's handling of his cavalry was not impressive. Though he possessed four Divisions he never employed them as a whole. Instead he used them individually, usually one on each flank, and one, or two, in reserve. Consequently when he ordered some big effort, such as the breaking of the line behind the Confederates, the cavalry generally failed him—as they did between Resaca and Allatoona.

Johnston must be credited with the brilliant stratagem of dividing and then reuniting his forces, in order to induce his opponent to divide his, and so offer an opportunity to strike them in detail. But for uncommonly bad " fortune of war " this stratagem would have brought its reward. But Johnston was himself partly responsible for his lack of success. A really great offensive general would have ignored the reported danger to his flank, once he had ordered his troops forward to the attack. Did Jackson hold up for a moment his flank march at Chancellorsville when he heard that his rear was being attacked?

Johnston cannot be acquitted of infirmity of purpose—except on the supposition that his heart was not in the attack and that he was only too glad of an excuse to call off the battle. The apparition of the flank force in the morning, and the difference with his Corps Commanders in the evening, afforded such an excuse. In either case, the morning episode is a first-rate example of the extreme sensitiveness of the flank of a retiring force.

It has been argued, with some force, that Johnston should have abandoned the Atlanta line and retreated through Rome towards the south-west. The contention is that Sherman would not have dared to push on towards Atlanta, leaving his right flank exposed; whereas if he pursued Johnston, the latter would fall back to the Selma–Meridian railway, which would feed him, while Sherman would not be able to exist more than 100 miles from his railway. Johnston does not seem to have seriously considered this course of action; and in the unlikely event of its appealing to him there would probably have been an outcry from Richmond, and from the Governor of Georgia, who would not relish the risk run. We shall see later how General Hood fared when he adopted this course.

A Note on the Cassville Affair.

Most historians seem content to leave this affair an open question, treating it as merely one man's word against another's. But it is difficult to see how there can be any doubt about the facts, when all the relevant statements in the Official Records and the various memoirs are considered. Taken together, they can be pieced into a perfectly coherent picture—the one that is given above.

As to the first point at issue,* namely whether there was a hostile force on the Canton Road, and Johnston's assertion that the report was " manifestly untrue," Hood's statement was, as we know, corroborated from the Federal side in 1874; the force in question formed part of Hooker's XX Corps. How it came to find itself on the Canton Road is not clear. Most probably, as I have already suggested, it had lost its way: it not infrequently happens that a force that has lost its way unwittingly contributes to the victory of its own side!   26

As to the conflicting versions of what happened at the famous conference at Cassville, Johnston declared in his " Narrative " that Hood urged a retreat " across the Etowah." Hood, however, was emphatic that the contention of Polk and himself was simply that the position selected was a bad one and that either it should be changed or that an offensive should be launched from it next morning. Johnston's Chief of Staff was not present, but years after the war the matter was happily settled when it was discovered that there had been a witness throughout the conference, one Captain Morris, Polk's Chief Engineer.† Morris exactly corroborated Hood's story, stating *inter alia* " these Generals (Polk and Hood) both advocating to the Commanding General to take the offensive and advance on the enemy from these lines." Hardee eventually joined the conference, but he

* Johnston's claim to have ordered an attack on the 18th is evidently a mistake for the 19th.

† General French, a divisional commander, was present at the start, but left before the salient part.

does not appear to have done much except express surprise at hearing that the other Corps Commanders did not like their position. As he had not seen it himself this does not amount to much. Morris, on the other hand, not only had seen it but had made a detailed plan of it and of the dispositions of each side. This plan and report are printed in Hood's book, and I as an artilleryman have no doubt that the centre portion of the position 27 would have been rendered untenable by the Federal artillery.

CHAPTER XI

From the Etowah to the Chattahoochee.

SHERMAN now decided to cut adrift from his railway for a time, and make across country for Marietta, and then the Chattahoochee. In his own striking words: " The Etowah is the Rubicon of Georgia. We are now all in motion like a vast hive of bees, and expect to swarm along the Chattahoochee in a few days." So, having provided his army with twenty days' supplies, he set out on May 23rd. The army marched in three columns, through a wild, mapless country. On the third day, while still fifteen miles short of Marietta, the centre column bumped into Johnston's Army, formed up in battle order, near New Hope Church. Again Johnston had blocked the way—again reminiscent of the Lee-Grant duel then in full swing 500 miles farther north. Johnston, again utilizing his interior lines had quietly slipped across to his left, and on the 25th occupied a position from Dallas to north of New Hope Church. On the 27th Sherman assaulted this position, 28 attempting to turn its right, but without success. He then decided to switch his army to the left; but next day Hardee on the Confederate left attacked McPherson so fiercely that the move was postponed.

Sherman had, for the time being, been foiled. But he still had 14 days' supplies in hand, and it was open to him to continue his movement to the right (just as Grant was doing in Virginia, and with such success). Why, then, did he decide to abandon it 29 and switch across to his left? From Dallas the Chattahoochee, along which he had hoped to be swarming, was distant twenty miles in an air line. Sherman gives the reason in his Memoirs, written eleven years later. From this it appears that his objective was the railroad, not Marietta. He therefore began edging towards it. On June 1st his cavalry occupied Allatoona, and the repair of the railway was at once put in hand. On June 4th Sherman moved his whole army across to the railway at Acworth. Whether he really expected to get round Johnston's flank by so doing is doubtful. At any rate, when he reached the railway he found that his opponent had simultaneously moved on a parallel course, and for the third time in a month was blocking his further advance.

The Confederate position was a strong one, ten miles in extent, with its centre in front of a commanding eminence called Kenesaw Mountain.

Heavy rain now fell, turning the roads into mud troughs, and making mobile operations practically impossible. Thus Sherman found himself in an *impasse*. He had in a month gained eighty miles of territory, and had certainly " kept Joe Johnston quiet." But the relative strengths of the two armies had changed to his disadvantage. Though his casualties had been under 10,000— only slightly greater than the enemy's—Johnston had received more reinforcements than himself, and owing to necessary detachments the respective strengths of the field armies were in a proportion of about 5 to 4. But on June 9th the position was improved by the arrival of Blair's Corps of 9,000 for the Army of the Tennessee. Probably Sherman regretted that he had been lured back to the railway, while the going was still good.

On June 14th, General Polk was killed and was succeeded by Loring, and shortly afterwards by Stewart. The same day the centre of the Southern line was brought back to Kenesaw Mountain itself. On the 21st Hood, having been rapidly switched across from the right to the left, made a counter attack on Hooker which, though unsuccessful, resulted in a division that was working round Johnston's left flank being recalled. It also resulted in a quarrel between Sherman and Hooker.

The rains still continued, but Sherman decided that something must shortly be done to prevent Johnston detaching troops to Grant. Movement round a flank was for the moment out of the question for it would involve leaving the railway. All that remained was to attack the Confederate position. Now this position was dangerously extended, and it was probable that it was held lightly in some parts. The centre, on the slopes of Kenesaw Mountain was by nature the strongest, and was therefore probably the weakest garrisoned. A further reason for attacking here was that up to date Sherman had eschewed a frontal attack; thus surprise was more likely to be effected here than anywhere. Now surprise was essential if such a strong position was to be captured. Sherman therefore gave orders for a surprise attack upon a narrow portion of the hostile centre. This attack took place on June 27th, and was a ghastly failure; 10,000 men took part in it, and they suffered 25 per cent casualties. The southern loss was trifling.

COMMENTS.

Sherman's move to Dallas was his most bold and enterprising operation of the campaign up to date. Whereas at Resaca he had left one corps guarding his railway, here he moved his whole army away from it. One must admire the conception, but the execution was not so praiseworthy. Troops lost their way, progress was disappointingly slow, and the Southern cavalry was able to detect and report the movement. It would in any case have been difficult to effect complete surprise, for a move by his right, situated as he was at Kingston, was the obvious one, and Johnston was bound to be on the look-out for it. Chances of surprise would, moreover, have been greater had Sherman left a skeleton but active force in front of Johnston, and employed his whole cavalry (now amounting to nearly 12,000 men) in screening his left flank during the march.

The danger to his communications was not in reality as great as might appear. The Southern cavalry might, it is true, cut the railway, but so also they might had he remained on the railway. Indeed, they frequently did cut it in his rear. The danger of Johnston taking advantage of Sherman's flank movement to push forward down the railway and cut him off from his base was little more than theoretical. Occasions when the weaker of two forces, being threatened by its opponents flanking move, itself pushes forward and threatens its opponent's own flank, are rare; only when the commander of the weaker force is the more daring of the two can it happen—and such was not the case here. Sherman was becoming more and more inclined to take risks, owing to his opponent's strictly defensive attitude. At Resaca he had said "I'll risk it." At Dallas he did not even trouble to mention the word " risk."

The crisis of the operation came on the 25th, when Sherman found his passage barred at New Hope Church. It was here that he seems to have failed. The fundamental fault seems to have been the same that he was guilty of at Resaca—that is to say, he formed too precise a picture of what the enemy would do. At Resaca it was a single picture—the railway cut, and Johnston streaming to the rear. At Dallas he formed two alternative pictures; in the first Johnston would remain at Allatoona; in the second he would retreat across the Chattahoochee. He was prepared for either of these eventualities. In the first case he would move on Marietta; in the second case he would move on Sandtown. But Johnston did not oblige by taking either of these courses; he took a third; and Sherman was accordingly non-plussed. Moreover, the course that Johnston took was the one that he might have been expected to take. It was childish to suppose that he would remain quietly sitting down at Allatoona; his past conduct should have shown that he was far too prescient a commander to do that. Sherman should therefore have said to himself: " Suppose I find Johnston across my path at Dallas, what then? " Not only having a fortnight's supplies still in hand, but being able largely to live off the country in that area, he should surely have widened his sweep and made for the Chatta-hoochee. Liddell Hart considers it almost inconceivable that he could have got round Johnston's flank in time to get to the Chattahoochee before he was again blocked, and that they would have remained in a locked embrace till supplies ran out; and this opinion must be treated with respect. But after all, it was only what Grant was doing at that very moment! The two cases were not in essence dissimilar. If Sherman was able, as he was, to sideslip 15 miles to his left, to the railway, why should it have been impossible for him to sideslip equally to his right, and reach the river? Had he succeeded in doing so there can be little doubt that Johnston, alarmed for his communications, would have fallen back across the river. At the very least, the Kenesaw Mountain position, which was destined to hold up Sherman for a month, would have been turned. The net gain of the operation was thus the turning of the Allatoona position, a good achievement in itself, but one that hardly required the flanking move of his whole army to bring about. Thus, ten days after the commence-ment of the operation, instead of swarming along the Chattahoochee as it very well might have, the Union Army found itself once more on the railway, still 20 miles short of the river, and con-fronted by a formidable entrenched position. " It is a race for Atlanta, and General Sherman hopes to win it," had written his Chief of Signals before the event.[1] But his opponent had won it.

Why then did Sherman abandon his original intention, and return to the railway? The element of fear is seldom entirely absent from a commander's conceptions. It may take the form of nervousness, or merely of prudent caution. But it leads to more opportunities being lost than the opposite quality of boldness leads to battles being lost. It is clear that Sherman was becoming nervous for his railway. Probably he was influenced in this direction by the cautious Thomas. He can scarcely have believed

[1] *M.H.S.M.*, viii, 405.

it possible to turn Johnston's right flank.   Whatever his reason, he lived to regret his action.

It should further be noted that throughout this operation the general conception seems to have been one of MANŒUVRING JOHNSTON BACK, rather than of dealing his army a blow.   Gradually and perhaps half unconsciously, Sherman was abandoning his first objective, "to knock Jos. Johnson," in favour of the second, "to get into the interior of the enemy's country."   And more and more he was interpreting this second objective as—the capture of Atlanta.

Sherman has been unmercifully blamed for attacking Kenesaw Mountain, but his reasoning seems to me to be perfectly sound. It was a fair gamble—once in a while.

In conclusion, it should be noted that, as twice previously, Sherman allowed the lines of his columns to sag outwards during the march, but drew them in again as he approached his objective, Dallas.

As for Johnston, there is little to criticise.   Steele considers that while the Union Army was " groping in the wilderness " he should have taken advantage of the better knowledge of the country possessed by his men to strike a blow at his enemy's columns.   Had he done so, the situation would have closely resembled Lee's blow at the beginning of the Wilderness Campaign.   It must suffice to point out that Johnston was not a Lee. Only once did Johnston fight an offensive battle—that of " Seven Pines," a battle that General Alexander describes as "phenomenally mismanaged."

On the other hand, Johnston's utilisation of interior lines both to block Sherman at Dallas, and to mount Hood's attack on the 22nd is deserving of high praise.   32

THE CROSSING OF THE CHATTAHOOCHEE.

Foiled at Kenesaw, Sherman had to make a fresh plan.   The weather was now improving, and getting very hot.   He decided to threaten Johnston's left flank once more.   Schofield was soon sideslipping to the right, and on July 3rd McPherson's Corps was transferred from the left to the right and pushed out boldly for the Chattahoochee.   Johnston countered by falling back 8 miles to a fresh position at Smyrna.   Then, finding that his flank was still threatened, he fell back still farther on July 4th to a curiously situated position with his back to the Chattahoochee. This was a precarious position, and surprised Sherman, who had remarked that " no general such as he would invite battle with the

Chattahoochee behind him." Johnston's position was, however, a strong one—no mere rearguard position. He would evidently have to be manœuvred out of it. Sherman sent his cavalry out on each flank. On the right, Stonemen was told to demonstrate, while on the left Garrard, having secured the ford at Roswell, was told to conceal his division. Thus the Confederate cavalry were enticed over to the western flank, all unsuspecting of the blow that was about to fall. On July 8th Schofield crossed behind Thomas, who was holding the enemy in front, and reached the river at Soap Creek, 8 miles in an air line from the centre of the Confederate position. By an extremely skilful piece of work pontoons were thrown across the river without being detected, and Schofield immediately crossed. Further up stream at Roswell Garrard also crossed. The surprise had been complete. Johnston had patrols along the river but they " let him down." Next day one of McPherson's Corps was transferred from the extreme right to the extreme left and occupied the bridgehead at Roswell.

Johnston, fearful for his right flank, fell back once more, and occupied a position behind Peach Tree Creek, with his right resting on the Decatur railway and his left on the Marietta railway.

So far so good, and Sherman's next problem was whether to approach Atlanta by the right or by the left. The latter involved traversing more difficult ground, but as he had already secured a bridge-head on this flank it was only natural that he should make use of his success, and we need not look about for additional reasons, though an obvious one was that he had been warned that Johnston might receive reinforcements by the Augusta-Decatur railway, which his Roswell move enabled him to cut. Sherman spent the next five days in amassing supplies, and on July 16th he put his new plan into operation. But before describing it we must refer to an important happening in the hostile camp.

General Bragg had just visited the army, where he saw Johnston and Hood. The latter complained of the Army Commander's defensive policy. Bragg returned to Richmond with an un-
33 favourable report. Davis and his government had already lost patience with Johnston's prolonged retreat, and Bragg's visit was no doubt in order to prepare the ground for a change of command. On the 16th the President wired asking for " Your plan of operations so specifically as will enable me to anticipate events." Johnston gave an evasive reply, and on July 17th Johnston received a letter from the President ordering him to

relinquish his command, handing it over to Hood, his chief accuser, although Hardee was his Senior.

Thus ended, on the banks of the Chattahoochee, the great duel between William T. Sherman and J. E. Johnston.

COMMENTS.

Most of the lessons of this period are of a tactical nature, and do not concern us closely. In this connection there is perhaps something to be learnt from the excellent work of the Union troops in effecting the crossing of the Chattahoochee. It is safe to say that they never did more brilliant work throughout the campaign.

Johnston's position on July 4th with the river just behind him provokes tactical criticism. But it should be noted in his favour that he had constructed a large number of bridges in rear of this position which should reduce the risk of disaster if he was driven back.

Sherman's successful sideslip to the right on July 3rd, with its instant effect upon Johnston, provokes the thought: Why could he not have done it on May 28th. We have already noted the suggestion that the attempt would have ended in a locked embrace, but it is not obvious why this would have been the result in May whereas a similar move had such a different result in July. A really enterprising opponent might have found the opportunity to strike McPherson during either attempt; but Johnston cannot be described as an enterprising opponent—Colonel Conger describes him as "the defensively minded Johnston"—and the actions of a commander must be appraised in the light of the character of his opponent. Sherman was prepared to take a greater risk in July than he was in May; the reason is obviously that he was beginning to discount his opponent's enterprise, and rightly. Sherman took increased risks against Johnston, culminating in his great right wheel with wide-flung columns, in just the same way as Wellington—knowing his men—gradually took increased risks against Soult, culminating in his most risky move of all at Toulouse. 34

GENERAL COMMENTS (Sherman v. Johnston).

When we cast our eye back over the prolonged duel between these two great commanders we find much to admire in each. The one had lunged, the other had parried—generally giving ground in so doing, it is true. But Johnston had never had to

cry " *Touché !* "   His army remained intact and after 2½ months'
fighting was—thanks to reinforcements—almost as strong as at
35 first.   Owing to the long retreat its morale had probably depre-
ciated, though the evidence on this point is conflicting. (How is
one to measure morale short of engaging in battle?)   Nor does
the confidence of the Army as a whole in its chief seem to have
been shaken.   But the confidence of the Government, and of
civilian opinion generally, had.   Thus do political considerations
react upon policy.   It is a valuable lesson.

Sherman had certainly increased his hold upon the affections
and confidence of his own army, and upon his immediate subordinates.   He had driven a difficult team with skill and determination.   Moreover, his army was daily increasing in moral superiority
over its opponent.   Johnston's continuous avoidance of battle
had increased their confidence.   A prolonged advance and
retreat cannot fail to have this effect.   Both French and English
learnt this inexorable truth in September 1914.   It is true that
Johnston (helped by the rains) had delayed Sherman longer than
Lee delayed Grant, but Grant had suffered much heavier casualties
in proportion to his opponent than had Sherman.   It must be
confessed, though, that Sherman had been singularly unsuccessful
in divining his adversaries' intentions and course of action.   On
four major occasions, Resaca, Cassville, Dallas, Chattahoochee, his
appreciation of the situation was sadly at fault.

Johnston's theory was that it mattered little what geographical
gains the Union made so long as he could keep " his army in
being."   It was much the same theory as that of " the fleet in
being " of which we heard so much in the Great War.   But this
was not the theory of the Government, and whether it was right
or wrong (it was probably right) the Government must have the
last word, and if the commander is not willing to implement the
wish of the Government it is his duty to resign.   It happened that
Johnston's doctrine and his natural propensity for retiring happened to agree. Moreover, it is generally observable that the
farther a general retreats the more difficult he finds it to screw
himself up to turn and meet the foe.   The Great War showed
this.   Moore showed it in his retreat to Corunna, though the
glamour of the battle of Corunna has tended to obscure the fact.
When all is said and done, it must be admitted that Johnston
had one great failing: in the words of a very discriminating
commentator, Cox, he " lacked enterprise."   A passive defence
never has secured results, and it never will.

A word must now be said about the replacement of Johnston

by his chief critic, Hood. A controversy afterwards raged on the subject, not dissimilar to that concerning the replacement of Sir John French by Sir Douglas Haig in the Great War. President Davis was afterwards accused of personal motives, Hood being his friend, and Johnston being disliked and distrusted by him. Johnston was much to blame for this, being unduly secretive and querulous in his dealings with the President. But Davis had little difficulty in showing that he had hesitated longer than his colleagues in coming to his decision. "From many quarters," he wrote, "including such as had most urged his assignment, came delegations, letters, and petitions urging me to remove General Johnston."[2] Finally, after Bragg's visit the President requested a specific plan. Johnston's reply was as follows: " As the enemy has double our numbers we must be on the defensive. My plan of operations must therefore depend upon that of the enemy. It is mainly to watch for an opportunity to fight to advantage. We are trying to put Atlanta in condition to be held for a day or two by the Georgia Militia that army movements may be freer and wider." The comment of General G. W. Smith (who commanded the Georgia Militia) on this project was: " Atlanta would in all probability have been taken by the enemy within 24 hours."[3] It is clear from the above that Johnson had no plan. There was even doubt whether he intended seriously to defend Atlanta, for he had asked that the prisoners at Andersonville, over 100 miles to the south, be removed "immediately." If it was essential to hold Atlanta the President was perfectly justified in removing Johnston at this juncture. Most critics, being "wise after the event " after their fashion, condemn the President for his action. But taking all the facts into consideration as they stood at the time, it seems to me that the President acted correctly.

As to the differences of opinion between the senior generals, it is always likely to happen in war. War is not an exact science, and the correct action at any moment is merely a matter of opinion. Opinions are bound to vary; and when the stakes played for are high, as they must be in war, this difference of opinion between the generals is likely to make itself evident in positive friction and even in estranged relations. It is an unpalatable, but inescapable fact, and is likely to be particularly prone in a "popular" army, a mixture of regulars and volunteers such as an American

[2] *Rise and Fall of the Confederacy*, ii, 556.
[3] *Advance and Retreat*, p. 147.

or British army is always likely to be.   Both armies suffered from it almost equally, both before and after this episode.

This is a convenient place in which to insert a general comment on the faulty organisation of the Union Army.   As we have seen, the three territorially designated armies of which it was composed were of very different sizes, that of the Cumberland being over four times as large as that of the Ohio.   One objection to this arrangement was that complications of command arose when (as often happened) the smaller had to be assisted by the larger. A further objection was that for most of Sherman's flanking movements the Army of the Cumberland was considered too large and unwieldy, while that of the Ohio was too small.   Consequently the brunt of the manœuvre fell upon Sherman's old Army of the Tennessee.   Apart from the objection that this constant use of his own army led to the suspicion of favouritism, and hence of jealousy in the other armies, it tended to put too great a strain on the Army of the Tennessee compared with the others.   Though to have broken up the territorial organisation would have been an unpopular move there is no doubt that one corps should have been transferred from the Army of the Cumberland to that of the Ohio.

36

CHAPTER XII

Sherman *versus* Hood.—Atlanta.

SHERMAN became aware of the supersession of Johnston by Hood on July 18th. As it happened the new Southern commander had been in the same class as McPherson and Schofield at West Point. Sherman therefore took the sensible step of enquiring from these classmates the character of Hood. From them he learnt of the bold and even reckless nature of his new opponent. Knowing also that Johnston had been displaced for failure to arrest his advance, he naturally expected a more resolute attitude by Johnston's successor. This expectation does not, however, appear to have had any effect on his plan which was then in course of execution—except to make the movements of his columns more slow and cautious than they would otherwise have been.

Sherman's plan was, as we have seen, to turn Johnston's right, cut the Decatur railway and approach Atlanta, his goal, from the east. For the turning movement he selected, as always, his old Army of the Tennessee. McPherson's troops were switched rapidly across from the extreme right to the extreme left, and occupied the bridgehead at Roswell. McPherson's orders were to make a bold sweep and cut and destroy the railway seven miles east of Decatur, then close in on Atlanta along the line of the railway. Thomas, on the right, or pivot of the movement, was to mark time at first, then cross Peach Tree Creek and attack Atlanta from the north. Schofield was to form the centre and a connecting link between the other two armies.

This plan involved a wide dispersion at the moment when McPherson reached the railway. This occurred at 2 p.m. on July 18th. At that moment he was twelve miles distant from Thomas in an air line, and considerably more by road. But Hood only assumed effective control that afternoon and could hardly be expected to take immediate action. So the operation went on. On the 19th the whole Union Army was on the move. Thomas started to cross Peach Tree Creek, encountering a good deal of opposition. Schofield approached Decatur from the north, while McPherson approached it from the north-east.

PEACH TREE CREEK, JULY 20TH.

On July 20th the move continued. McPherson and Schofield in combination advanced south-west straight towards Atlanta, their advance being vigorously resisted by Wheeler's cavalry. Thomas continued to cross Peach Tree Creek, and by 4 p.m. had got practically his whole army across.

And then the blow fell. A long line of Confederate infantry dashed forward out of the woods against Thomas, and struck his left flank. At that moment there was a gap of about two miles between his left and Schofield's right. The situation was critical. But before describing the fortunes of the battle we must explain Hood's plan.

We must preface this with a description of the man who was now entrusted by the President with the task of defeating the redoubtable Sherman. Among the many notable and remarkable Generals whom the Civil War brought into prominence in some respects the most remarkable of them all was General John B. Hood. Coming of an old Devonshire family, and educated at West Point, he served in the Texas Wars of 1856, where he showed that boldness and dash that afterwards became his distinguishing characteristic. Early in the Civil War he became one of Stonewall Jackson's young men, and soon earned rapid promotion. But wounds came too. First at Gaine's Mill, then at Gettysburg one arm was shattered, and at Chickamauga he lost a leg, high up near the joint. Yet even so he continued to serve. Strapped into the saddle, he was able to get about much better than might be expected, though it must have crippled his activities appreciably. But nothing could cripple or tame his proud spirit. Snow describes him as " one of those whom no disasters or physical ailments—not even the partial dismemberment of his body—nor any amount of external trouble, annoyance or ill will can crush."[1] When appointed to the command of the army he was only 33 years of age, 11 less than Sherman, and 24 less than Johnston.

After this description of the new Commander, the reader may expect to see some " sparks " introduced into the campaign. He will not be disappointed. Realising, directly he had taken over the command, the necessity for delivering a powerful blow before his enemy closed in on Atlanta he ordered an attack to be launched on the following day, the 19th. But it proved to be too short notice, and had to be postponed till the 20th. The

[1] *Southern Generals*, 393.

plan was for Cheatham's (Hood's) Corps on the right to hold McPherson and Schofield while Hardee in the centre and Stewart (Polk's successor) on the left delivered a combined attack on Thomas while in the act of crossing Peach Tree Creek. The 38 plan was an excellent one. Johnston, writing eleven years after the battle, claims to have been the originator of it; if this be so Hood was not generous enough to acknowledge his debt. In fact, he denies having received the plan from Johnston. As we have seen, Hood was not able to mount his attack as soon as he desired; which was unfortunate, for it would have struck Thomas in the act of crossing the creek. Further delay was occasioned on the 20th by the necessity of moving the whole army a short distance to the right, as McPherson's advance was becoming threatening. Instead therefore of the attack starting at 1 p.m. it had to be postponed till 4 p.m. The clash, though unexpected, was fiercely contested by the Union troops, and Hardee's progress was slow. Successive attacks were driven back, and eventually, when one seemed really like succeeding, General Thomas in the nick of time ordered forward some batteries which managed to take the attackers in enfilade and bring the assault to a standstill. Hardee was about to put in yet another attack when he received an order from Hood to send a division to the help of Cheatham, who was being hard pressed by McPherson. The division sent arrived in the nick of time; but its detachment put any further attack by Hardee out of the question. His troops therefore returned to their own trenches, having suffered very heavy casualties. Hood's first blow had proved a complete failure.

On July 21st McPherson on the left made slight progress, capturing a bare hilltop, only two miles east of Atlanta, and dominating the town.

BATTLE OF ATLANTA, JULY 22ND (*Sketch Map* 15).

Patrols were pushing forward all along the line, and on the early morning of the 22nd the exciting intelligence reached Sherman that the enemy had abandoned their position and disappeared. On receipt of this news he issued some orders for pursuit. Sherman does not mention the fact, and they are not included in the Official Records, though all three Army Commanders stated that they had received them. Their purport can, however, be gleaned from the following despatch from McPherson to one of his Corps Commanders, timed 6 a.m.: " The supposition of General Sherman is that the enemy have given up Atlanta, and are retreating in the direction of East

Point. . . . He desires and expects a vigorous pursuit." That evening Sherman's cipher operator wrote to Washington: " At day-light . . . General Sherman announced the occupation of Atlanta by Schofield, and ordered pursuit by Thomas and McPherson. Vigorous pursuit was made and the enemy found in the fortifi-cations of Atlanta, and not Schofield."[2] Thomas and Schofield took up the pursuit and were soon closing in on the city from the north and north-east. But McPherson, who was already in an advanced position, did not immediately move forward, contenting himself by making some minor but important adjust-ments in his army. He had two corps in line, Logan (XV) on the right, Blair (XVII) on the left; and he placed Dodge (XVI) in rear of them, Fuller's Division on the left and Sweeny's on the right. It had now become clear that the enemy still held Atlanta. McPherson accordingly rode over to see Sherman who was at Howard House, and they discussed the situation together. Suddenly gunfire was heard from the Decatur direction, and McPherson galloped off to see what it could mean. For Decatur was right in the rear of his army. The sound of battle steadily rose to the south-east, when in what seemed like a few minutes (in Sherman's own words) " one of McPherson's staff, with his horse covered with sweat, dashed up to the porch, and reported that General McPherson was either 'killed or a prisoner.' . . . I ordered the staff officer to return at once, to find General Logan . . . and to instruct him to drive back this supposed small force, which had evidently got round the XVII Corps behind the blind woods. . . ."

We must now follow the fortunes of this " supposed small force." In truth, so far from being a " small force " it con-sisted of no less than one-third of Hood's Army! It was attacking McPherson's left rear, and was threatening to roll up his whole line. Already it had captured numerous guns, colours and prisoners. It was Hardee's Corps, and Wheeler's cavalry. But how had it got round McPherson's rear in that astonishing manner? Only thirty-six hours before, this same corps had suffered a heavy defeat on the northern front of the battle line, yet here it was, apparently approaching from the south-east and striking the extreme southern end of the line! To explain this astonishing situation, surely one of the most remarkable, in the circumstances, in the annals of war, we must go back to the Confederate camp on the previous evening.

Here the situation was gloomy in the extreme.

[2] *Sherman's Historical Raid*, by H. Boynton, p. 117.

The blow, on which so much had been expected, had proved a ghastly failure, and Sherman was tightening his remorseless grip upon the seemingly doomed city. But Hood believed that the mantle of Stonewall Jackson had descended upon him. He thought of past occasions when the situation had appeared equally desperate but when some bold action had restored matters. In particular he thought of that most risky yet most successful of all Stonewall's operations, the flank march and attack at

SKETCH MAP 15

BATTLE OF ATLANTA, July 22nd

Chancellorsville. Hood determined to emulate this. Owing to the propinquity of the Chattahoochee on his left, the only flank that there was room to manœuvre round was the southern flank. This flank therefore was selected. But Hood added a striking feature to the operation that was not present at Chancellorsville: one quite unique in its way. Simultaneously with, or rather immediately prior to delivering his new blow, he staged a retreat by his whole army. This striking stratagem presented three advantages: it would tend to put the enemy off his guard, it would enable Hood to withdraw his striking force out of the line of battle without discovery (because his whole line would be on the move), and thirdly, it would make it the easier for Hardee to get round the hostile flank because that flank would probably be closing in on Atlanta. Hood's " battle of Chancellorsville " was therefore thus mounted.

Under cover of darkness, on the 21st, then, the Confederate Army quietly fell back. But whereas Stewart's and Cheatham's Corps entrenched and occupied a new line just outside the city Hardee, accompanied by Wheeler's cavalry, marched straight through the town and out to the south. His orders were to get completely in rear of the Union line, even if this involved going right round to Decatur. A big detour was found necessary, and it was not till 15 miles had been traversed that Hardee considered himself in the required position. The road he was following headed in a north-easterly direction towards Decatur. Sending the cavalry straight on to Decatur, Hardee halted his infantry, rested them, and turned square to his left. This action brought his four divisions in line abreast, facing north-west. (See Sketch Map 15.) The whole line then advanced straight to its front. So far, fortune had favoured the Confederates. Garrard's cavalry, which might have discovered this move, had been sent east of Decatur to deal further destruction to the railway. (Such work appears to have been almost an obsession with Sherman.) Hardee had guided his column skilfully, and though he had not got completely in rear of the enemy he had reached an advantageous position for the attack; indeed Hood is reported as saying at the time that it was exactly where he wanted him.

The next piece of good fortune fell to the Northerners. It will be remembered that Dodge's Corps had just been placed in rear of the other two corps of the army. Thus, the right of Hardee's line, instead of striking the rear of McPherson's entrenchments found itself confronted by Dodge's intact Corps. The latter, after the first moment of surprise, accounted for itself extraordinarily well. A line was rapidly formed, facing the rear, and—another piece of good fortune—two batteries happened to have bivouacked on the bare hill captured by McPherson on the 21st. These batteries were able to engage the oncoming Southerners at short range with great effect. The attack, judging from General Fuller's own account, does not seem to have been pressed with much determination. But it was repeated; and it was during the second attack that McPherson galloped forward unsuspectingly into the front line and was immediately shot dead. This was an irreparable loss to the Northerners, for McPherson 39 was one of their best commanders. Things fared badly for them, also, on the extreme south of their line. Here there was no protection for the front line troops, and Blair's men were constrained to jump out of their trenches, over the parapet, and engage the enemy from the front side. Hardee's men met with great success in this quarter, rolling up about 900 yards of trenches and capturing 13 guns and numerous prisoners. The scene was as remarkable as that at the Bloody Angle at Spott-sylvania. " The flags of two opposing regiments would meet on opposite sides of the same works and would be planted by their respective bearers in each other's faces. Men were bayonetted across the works."3 Hood was watching the progress of the attack from the southern end of Cheatham's line, waiting for the psychological moment to throw Cheatham's Corps into the attack from the west. At 3 p.m. he judged that the moment had come. He gave the word and Cheatham's men were unleashed to the attack, whilst Smith's Georgian militia* attacked Schofield's 40 Corps farther north. Blair's men, who had just repelled an attack by Hardee, jumped back into their own trenches in order to face the new foe from the orthodox direction. The situation at this moment, if set out in a war game, would result in the director stopping the game and announcing Hood the victor. But the course of battle is unpredictable. In this case, though Cheatham gained considerable success on the left, capturing guns and prisoners, and making an ugly breach in the hostile line, the situation was restored in the nick of time by Sherman himself. Once again it was the artillery that turned the scale. From his position at Howard House he witnessed the setback to the south of him. His quick eye saw what was required, and he immediately called on Schofield for a portion of his artillery. As the guns came up Sherman himself placed them in a position whence they could enfilade Cheatham's men. In a few moments a formidable mass of Schofield's artillery came into action and struck Cheatham's victorious troops in flank with " a terrible raking fire." The attack was checked with " terrible carnage " and the Confederates forced to fall back again. Further attacks merely added to the carnage. The Northerners had now clearly attained the upper hand, and at dusk the attack was called off. Hardee drew back his right flank through 90 degrees, but the

3 *S.H.S.P.*, viii, 230.
* These troops, about 5,000 strong, had recently joined the Army.

remainder of his corps held fast on the line they had won, and entrenched it during the night. The Confederates had captured 13 guns and nearly 2,000 prisoners, and they had frustrated any attempts at turning their right flank. But they had suffered twice as many casualties as their opponents.

While the battle was raging Thomas's Army, four miles to the north, remained inactive. To quote Stone: " During the whole of this day's battle—the most serious, threatening, and hotly contested of the campaign—over 50,000 soldiers of Sherman's Army stood auditors and spectators of the doubtful conflict, almost within gunshot of the scene, anxiously awaiting some order from the commanding general to aid in the work. Such order never came. In his *Memoirs* he explains this extraordinary failure to utilise five-eighths of his army by the astonishing declaration: " I purposely allowed the army of the Tennessee to fight this battle almost unaided. . . . if any assistance were rendered by either of the other armies, the Army of the Tennessee would be jealous."[4] Stone, commenting on this, enquires what would be thought had Wellington had Blucher under his command at Waterloo and refused to use him for fear the British Army would be jealous! Schofield asserts: " My impression was, and is, that they would have been very glad of assistance and that timely help would have increased the fraternal feeling between the armies, instead of creating unworthy jealousy." He considers that by neglecting to use the other armies Sherman " lost a great opportunity that day."[5]

EZRA CHURCH (*Sketch Map* 16).

After the battle of Atlanta various changes took place in both armies. Although Logan was the senior general in the Army of the Tennessee Sherman did not recommend him for the succession to McPherson. Logan was not a regular, which may have influenced Sherman. At any rate, he recommended Howard, and Lincoln approved. This caused Hooker to resign in umbrage. He was the senior Corps Commander, and Howard, serving under him, had been in his opinion responsible for the defeat of Chancellorsville. His indignation was therefore natural. In any case, Sherman and Hooker did not hit it off together. All this shows how important a part in war is played by the personal relations of the senior officers. Slocum succeeded Hooker. In the Confederate Army S. D. Lee replaced Cheatham. There

[4] *M.H.S.M.*, viii, 447.
[5] *Schofield*, p. 148.

were thus three changes in the four principal posts in the Confederate Army in the space of ten days.

To resume the narrative, Sherman, having been foiled on his left, now decided to approach Atlanta by his right.   By July 25th the railway bridge over the Chattahoochee was restored, a very fine feat; the Union engineers were a splendid help to Sherman throughout the campaign.   On the 27th Howard's Army was transferred once more from flank to flank.   It was just taking up its new position near Ezra Church when, on the 28th, it was again attacked.   Hood, taking advantage of his interior lines,

SKETCH MAP 16

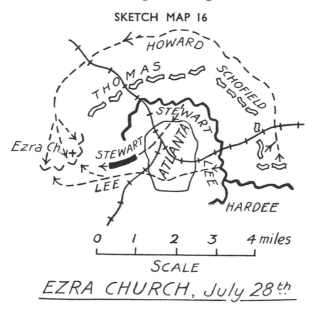

EZRA CHURCH, July 28th

suddenly switched Lee across the base of his salient in order to attack Howard's right flank before it had properly settled in.

The plan for this attack was almost as ambitious and striking as that of the 22nd.   But the procedure was reversed.   Stewart's Corps was this time to take the enemy in reverse but instead of opening the proceedings with this manœuvre, it was to remain in a waiting position on the first day of the battle, and was only to execute its turning movement on the second day.   This is quite a novel plan for a battle, and it would have been interesting to see how it prospered.   But unfortunately it did not have the chance, for things went so badly with Lee's attack on the first day that Stewart was called to his support.   Even so the attacks, though repeatedly renewed, were beaten off with ease, and with great slaughter, for Howard's men had just had sufficient time to throw back their right flank and run up some rough stockades. But once again it was a case of " touch and go." The attack was held by artillery hastily rushed up, and by the fire of repeating rifles. Moreover, the Confederate attacks lacked sting. The fact seems to be that Hood's weapon had been blunted by the apparently unavailing losses and exertions of the past few days: the Confederate infantry would not go " once more unto the breach " with the unquestioning confidence and dash that had characterised them of old. It was an almost exact counterpart of Coldharbor—with the roles reversed. Nevertheless the attack had foiled Howard's flanking movement. The latter, to do him justice, had expected that Hood would attack him before he got settled into position, and told Sherman of his fears, knowing what sort of a tornado he had to deal with from West Point days. But Sherman refused to believe that Hood would dare to attack again so soon after his setbacks on the 20th and 22nd. Hood took another unorthodox but imaginative step in this battle. Two corps were engaged in the same operation. It is an axiom of war that troops so engaged should have a common commander —an axiom that was seldom observed in Sherman's Army. Hood therefore placed Hardee, whose corps was not actively engaged in command of the other two. Unfortunately by the time the change of command was effected, the crisis of the battle 41   was past. But the conception was a sound one.

COMMENTS.

I hope my readers agree that General Hood provided the necessary " sparks " during the past ten days. It would be difficult to find, in the history of any campaign, a more dazzling series of blows so rapidly delivered by a retreating and discredited army. The conception of each was sound—even brilliant. In every case the enemy was struck either on the move or before he had had time to throw up adequate defences. In each case there was little or no warning of the impending blow. In the case of Peach Tree Creek, Hood was right to strike at the force nearest to him. To give direct support Schofield would have had to recross the Creek, involving a march of several miles. General G. W. Smith, who commanded the Georgia Militia, afterwards wrote: " If Hood's orders had been promptly obeyed this attack would probably have resulted in a staggering blow to Sherman."[6]

   [6] *M.H.S.M.*, viii, 334.

In the case of Atlanta, Hood's blow was bold and brilliant—almost breath-taking in its brilliance and boldness—coming hard on top of a bloody defeat. Hardee's execution of it was also brilliant. General Blair, the Northern Corps Commander, admitted that " the movement of General Hood was a very bold and brilliant one, and was very near being successful."[7] General Dodge, the other Northern Corps Commander most closely concerned, describes it as " one of the best planned and best executed attacks."[8]   Chamberlin, yet another Northerner, wrote: "Upon what a slight chance hung the fate of Sherman's army that day.[9]   This refers to the fluky chance by which Dodge's Corps happened to be at the critical point at the critical time.

If McPherson's troops had not managed to hold their ground their retreat would have been precarious, for Wheeler's cavalry were at the gates of Decatur.

As for Ezra Church, Cox, who was not kindly disposed towards Hood, concedes, somewhat grudgingly: " Since the thing was to be again tried, it must be admitted that Hood was right in determining to strike Howard's right while in motion and before it could intrench."[10]   The effective use made by Hood of interior lines is also to be noted. Summarising the whole, General Smith asserts: " As an army commander (Hood's) orders were judicious and well timed."[11]

Hay's comment is: " That (Hood) came so near to success is a tribute to his indomitable faith and courage, and to the real ability displayed in a campaign that on several occasions put him within reach of victory."[12]

Why then, it may be asked, were all three blows so barren in results?   There are several reasons, but the chief one may be stated in general thus: *Hood's weapon was becoming steadily blunter, whereas Sherman's was becoming steadily sharper.*   The heavy casualties sustained by the Confederates were having their inevitable effect upon the troops, who could no longer be counted upon to attack with their old-time dash and devilry.   Added to this, Hood's plans were hasty and somewhat sketchily worked out. The staff work was bad at Headquarters. (When Hood assumed command he spent a long time in ascertaining the position of the other corps.   A good staff should have been able

42

---

[7] *Advance and Retreat*, p. 190.
[8] *Personal Recollections*, p. 156.
[9] *Ibid.*, p. 326.
[10] *Atlanta*, p. 184.
[11] B. *&* L., iv, 335.
[12] *Hood's Tennessee Campaign*, p. 21.

to inform him at once.)   Next, the luck was almost all on the other side.   Hood was an " unlucky general," and though it seems childish to advance such a reason, and though in the long run luck cancels out, Hood did not have a long run—his run against Sherman was all too short.   In after years controversy arose between Hood and Hardee respecting the battle of Peach Tree Creek.   Hood said that if his orders had been carried out the battle would have been won, and it is a fact that Hardee extended $1\frac{1}{2}$ miles to his right instead of the half division front as ordered.   The relations between these two were not of the best.   Hardee, on being passed over by Hood, had asked to be transferred.   There were also special reasons for the lack of success in the case of July 22nd.   The Confederates fought the battle on exterior lines.   In such cases it is always difficult to co-ordinate the attacks.   The result in this case was that Cheatham's attack was launched too late.   It may also be said that the Union troops, both leaders and led, never showed their veteran qualities better than on that trying 22nd of July.   The coolness and promptitude of Generals Blair, Dodge and Fuller, saved the situation time and again.   At Ezra Church the prescience of General Howard and the speed with which his troops entrenched themselves saved the day.   They remind one of the picture of the Jews, returned from exile, hastily fortifying themselves, with sword in one hand, trowel in the other.

Nevertheless the successive blows delivered by Hood were not so entirely fruitless as appeared on the surface.   Their effect on the operations will appear in the following chapter.   Their effect upon the political situation was, according to Rhodes, to increase the gloom and despondency that was then spreading over the Union. Sherman's advance had been brought to an abrupt halt just at the moment when he seemed within sight of his goal.

It is usually held that this partial success was too dearly bought, owing to the blow it dealt to Confederate morale.   But this decline in morale was of *gradual* growth.   On July 25th an officer wrote: " The army is in good spirits and confidence in General Hood is unabated."[13]

Of Sherman there is not so much to be said.   His wide wheeling operation against Atlanta was well designed to defeat Johnston; but when the Southern command was changed the Northern plan might also have been.   If Sherman had then suddenly reverted to the defensive, and entrenched furiously, Hood would not have had the openings that were presented to him.   Sherman

[13] *Battle of Franklin*, by R. W. Banks, p. 18.

has also been criticised for losing an opportunity on July 22nd. In spite of his excuse for not using the Armies of the Cumberland and the Ohio on that day there is evidence that he did contemplate employing them. He was probably put off by gloomy reports 43 from Thomas. If so, he showed the same infirmity of purpose that Johnston had showed at Cassville. He also no doubt lived to regret the frittering away of his cavalry beyond Decatur while Hardee was attacking McPherson.

Tribute must, however, be paid to Sherman for his coolness and quick grasp of the situation at the crisis of the battle of Atlanta. His promptness probably saved the day. Once again: " It was a damned nice thing." Cox brings out this trait in his character well: " He had the rare faculty of being equable under great responsibilities and amid scenes of great excitement. At such times his eccentricities disappeared. . . . His mind seemed never so clear, his confidence never so strong, his spirit never so inspiring, and his temper never so amiable as in the crisis of some fierce struggle like that of the day when McPherson fell in front of Atlanta."

CHAPTER XIII

Jonesborough.

SHERMAN had now been held up for over a week in front of the town that he had believed the enemy to be evacuating on July 21st. On July 29th, fertile in his resource as usual, he ordered a double enveloping movement against the railway at East Point by two of Thomas's Divisions on the west and of Schofield's Corps on the east. But both forces moved with such excessive caution that the movement ended in fiasco. Herein is early evidence of the nervousness that Hood was engendering in the hostile commanders by his rapid and successive blows—centre—right—left. They might be excused if they advanced " with all military precautions " for the remainder of the campaign. With their mouths they belittled Hood, but deeds are more eloquent than words.

Sherman had to admit himself foiled to right and to left. But his versatile and active mind immediately set to work conjuring out fresh devices for the capture of the prize that lay so close to his grasp. But it was not easy. Hood had by now extended his entrenchments till their left rested on the Macon railway. There appeared to be no joint in his armour. Sherman had scarcely enough men to invest the town. But he had other means of starving it out. That was by his favourite device of railway destruction. Already he had destroyed many miles of the Augusta railway, beyond Decatur. He now determined to destroy the Macon railway with his cavalry. One half pushed out to the east and the other half to the west. But both raids proved expensive failures, and the commander of one of them was captured.

Sherman therefore had recourse once more to his infantry. From August 3rd to 5th he carried out a bold flanking movement by two corps, the XXIII and the XIV. Schofield was in command, but Palmer ranked senior as a general and refused to accept orders from Schofield. The result was, as might be expected, chaos, and the force failed to reach the railway, its objective. This emphasises the faulty system of command in the Union Army, to which reference has already been made.

Once again Sherman had to change his procedure. This time he decided to see what a bombardment would do. Some heavy 44 Parrott guns were brought up and bombarded the town for several days, but without effect. Taking advantage of the absence of Wheeler's cavalry on a raid to the North, another raid on the railway was made by Kilpatrick's cavalry. But this raid also was abortive, which forced Sherman to the conclusion that only infantry could accomplish really thoroughgoing destruction. Once again therefore he had resort to his infantry.

In an important order issued on August 16th Sherman foreshadowed the nature of his new plan. The wording of the following phrases should be noted: " The move of the Army against the Macon railroad," and " During the movement, and until the Army returns to the river. . . ."

The new plan resembled the Dallas manœuvre in so far as it involved almost the whole army cutting adrift from the railway for several days.

Slocum's (Hooker's) Corps was withdrawn to the Chattahoochee to defend the railway, while the remainder of the army swung out to the south-west, pivoting on Schofield's Army, which was now opposite East Point. (See Sketch Map 17.)

On August 25th the new operation started, Howard on the right, and Thomas in the centre. Moving somewhat leisurely and cautiously, the Montgomery railway was reached from five to ten miles south-east of East Point, on the 28th at noon. So far, Hood had not moved. It happened that he had sent off Wheeler's cavalry on a raid against Sherman's communications—perhaps catching the bad habit from his opponent—and when he discovered that the enemy had disappeared from their entrenchments and that Slocum's Corps was apparently guarding the rear at the Chattahoochee he not unnaturally came to the conclusion that Sherman had raised the siege. There was jubilation in the 45 Southern camp—but not for long.

Sherman's plan had in fact succeeded beyond the most sanguine anticipations. The Montgomery railway was cut, and there appeared to be nothing between him and the Macon railway, six miles away at its nearest point, and Hood's whole army was sitting serenely in Atlanta, fifteen miles to the north-east! What action should Sherman now take? Even the wildest guess of the student will probably be wide of the mark. The answer is— he did nothing, except sit down and with his whole army devote himself to destroying the railway. Not only was that afternoon devoted to the congenial task, but the whole of the following day.

Sherman's propensity for railway destruction took its fill.   The amazing situation on August 29th, when both armies were stationary, one within a few miles of the line of communications of the other, is shown on Sketch Map 17.   It was not till the morning of the 30th, thirty-six valuable hours having been wasted, that his whole army (Schofield having by now connected up) resumed the advance eastwards.   But Hood had learnt of the railway destruction, and though he only believed it to be a minor raid, he sent two brigades to Jonesborough and three to Rough and Ready Station.   On the evening of the 30th, realising that there was a considerable force in his rear (estimated at about two corps), he sent off Hardee's Corps, followed by Lee's, to Jonesborough.   Hardee arrived at 9 a.m. on the 31st, and Lee shortly afterwards.

Meanwhile Sherman was continuing his slow advance.   On the night of the 30th he halted about two miles from the railway, right flank on Jonesborough, left just south of East Point.   The situation was becoming tense.

AUGUST 31ST.

The dawn of perhaps the most remarkable day in the campaign found the Union Army continuing its slow advance.   But the corps of Hardee and Lee had formed a line covering Jonesborough, and when Howard's army approached early in the afternoon it was sharply attacked.   The battle-line then became stationary on this flank, but on the northern flank Schofield continued to advance till, at 3 p.m., he cut the railway just south of Rough and Ready.   A train was approaching, but hastily reversed and took the alarm with it back to Atlanta.   Hood had not heard of Hardee's action farther south, and supposed that Sherman was about to attack Atlanta from the south and west.   This would be the worst that could happen, for the bulk of his army had quit the town the previous day.   Was it too late to recall a portion of his detachment?   If it was, there was nothing left but to retreat while yet there was time.   But Hood had not abandoned all hope, though he seemed to be in a parlous position.   Not only was the hostile army astride his line of communication, but his own army was split in two, and risked being defeated in detail by the superior army of the enemy.

Urgently Hood sent orders by a necessarily circuitous route that Lee's Corps should return to Atlanta, starting at 2 a.m. on September 1st, while Hardee was ordered to cover the Macon railway as well as he could.

At about 2 p.m. Sherman had become aware of Hood's dispositions, and gradually he evolved a plan. Writing to Howard that evening, he expressed it thus: " I think we now have a good game. Break [rail] road down towards Jonesborough. The bulk of the enemy's good troops are there. . . . We will push Hardee and Lee first, and then for Atlanta."[1] I shall have something to say of this message later.

SKETCH MAP 17

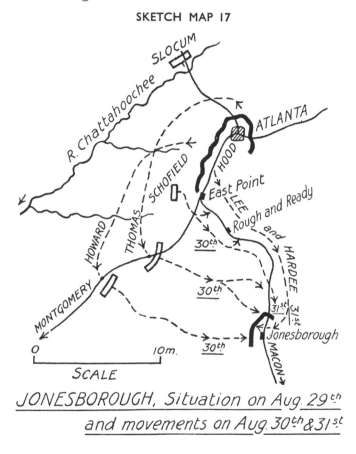

JONESBOROUGH, Situation on Aug. 29th and movements on Aug. 30th & 31st

The end of that day therefore witnessed the extraordinary spectacle of the whole of the Union Army preparing to push the bulk, if not the whole of the Confederate Army southwards from Jonesborough, whilst the bulk of the Confederate Army was preparing to concentrate at Atlanta, twenty miles to the north! The situation was such as to promise exciting events next day!   47

[1] *O.R.*, XXXVIII, Pt. 5, August 21st.

SEPTEMBER 1ST.

In the early hours of the morning Lee's Corps started to retrace its steps, pursuant to order, to Atlanta. But the men were weary after their long march, followed by a battle, and progress was slow. It was however sufficiently rapid to prevent interception by Schofield, who had orders to work round to the east of Jonesborough, whilst Thomas pressed it from the north and Howard from the west. By this means Sherman hoped to " push Hardee " southwards. The advance was slow, but this did not seem to disturb Sherman, until he heard in the afternoon that Lee's Corps had disappeared and Hardee's was left isolated and alone. Then at last he awoke to the opportunity that was presented to him, and he bent all his energies to speeding up the advance. But troops and commanders were dreadfully slow and " sticky." Sherman had already complained " I cannot move the troops a hundred yards without their stopping to entrench." Is it fanciful to attribute this " stickiness " to the heavy blows that Hood had recently aimed at the Army of the Union? Hardee was isolated at Jonesborough. Sherman decided to attempt to surround and destroy his corps. Howard was ordered to work to the south of Jonesborough, cutting the railway, while Thomas, supported by Schofield, enveloped and attacked the northern end of Hardee's position. Howard did not succeed in cutting the railway, but Thomas won a partial success on the other flank—a success which might have been greater but for the hesitation of one of his corps commanders.

The situation at nightfall was thus that the whole of the Union Army was closing in on Hardee's devoted corps from north, south and west, while Lee was marching to join Hood in Atlanta. Slocum was at the same time feeling forward towards the northern edge of the town, in case Hood should have evacuated it. The fog of war was in full evidence this day; perhaps more so than on any previous day in the campaign.

SEPTEMBER 2ND.

During the night Hardee, who had the independent mission of covering the railway to Macon and the south, felt that he could hold out at Jonesborough no longer, and under cover of darkness quietly slipped out to the south. His move was undetected, and he was able to take up a fresh position at Lovejoy Station, six miles to the south, not only without molestation but with several hours in hand in which to fortify his new position.

Meanwhile, from 1 a.m. onwards, Sherman could hear either gunfire or a series of explosions from the direction of Atlanta. What did it mean? Was Slocum engaged with Hood, or was the city being blown up? If the latter, Hood might be bearing down upon his rear, in an endeavour to join up with Hardee. That at any rate seems to have been Sherman's line of reasoning, for he sends a long message to Thomas purely defensive in tone, while Schofield is told to be prepared either to face to the north or to attack Jonesborough from the east. But either task was a futile one, for Sherman had misjudged the situation as badly as Hood had on the previous day. Hood was not bearing down on his rear; neither was Hardee still in Jonesborough. At 9.15 a.m. Sherman, having learnt of Hardee's escape, ordered a pursuit to the south, leaving one corps facing north, against the unknown danger from that direction. In the course of the day touch was obtained with Hardee's new position at Lovejoy Station, while Schofield watched the eastern flank. Rumours were accumulating that Atlanta had been evacuated, but Sherman did not care to place too great faith in them, and his action was accordingly considerably paralysed.

Meanwhile what had really happened in Atlanta, and where was Hood and the bulk of his army? The explosions heard in the night had been the blowing up of ordnance stores in Atlanta; for Hood had decided, on hearing of Hardee's repulse, that he could hold his position no longer. Under cover of darkness, therefore, he had evacuated the town and marched away towards the south-east, completely unmolested. He had previously halted Lee's Corps outside the city limits, and stationed it as a flank guard to the rest of his army. Apart from a slight brush with cavalry, it also was unmolested. Marching through the day, both corps succeeded in reaching McDonough, where they turned west and joined Hardee during the following night.

COMMENTS.

Atlanta had fallen at last! The effect in the North was electrical. It turned the forthcoming Presidential election in favour of Lincoln. " It is hard to exaggerate the effect of this news. To the average Northerner, weary with hope deferred after years of frightful loss, it seemed the most important achievement of Union arms in the year 1864. To Lincoln. . . it was a godsend." Thus Professor Randall in *The Civil War and reconstruction*.[2] Captain Liddell Hart puts it neatly: " Sherman had saved

[2] *Op. cit.*, p. 554.

Lincoln, and by saving him sealed the fate of the South."
This is the generally accepted view; but Professor Randall
dispels the "stereotyped picture that Lincoln and McClellan
were opposites . . . that Democratic victory would have brought
defeat in War. . . . The patent fact however is that all parties
in the North in 1864 were Union parties."[3]

This is a political question that we will not pursue further.
The most interesting military point is, again in Randall's words,
that "the failure of Sherman to capture Hood's Army showed
that his main objective had not been won. That army . . . had
caught something of Hood's confidence, as he dreamed of drawing
Sherman after him into Kentuckee and Tennessee."[4] This raises
the question as to whether Sherman was justified in pursuing
a purely geographical objective—quite apart from what Grant's
orders to him were. We will defer discussion of this question
till the end of the following chapter.

The operation of Jonesborough raises several other questions
which it will be convenient to deal with here.

Why did Sherman halt on the 28th and 29th, when almost
completely in rear of his opponent?

Why was his advance so slow on the 30th and 31st?

Why did he not cut off Hardee's retreat on September 1st?

Why did he not strike Hood in flank while he was retiring on
September 2nd, or, at least, keep him separated from Hardee?

To find the answer to these puzzling questions we must go
back to the wording of his original order of August 15th. "The
move of the army is *versus* the Macon railway . . . until the
army returns to the river. . . ." This seems to suggest that the
move was only to be a temporary one, to the railway and back:
in other words, merely a raid. If that was all that Sherman had
in mind the above questions receive an obvious answer; everything becomes crystal clear. Let us see whether this theory is
supported by Sherman's orders during the operation. Here
are a few samples:

September 31st. *Sherman to Thomas*: "I don't believe anyone recognises how important it is now to destroy this railroad."

Sherman to Howard: "We must have that railroad and it is
worth us a heavy battle."

Sherman to Halleck: "To-day I press at all points, but expect
to make a lodgment on the [rail] road at or below Jonesborough,

[3] *The Civil War and Reconstruction* p. 622.
[4] *Ibid.*, p. 554.

when I propose to swing the whole army upon it and break it all to pieces."

At 2 p.m. that day, when he has become aware of Hood's correct disposition, Sherman is still talking of Schofield "doing infinite mischief" to the railroad.

As late as September 2nd, when Hardee had retreated to Lovejoy, he orders the IV Corps to break the railway that night and press the enemy next day. Finally comes his wire to Halleck sent off at 6 a.m. on September 3rd: " I shall not pursue much further *on this raid* " (my italics).5

Thus it was purely a raid all the time. The railway was to be destroyed; the army would then return to the river, and await the inevitable result—the evacuation of Atlanta by Hood. Evidently there was to be no pursuit, else Sherman would hardly have destroyed the railway so thoroughly, only to have to repair it a few days later. The fact that in the course of it Sherman tried to seize the opportunity to strike one of Hood's Corps when it was isolated did not turn Sherman from his main object, though the fact that he proposed merely " to push Hardee and Lee " away from Atlanta shows that he was not proposing to defeat these two corps, but would be satisfied with driving them away. Sherman seems to have had an absolute obsession for the destruction of railways—to the neglect of everything else. On this point Schofield has some caustic things to say. " Had Sherman divided his army . . . and struck at Hood's rear, he might have found a chance to destroy that army as well as the railroads in Georgia."6

Stone sums up the matter in a neat phrase: Sherman's operation " failed of overwhelming success only because, after it was fairly under way, Sherman expended his energies in breaking up the railroad, instead of breaking up Hood's Army."7

There can be few more extraordinary spectacles in war than that of a whole army sitting upon a railway in rear of its opponents, engaged in " breaking it all to pieces "!

It should further be noted that when, on September 1st, Sherman did try to drive his army forward rapidly it refused to be driven. This was probably due to two causes. After all the emphasis that had been placed upon railroad destruction, and after a leisurely two days spent in that congenial task, the troops would find it hard to believe that there was really cause

---

5 All these despatches are contained in *Official Records*, vol. 38, v.
6 *Schofield*, p. 146.
7 *M.S.H.M.*, viii, 490.

for extreme exertion. The other reason is the caution that Hood had driven into the Union commanders by his rapid rapier thrusts.

In his report of September 15th, Sherman explains that he was in a hurry to get to the Macon railway, since it would give him the "interior lines," owing to its sharp bend to the east south of Rough and Ready. But did he forget when he penned this passage that he had halted for thirty-six hours on the Montgomery railroad before moving forward to this "interior lines" position? Probably he did, for his report proceeds: "The several columns moved punctually on the morning of the 29th," whereas we know that they remained halted all day.

Sherman displays throughout this campaign a curious mixture of boldness and caution. He is frequently impressing upon his subordinates the need to take risks, and many of his projects involved the taking of risks, yet when an operation was in full swing we seldom find him taking risks himself. The Jonesborough operation is a conspicuous example of this. On September 2nd, when he got an inkling of the fact that Hood was trying to escape from Atlanta, his first instincts and his first orders were of a defensive nature. Though all the omens pointed to the fact that Hood was quitting, he professed to hold doubts of it throughout that vital day. He had recently lectured Schofield on the necessity for taking risks, yet when that general "offered to go with two corps, or even with one, and intercept Hood's retreat . . . we remained quietly in our camps for five days, while Hood leisurely marched round us."[8] Sherman no doubt told the exact truth in a letter home: "(Grant) don't care a damn for what the enemy does out of his sight, but it scares me like hell."[9]

In fact, Sherman seems to have reversed Bacon's famous adage: "In counsel it is good to see dangers, and in execution not to see them except they be very great." Shortly after the war he proclaimed in a speech: "You cannot attain great success in war without taking great risks," which is perhaps one reason why he never won a great battle.

Hood has been universally blamed for his misreading of the situation in the early days of the operation, and on August 31st when he recalled Lee's Corps. Yet the fact has been overlooked that Sherman was almost equally at sea on the 31st, and again on the 2nd, and he had not the excuse that he was deficient of

[8] *Schofield*, p. 156.
[9] *Home Letters of General Sherman*, p. 424.

cavalry. Hood was certainly in an unenviable position. He had divested himself of his " eyes," like so many other leaders in the Civil War, and like them he lived to regret it; and latterly he was cut off from direct communication with Hardee. But he did not adopt the supine and inert attitude on August 30th of which he is generally accused. The *Official Records* contain no less than twenty-seven messages sent out to his corps commanders that day, betokening his anxiety and wideawakeness. Several minor movements of troops were made. For instance, at 2 p.m. on that day Hood's Chief of Staff wrote to Hardee: "General Hood desires you to take whatever measures you may think necessary to prevent the enemy gaining Jonesborough or Rough and Ready this afternoon." But no number of messages could compensate for the absence of Wheeler. Hood's surprise is as directly attributable to this as McPherson's surprise on July 22nd was attributable to the absence of Garrard's cavalry.

A word must go out in sympathy to General Hardee in his lonely uphill battle against the bulk of the Union Army at Jonesborough. The march to Jonesborough had been a very trying one. Lee, in his report, speaks of " a wearied and jaded column," and says that straggling was widespread. And Hardee reports that the troops advanced to the attack " with reluctance and distrust." After Lee had been taken away from him and he was left to face the Union Army single-handed, his line was so extended that in most places it consisted of but a single rank. We may believe him when he says: " It is difficult to imagine a more perplexing or perilous situation."[10] The fact that, despite the low morale of his troops, he was able to extricate them and withdraw to Lovejoy, and there beat off an attack, speaks well for his generalship.

48

The reader may be surprised to read so many adverse criticisms of General Sherman, at a moment that proved the zenith of his career. But students of war must not allow themselves to be dazzled by the blaze of glory that has encircled the Union commander, consequent on his capture of Atlanta. To err is human, and even Napoleon made glaring mistakes in the midst of his most famous campaigns. After the lapse of three-quarters of a century we ought to be able to look the facts unblinking in the face, and sort out the chaff from the good grain. There was not much chaff in Sherman, and his reputation will stand the chaff being exhibited as well as the good grain.

In conclusion, it is instructive to note how the main objective

[10] *S.H.S.P.*, viii, 344.

gradually changed in Sherman's eyes, from the destruction of his opponent's army to the capture of a particular town. He achieved this object cleverly and at times brilliantly, and at a cost of only 40,000 casualties (about the same as his opponents). But he had not carried out the primary task assigned to him. The Confederate Army, though shaken, was still intact. Was Sherman justified in now leaving it to its own devices, as he did, and in sitting down in a defensive position in the city he had just captured? What would Grant think of it? The opening stage 49 in the campaign thus ends on a large note of interrogation.

CHAPTER XIV

The Rebound.

"THE enemy, I think, will take position at East Point, Atlanta and Decatur, to recruit his army and prepare for another campaign." If Sherman had himself penned those words they could not more exactly describe the actual course of events. But they happened to be penned by his opponent, General Hood—a remarkable example of correct appreciation of the situation. Sherman withdrew to Atlanta, rested and refitted his men, and began to debate what his further action should be.

His situation was a difficult one. He had " scotched the snake, not killed it." The opposing army was still intact, if disheartened and weary. But the breathing-space vouchsafed to it by Sherman was of greater comparative value than that accorded to his own army, which was in less need of it. Sherman's idea had been to strike south and join forces with Canby who should be advancing from Mobile on the Gulf of Mexico. But the troops that were earmarked for this purpose had been detached into Missouri, and the plan had to be abandoned. Meanwhile, the Union Army found itself reduced by 30 per cent owing to the time expiry of many of the regiments. Instead of making them up with recruits, fresh units were formed. Thus the experience and prestige gained by the old regiments was lost with them. Moreover, 50 the lines of communications with the base, Louisville, had stretched to 475 miles, and was in continual danger of being broken by the superior Southern cavalry. The Northern historian Ropes writes: " General Sherman thus found himself in a very difficult position. . . . He knew perfectly well that he had not set out from Dalton with the object of getting possession of Atlanta, but with the object of destroying the main Confederate Army in the west; and he knew also that he had done practically nothing towards carrying out his intention."[1]

The idea now occurred to him to make a raid of about three months into Georgia, " to smash up things " and, in his own elegant phrase, " to make Georgia howl." It would be tedious and profitless to trace out in detail the long correspondence that

[1] *M.H.S.M.*, x, 136.

he had with Grant on the subject. Apart from occasional allusions to it, I must leave the reader to picture to himself the idea steadily growing in Sherman's mind during the next few weeks, whenever a pause in the operations occcurred.

The Confederates also had their difficulties. Hood's appointment had never been popular with the army, and the heavy casualties incurred, coupled with a lack of success, had shaken the confidence of the troops in their commander. When the President visited the army on September 25th, some of the men were heard to cry out: " Give us back Joe Johnston." The President, however, remained faithful to Hood; but probably in deference to the murmurs he heard from various quarters, he brought in General Beauregard over Hood's head, to command the " Military Division of the West." Beauregard's instructions were somewhat equivocal, and according to Roman, Beauregard interpreted them to mean that he was merely sent in the capacity of adviser to Hood. Hood seems to have had the same impression, and being of an independent disposition he paid scant regard to Beauregard's views. In fact, the latter had no appreciable influence on the forthcoming campaign, and though he frequently visited Hood, he will but seldom be referred to in these pages.

Hood, in spite of his early lack of success, had no intention of reverting to the passive defensive, and was soon debating a new plan. This plan, which was approved by the President, can be given shortly in his own words: " I shall, unless Sherman moves south . . . cross the Chattahoochee river . . .; this will . . . force him to drive me off, or move south, when I shall fall upon his rear."[2] A Northern general comments on this: " Hood had now grown tired of inaction and formed a most sensible plan."[3] But before carrying it out, various changes were made in each army. On the Northern side Thomas had been sent to Nashville to organise the defence of the Tennessee, and had been succeeded by Stanley. Schofield had gone on leave, and was temporarily replaced by Cox (the future historian of the campaign). Two corps commanders, Logan and Blair, had also gone, and the XVI Corps had been broken up. It will be convenient, therefore, to recapitulate the new order of battle.

Army of the Cumberland (Stanley)
IV, XIV, and XX Corps.

[2] This and the other quotations in this chapter are taken from O.R. XXXIX, Parts 1 and 3, unless otherwise stated.
[3] M.H.S.M., viii, 506.

Army of the Tennessee (Howard)
XV and XVII Corps.

Army of the Ohio (Schofield)
XXIII Corps.

In the Confederate Army Hardee had, by Hood's request, been replaced by Cheatham. This was in accordance with Hardee's wishes, as he disliked serving under Hood, who was his junior. The three corps commanders were, thus, Lee, Stewart, and Cheatham.

Sherman had incurred great odium in the Southern ranks by removing all the civilian population from Atlanta. "I want it a pure Gibraltar," he explained to Halleck.* He had obtained an inkling of Hood's plan from some indiscreet speeches by the President: and in addition to sending Thomas to Tennessee he sent two divisions to Chattanooga and Corse's Division to Rome.

On September 20th Hood set out upon his new move, by transferring his army to Palmetto on the Montgomery railway twenty-four miles south-west of Atlanta. On the 29th he crossed the Chattahoochee without opposition and by the 2nd of October was concentrated at Lost Mountain midway between Dallas and Marietta. On October 1st Sherman got wind of this move, but fancied that Hood was making for Tennessee. He formed the intention, in that event, of advancing on Savannah himself; if on the other hand Hood's objective should prove to be the railway in his rear, he would turn upon him. But before issuing any orders Sherman waited till the 3rd, in order to make quite certain that Hood was moving. (Sketch Map 18.)

On the 3rd Sherman set out in pursuit with his whole army, less the XX Corps, which was left to garrison Atlanta and hold the Chattahoochee Bridge. This move was expected by Hood who, on taking up his position at Lost Mountain had written to Bragg: "This will, I think, force the enemy to move on me or move south."

On October 4th Hood sent Stewart's Corps to destroy the railway between Big Shanty and Acworth. This was successfully achieved and prisoners captured, and the corps returned to Lost Mountain on the morning of the 5th, less French's Division, which was sent to Allatoona. Hood's instructions were that it should " fill up the deep cut at Allatoona, with rails, logs, dirt,

---

* Eventually he abandoned it himself, and this proud city of the South became for some time an empty shell.

brush, etc., and destroy the Etowah bridge if possible and then rejoin."

BATTLE OF ALLATOONA, OCTOBER 5TH.

This battle is described by Ropes as "one of the most memorable occurrences in the whole war"; and it merits detailed examination by the student—but not for the reason that made it memorable to the Northern public.

Early in the morning French set off on his mission, but on approaching Allatoona he found it occupied and entrenched. The small garrison had by Sherman's orders been reinforced in the nick of time by Corse's Division from Rome. At 9 a.m. French attacked, and soon captured a portion of the position, together with prisoners and colours. But the resistance was sturdy. After three hours hard fighting preparations were made for a final assault. General Sears, who was in charge of it, reported to French at 12.30 p.m.: "Will get up a grand charge as soon as the men rest a little. We will take this work if possible." But the charge was never made. Instead, French ordered his whole division to retire. What had happened? Let French himself explain. "At 12.15 I was informed that enemy infantry was moving on the railroad and entering Big Shanty at 9 a.m., and that his cavalry was moving up on the east side of the railroad. Ammunition too, being nearly exhausted . . . I resolved to withdraw my forces." He says in further explanation: "By noon the enemy could reach Acworth and be within two miles of the road by which I was to reach New Hope Church." French's reasoning was sound, always provided that his information was correct. However it was incorrect. No hostile infantry entered Big Shanty that day. At the most it was a cavalry patrol. Meanwhile, Sherman was himself watching the fight from the top of Kenesaw Mountain, and his signal station there was exchanging some dramatic messages with the stricken garrison, which have tended to give the colour and fame to the engagement that was soon attached to it by civilians. On the evening of the 4th the garrison spelled out this message. "General Sherman says hold fast, we are coming."*

After anxious hours on the morning of the 5th Kenesaw received this message: "We hold out. General Corse here." Later: "We are all right so far. General Corse is wounded. Where is General Sherman?" To which the signal officer replied:

* This became the inspiration of the popular hymn: "Hold the fort, for we are coming."

MAP 18

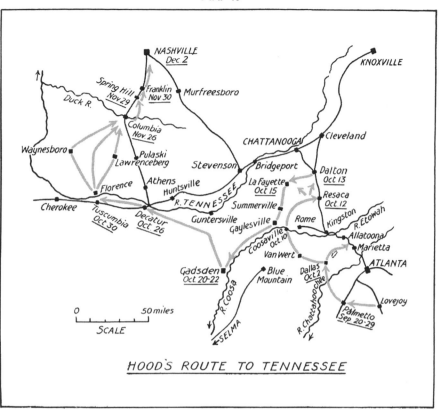

HOOD'S ROUTE TO TENNESSEE

" Near you "—a polite lie. This was followed by a message, evidently on Sherman's instructions: " Tell Allatoona hold on. General Sherman says he is working hard for you."

Now let us see what hard work Sherman was doing for Allatoona. The situation at 8 a.m. when he arrived on the mountain

SKETCH MAP 19

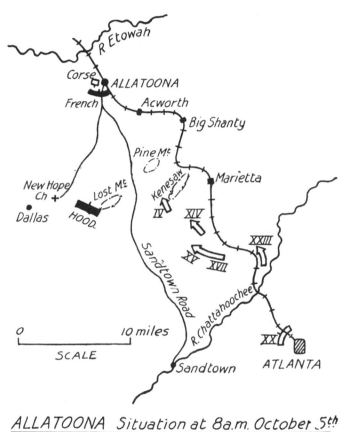

ALLATOONA Situation at 8a.m. October 5th

is shown on Sketch Map 19 (cavalry dispositions omitted). The IV Corps had reached Kenesaw overnight. The remaining four corps were strung out a dozen miles to the rear on the march. The cavalry was scouting forward towards Allatoona. In his official report Sherman afterwards claimed to have caused the abandonment of the attack by French. " The distance, 18 miles, was too great for me to make in time to share in the battle, but I

directed the XXIII Corps . . . to move rapidly . . . due west
. . . threatening the rear of the forces attacking Allatoona. . . .
The move of General Cox had the desired effect of causing the
withdrawal of French's Division rapidly in the direction of Dallas."
In his *Memoirs* he adds another claim: " The rest of the Army was
directed straight for Allatoona."[4] Unfortunately for Sherman's
reputation as a reporter, not one of these statements can be
substantiated.

1. The distance Kenesaw to Allatoona is thirteen miles in an
air line, and there was a fairly direct road.   But Sherman's troops
would have exerted some influence on the battle while still two
or three miles short of the place.

2. The IV Corps moved at 7.30 a.m. to make a feint on Pine
mountain.   On arrival they were ordered by Sherman to take
up a defensive position.   They could easily have reached the
fringe of the battlefield by 2 p.m., one hour before French broke
off the battle.

3. The XXIII Corps received no such orders.   It did receive
orders to advance north-west twenty-four hours later (but there
was no mention of " rapidly "), long before which time the
battle was over.

4. French withdrew, not as the result of any infantry movement
in his rear, but as the result of a false report—so common in war!
Possibly Stone had this passage in mind when he spoke of " Sherman's amazing indifference to historic truthfulness."[5]   The
fact is, of course, Sherman was not deliberately untruthful;
but generals, and other ranks too, are apt to become hazy and to
suffer delusions as to the course of events in battle in after days.
Did not the Duke of Wellington stoutly declare that the British
artillery ran away at the Battle of Waterloo!   But the episode
conveys a useful lesson for the student.   It is this: *accept no
statements made after a battle unless they are either inherently
probable or are corroborated from another source.*

The blunt fact is that in spite of the reassuring messages:
" We are coming," " working hard for you," etc., Sherman took
no direct steps to intervene in the battle.   The IV Corps had on
the previous evening been ordered to " make a feint on Pine
Mountain in the morning with a view to preventing an attack on
Allatoona which I want to avoid."   But when the morning came,
and it was evident that the attack was already being made on
Allatoona, the feint movement was not converted into a real

4 *Op cit.*, ii, 147.
5 *M.H.S.M.* x, 190.

advance on Allatoona. Indeed, at 2.30 p.m., Sherman ordered his army to take up a defensive line facing south-west.

What is the explanation of all this? It is a simple one—*the presence of Hood's Army at Lost Mountain.* The Confederate Army was concentrated and ideally situated to threaten Sherman's left flank if he advanced up the railway. Until his scattered corps should be concentrated Sherman did not dare to take the risk which he might have taken against Johnston. The result was that Allatoona was left to its fate. The attack on it was abandoned, not as the result of any Northern move but by the false report of a Southern scout!

That evening Sherman concentrated his army round Kenesaw, and sent a cavalry brigade forward to try and find out the situation at Allatoona.

COMMENTS.

Of few episodes in the war can so much misconception have arisen as of the Allatoona affair. This is due to the fact that historians who should have known better have accepted the literal truth of Sherman's report without verifying it.* The sober fact is that Sherman not only took no steps to relieve Allatoona on the 5th, but made no appreciable effort to hasten the forward move of his infantry. Cox's orders to his 2nd Division contained the words: "Do not hurry your men too much"—a clear indication that no special effort had been required by the commander.

It has also been asserted that Sherman intended to hammer Hood's force against the anvil formed by the River Etowah. I can find no support for this assertion in the recorded writings of Sherman himself. On the contrary the whole purport of his orders was that he should first concentrate and then " move upon the enemy *wherever he may be.*" Sherman had in fact learnt by experience that it does not pay to make too cut-and-dried plans in advance. It takes two to make a fight, and even when one possesses the initiative (which Sherman did not now possess) the enemy's future action cannot be assumed.

It is true that the Union Commander was badly served by his cavalry (his caustic comments on their " stickiness " elicited a spirited protest from Elliott, their commander), but he failed to give them explicit orders to relieve Allatoona. Even next day, when he was still uncertain whether the town had held out, he merely directed them to ascertain what the situation was.

* Even that careful historian T. R. Hay writes: " Sherman had set his troops in motion for the relief of the fort." *Hood's Tennessee Campaign,* p. 44.

The interesting point to discuss is, could and should Sherman have sent relief to Allatoona when he realised it was being attacked on the morning of the 5th? A study of Sketch Map 19 will show that (*a*) the IV Corps could have intervened in the battle, but that (*b*) it would have entailed unjustifiable risk to have sent such a large force at that juncture. Hood's Army was concentrated and within striking distance. Sherman had evidently imbibed a wholesome respect for the lightning blows that Hood had shown himself capable of delivering, and under the circumstances he was justified in concentrating at least the bulk of his army at Kenesaw before despatching a large force towards Allatoona. The fact is, Hood was enjoying those advantages that the possession of the initiative imparts. He had sprung a march upon his opponent, and was calmly sitting in an admirably selected "spider's nest" waiting for the chance to spring out on any isolated force of the enemy that might venture within range. But Sherman was too experienced a general to be caught. Hood's decision deliberately to open the road into Georgia to his adversary and to abandon his own lines of communication was an exceptionally bold one, even for him. But it was justified up to the hilt. In fact, both commanders show up in a favourable light in the first stage of the Rebound. But the fact remains that Allatoona was saved for the Union more by good luck than good management.

October 6th.

Sherman's orders for this day are worth recording. The infantry, less Cox, was to form a defensive line with its right on Pine Mountain, facing south-west. Cox was to advance north-west to the Sandtown road, presumably to cut off any enemy who might be in the vicinity of Allatoona. As for the cavalry, " General Elliott will send cavalry to-day to Big Shanty, Acworth and Allatoona, and bring back official reports." That is all! There is no hint of any offensive action, although his army was now concentrated. Cox advanced carefully to the Sandtown road, but could find no enemy. No reports came in from Allatoona, but two signal messages were got through in the afternoon. The first was from the gallant Corse: " I am short a cheek bone and one ear, but am able to whip all hell yet. My losses are very heavy. A force moving from Stilesborough on Kingston gives me some anxiety. Tell me where Sherman is." The second message merely asked, " Where is General Sherman?" The reply sent by an A.D.C. said: " Have sent you assistance (another polite lie). . . General is mindful of you." The general himself also sent a message, evidently meant to be reassuring: " All is right with you.   If possible keep the enemy off your lines . . . " but no reference to having " sent assistance."   Considering that he had earlier in the day admitted to Slocum that he was not yet positive of the fate of Allatoona his neglect to send this assistance on the morning of the 6th is remarkable—if not callous.

By the evening it became evident that Hood had withdrawn in the direction of Dallas.   He accordingly sent Corse a message ordering him back to Rome and adding: " I will to-morrow continue to demonstrate against [Hood] and make him keep his people together."

Next morning, the 7th, it appeared that the Confederate Army had gone south, and Sherman duly warned Slocum: " I will watch Mr. Hood good. . . . Hood has gone off south and may swing round on you."   Sherman intended to follow up but postponed the order pending the receipt of further information.   But a brigade was at last sent to Allatoona (as escort to a message to Corse), and Cox was sent out to the north and west in observation.   Thus the day was frittered away on the Union side.

Meanwhile, what had happened to Hood? So far from going back south, he had pushed on to the north-west, and by evening of the 7th had reached Van Wert (see Sketch Map 18).   There for the moment we will leave him.

Sherman was frankly puzzled.   Writing to Corse he unconsciously paid his opponent the greatest compliment in his power: " But [Hood] is eccentric and I cannot guess his movements as I could those of Johnston, who was a sensible man and only did sensible things."   Then, as if to encourage himself he added: " If Hood does not mind I will catch him in a worse snap than he has been in."

On October 8th, bar sending Cox to Allatoona, he did nothing. It was raining heavily, which he declared made an attack impossible. (It did not prevent his opponent marching.)   Sherman had by now learnt of the true direction of Hood's march.

On October 9th, still stationary, he sent Grant a dispatch which afterwards became famous: " It will be a physical impossibility to protect the roads now that Hood, Forrest, Wheeler, and the whole batch of devils are turnèd loose without home or habitation. I think Hood's movements indicate a diversion to the end of the Selma Road . . . [He then proposes to march to Savannah, adding the remark]. . . . I can make this march, and make Georgia howl."   Sherman was fretting increasingly at his loss of the initiative, and at the humiliation of being forced to dance to Hood's piping.

But on October 10th alarming news came in which banished all idea of making Georgia howl for the time being. Hood was reported crossing the Coosa ten miles west of Rome, and troops were approaching that town. It looked as if a swoop on Rome was intended. Instantly Sherman was galvanized into action. Orders were issued for the whole army to march at once on Rome, and Thomas was ordered to guard the Tennessee river to the west of Chattanooga in case a raid on Tennessee was intended. To Stanley he wrote in a slightly contemptuous vein: " Hood's whole movement is inexplicable to any commonsense theory." But his messages belie this attitude. For example, to Howard, who had asked to be allowed to march next morning: " It is all-important that you should make a forced march to-night." And to Corse at Rome: " Orders are all out and the troops are marching for Rome and will make it in time if it is possible." Evidently Corse was not to be left to fight his own battle this time! Help was indeed coming. Sherman showed himself at his best this day. His tireless energy and active mind is reflected in his correspondence. The *Official Records* contain no less than 35 letters written by him this day, and all very much to the point. So the army marched that afternoon and through that anxious night, and on the morning of the 11th was just short of Kingston.

That day the army reached Rome, but Hood had again vanished! Where had he gone to this time? Sherman made a series of guesses during the day which can be summarised thus: 1, To Resaca; 2, To Blue Mountain (i.e. south-west); 3, to Tennessee, " Doubtless Hood has gone up to the Tennessee and I will go to Rome and get behind him." 4, "Hood . . . may swing back to Georgia."

Sherman on this day reminds one of the Duke of Buckingham who " was everything by starts, and nothing long." Thomas collected what troops he could and sent them off to guard the river. Meanwhile anxiety, even consternation, was increasing, as is evidenced by the tenor and tone of the messages.

On October 12th there was still no news of Hood, and Cox was sent to Coosaville where the enemy had crossed the Coosa to destroy Hood's pontoon bridge and gather information.

On the 13th news at last came in that Hood had gone still farther north. All was once again feverish activity. This time Resaca might be the objective. All troops (less Cox, who was told to follow as soon as possible) were hastened towards Resaca, and Sherman wired to the commander of the garrison: " Hold Resaca to the death. I will send you reinforcements by cars and will come up." It was becoming quite a familiar story.

The alarm had now spread to Washington and Halleck wired to Schofield who was near Chattanooga and was trying to rejoin his command: " All forces that can possibly be spared from Kentucky should be sent to General Thomas at Nashville to enable him to meet any forces that Hood may send north."

Thomas was now concentrating every available man at Chattanooga.

We must now return to that phantom, General Hood. The Confederate Commander had not originally contemplated advancing so far north. But he was encouraged thereto by his opponent's reactions to his first manœuvre. On withdrawing from Lost Mountain he had ideas of attacking Rome, but thinking better of it, he turned it by the west and marched straight on Resaca. Lee's Corps was sent against that place on the 12th. Lee summoned it to surrender, but receiving a defiant reply and finding that it was strongly held he withdrew. On the 13th Hood attacked and captured Dalton after a brief cannonade. He then destroyed no less than fifteen miles of railway in the vicinity —and once again disappeared!

This brings us to the 14th. Sherman had now reached Resaca, but once again he had lost touch with Hood, who was believed to have gone north. Consternation in Tennessee was intensified, and Kentucky was combed for men. Grant, at a greater distance, was cooler, and wrote to Halleck: " It looks to me that Hood has now put himself in a position where his army must be to a great extent destroyed." No doubt Grant had been studying the map and saw that Hood was apparently between two fires, that of Sherman and that of Thomas. Sherman's views at this juncture are not so clear. According to Thomas's biographer, the Union commander had not anticipated such a move on the part of Hood; his messages become less voluminous, and he abandons conjecture and confines himself to the task in hand, which is the forcing of the Snake Creek Gap. This was accomplished without difficulty on the 15th, and Villanow* reached by the leading corps. It now appeared that the enemy had gone west, and on the 16th Sherman reached Ships Gap, on the road to La Fayette. From here he wrote: " As soon as I know where the enemy is I will follow." And then reverting to his old love, he

* Midway between Resaca and La Fayette.

adds: " I want to make a raid that will make the South feel the terrible character of our people." Schofield was manœuvring round Chattanooga, and to him Sherman wrote: " I am pushing straight for Hood, wherever he may be; do the same with whatever force you have, and let us run him down." This is evidently the contingency that Grant had pictured, but Sherman's next letter shows an abrupt change of policy: " I want the first positive fact that Hood contemplates an invasion of Tennessee. Invite him to do so. Send him a free pass in."

But apparently Hood contemplated no such thing, for on the 17th Sherman heard that he had gone south. Meanwhile the difficulties of forces working on exterior lines was being strikingly exemplified. Co-operation between Sherman and Schofield was proving difficult; Thomas and Sherman were each giving Schofield conflicting orders.

Ordering Schofield to join him, Sherman now resumed his march in a leisurely fashion after Hood. Passing Summerville on the 19th he reached Gaylesville on the 20th, and there he halted. On the same day Hood reached Gadsden, sixty miles to the south-west. He had gained twenty miles on his pursuer. His greater speed in marching was partly due to the fact that he had detached his train and reserve artillery to Gadsden after quitting Dallas.

Before turning south from La Fayette on the 17th, Hood had, as he himself admitted, spent some time in " serious thought and perplexity." He wished to turn and attack Sherman, but his corps commanders asserted that the morale of the army was not yet sufficiently high. He next considered advancing into Tennessee, and referred the matter to Beauregard. After further discussion at Gadsden, it was decided that he should undertake the operation, and on October 22nd he marched north with that object. A week later Sherman withdrew to Rome. Thus the two main armies of the West fell apart, never to meet again, a phenomenon that has rightly been described as " one of the curiosities of the war."[6] The duel between Sherman and Hood was over, and it only remains to examine their respective achievements.

COMMENTS.

In this campaign of what I have called "The Rebound," the limelight is switched from the colourful Ohioan to the equally colourful Texan. Hood's conduct of this campaign was practi-

6 *The Civil War and Reconstruction*, by J. G. Randall, p. 554.

cally flawless. In what respect could he have bettered it? Consider what he had achieved. At very slight cost in men he had drawn Sherman back over one hundred miles; he had wrested from him the initiative, and reduced him to hurriedly parrying a series of blows, none very great in themselves, but considerable in their cumulative effect; he had improved the morale of his own troops, and dampened that of his opponents; finally he had created alarm as far as the Northern capital, and had delayed Sherman's march to the sea by a month. The strength of Hood's strategic position lay in the fact that if he was attacked he could fall back on the railway from Blue Mountain to Selma; its beauty lay in the fact that while threatening his opponent's communications he was covering his own. Many people think that Johnston should have adopted the same course instead of retreating on Atlanta; and Hood's success seems to justify this view.

Sherman's conduct of the campaign is not particularly impressive. Though frequently boasting that he would " whip " Hood he never looked like doing so. Instead he had, in Liddell Hart's expressive phrase, " trailed in his enemy's wake until he had been drawn over a hundred miles back from Atlanta."[7]

Hood had calculated that his movements would have this effect, and they had. He was distinctly more successful in divining his adversary's movements than was Sherman.

The latter's task during this campaign had been a difficult, almost a humiliating one. One would feel sympathy for him were it not for the fact that he had brought his troubles on himself by ignoring his instructions—" to whip Joe Johnston." He had allowed the glamour of Atlanta to blind his gaze and distort his sense of proportion. After Jonesborough, the Confederate army was almost at the end of its tether. Another heavy blow and it might have disintegrated altogether. But Sherman never struck with his whole force. It has been observed that he never once in the whole war commanded in a battle in which he engaged his whole force. The result was that he never won a resounding victory; and he was to learn the truth of the adage, " He who fights and (is allowed to) run away, will live to fight another day." Sherman's withdrawal from in front of his opponent after Jonesborough is described by that sound and fair-minded Northern critic, T. R. Hay, as " a cardinal mistake." It was probably the greatest mistake of his military career. Apart from conceding to Hood the initiative, it gave him the opportunity of detaching troops to Lee. Yet one of Sherman's tasks had been to keep his

7 *Sherman*, p. 338.

opponent busy, and thus prevent detachments. If the war had ended with this campaign there is no doubt where the military laurels would have rested. But having made that mistake, Sherman did his best to retrieve it—or nearly his best. His opponent was a slippery customer: " Hood can turn and twist like a fox," he ruefully admitted. To have caught his fox he would have required to be well served by his cavalry and to take risks with his infantry. But his cavalry served him badly, and he took no risks with his infantry. Even when opposed by the passive Johnston he admitted: " My operations have been rather cautious than bold." Hood's vigorous if costly blows at Atlanta had had their harvest in imposing still greater caution. But assuming that caution was necessary, Sherman's handling of his forces was masterly. Except when Cox was detached to Coosaville the army was always within a day's march of concentration. Hood admitted as much. " It had been my hope that my movements would have caused the enemy to divide his forces that I might gain an opportunity to strike him in detail. This, however, he did not do." Neither did Hood give Sherman an opportunity to strike him in detail. In this respect both commanders conducted this most interesting campaign with unusual skill.

A note may be added here on the policy of cavalry raids. Occasionally these had material results, especially those of Forrest. But usually their effect was only ephemeral. They wasted horseflesh, and frequently they entailed the absence of the cavalry when their presence was urgently required. This continued to be the case in the campaign next to be described. In general, such raids were a mistake.

CHAPTER XV

Sherman and Hood Part.
Nashville and Savannah.

ON October 22nd Hood started off on his Tennessee campaign, disappearing once more from Sherman's ken. The latter had described Gaylesville as "a position very good to watch the enemy"; but Stone drily comments: " In spite of this ' watch ' Hood suddenly appeared on the 26th at Decatur, 75 miles away. This move was a complete surprise."[1] The crossing at Decatur was guarded, so Hood pushed farther west to Tuscumbia, where he was able to cross to the northern bank of the Tennessee at Florence. Sherman did not attempt to pursue. The fact is, the Confederate army could move more speedily than the Northern and it is rather hopeless, as Sherman now recognised, for a battleship to " watch " a cruiser, or to attempt to pursue it. He therefore fell back to Rome, hoping that Hood would follow. He also detached the IV and XXIII Corps to join Thomas, for the protection of Tennessee, while with the remaining four corps he prepared to march through Georgia to the sea.

Hood's intention was to advance rapidly into Tennessee before Thomas could collect sufficient force with which to oppose him. Hopes were also entertained of planting the Confederate banners on the banks of the Ohio. Beauregard joined him at Tuscumbia, and gave his approval to the plan. The anomaly of Beauregard's position is shown by a question he addressed from this place to the President: " Please inform me whether my presence with any army in the field imposes on me the necessity of assuming command." According to the strict letter of his orders it undoubtedly did, and Beauregard took good care to absent himself while active operations were taking place. The part played by him in this stage of the war is unimpressive.

Hood met with a double disappointment at Tuscumbia; the supplies that he had ordered were late in arriving, and the rains were so bad in November as to prevent any movement. As a result, instead of pushing straight on into Tennessee he was obliged to halt for three weeks. Thomas put these three weeks

[1] *B. & L.*, iv, 441.

to good account. He had over 70,000 troops at call, but they were badly scattered, and many of them were practically untrained. He set to work welding them into an army, and was in the middle of the task when the blow fell.

It is not possible here to give more than a brief account of the ensuing campaign. Hood started out, in vile weather, on November 20th, with about 40,000 infantry and 8,000 cavalry under the redoubtable Forrest who had by now joined him from his raid in west Tennessee. Schofield, in command of the IV and XXIII Corps, was at Pulaski, 50 miles to the north-east. Thomas was endeavouring to collect the remainder of his army at Nashville, 80 miles farther north. Two divisions from Missouri under Smith were daily expected; in the meanwhile Schofield was to delay the enemy as much as possible.

Hood advanced to the north on a very broad front. Cheatham towards Waynesborough, Stewart towards Lawrenceburg, and Lee between the other two. Schofield saw that if he remained at Pulaski his right flank would be turned, and on the 23rd he fell back to Columbia, midway to Nashville. In so doing, Stone is of opinion that he saved his army from utter destruction. Be that as it may, Hood came up with his main army on the 26th, and prepared to attack on the 29th.

His plan was, as usual, a bold one. While Lee held the enemy in front the remainder, led by Hood in person, made a wide sweep round to the east, thus turning Schofield's right flank. The battle which ensued is known as that of Spring Hill. For at that spot, 11 miles in rear of Columbia, the leading corps, Cheatham's, struck the road to Nashville. Only a thin line of Federals guarded it. Hood promptly gave the order for attack. Exactly what happened after that has been argued ever since, chiefly in Southern periodicals and collections. An amazing amount of conflicting testimony has been adduced. The one agreed fact is that the two leading divisions, Cleburne's and Brown's, failed to attack. Hood blamed Cheatham, Cheatham blamed Hood and his subordinates. Amid the maze of testimony on the subject one statement, made in the *Missouri Republican*, September 12th, 1885, and reprinted by Hay,[2] seems to clinch the matter. It is made by Cleburne's A.A.G., and states that he was present when an order was received from Cheatham to halt, just as the attack was getting to close quarters. Cleburne was a dashing Irishman (who had been in the British service) and was reckoned one of the best divisional commanders in the army; and it is hardly

[2] *Hood's Tennessee Campaign*, p. 231.

likely that he would have suspended his attack without definite orders.

Whosesoever the fault, the whole of Schofield's army was enabled to retreat down the road during the ensuing night and get clear away to Franklin. A Northern writer opines that " A single Confederate brigade . . . placed squarely across the pike, would have effectually prevented Schofield's retreat." Hood lost a "golden opportunity," and the consensus of military opinion is that he was himself primarily to blame, for he should have seen that his orders were carried out. This may be fair criticism, but it is a fact that Hood, writing only 13 days after the battle, stated specifically that his orders were " frequently and earnestly repeated." Writing years after the war, Hood made many statements that cannot be substantiated, but to state a deliberate untruth immediately after the event is unthinkable in one who was the soul of honour. No doubt if he had been an active man like Sherman he would have gone to the spot himself. But Hood was a cripple. The moral seems to be, *never place a cripple in command of an army*.

Schofield, having executed a most skilful night retreat, halted at Franklin next morning, November 30th, and hastily entrenched a position. Hood pursued vigorously, his troops and himself burning to make amends for the fiasco of the previous day. He reached the new position in the afternoon, and the age-long problem presented itself: should the attack be launched at once, before the enemy had time to strengthen their position, or should it be delayed till adequate preparation had been made? Hood decided for the first alternative, and his decision has been justified on the grounds that unless he attacked at once he would miss the chance of destroying Schofield's army before it could join forces with Thomas at Nashville. Schofield himself held this view. Hood therefore abandoned his usual method of making a wide flanking movement, and decided in favour of a direct frontal attack.

The attack was launched; its feature was the extreme gallantry of the attackers—probably unsurpassed in the annals of the Confederacy. This is at least evidence that Hood's army had recovered its lost morale. But alas, it was fruitless gallantry and sacrifice; few guns were up, and the Union predominance in artillery was overwhelming. After an initial success the Southerners were held all along the line. They had suffered over twice as many casualties as their opponents. A heavy price had been paid for this set-back, the heaviest being the death of General Cleburne.

The Confederate morale was once more broken. An officer wrote bluntly: "We had lost confidence in General Hood."[3]

Schofield had already received orders to withdraw next day, and this he did during the night. By noon of December 1st he was within the defences of Nashville. Hood, despite his heavy losses followed up, and encamped before the town. He hoped while in this position to gain recruits from the surrounding friendly country.

But his position had become an impossible one. Smith's divisions, and others, had arrived, and by December 10th Thomas had an army of over 50,000 men. Against this Hood could only put 23,000 infantry into the field. Hood's advance had created intense alarm all over the North. But he now seemed at the end of his tether.

But the difficulties were not all on one side. Hood had entrenched his position, and Thomas did not dare to attack it until his heterogeneous collection of troops had been formed into some sort of order. But Grant was impatient, and plied him with exhortations to attack at once—an eloquent tribute to the consternation that Hood's advance had created. The weather turned bad and Thomas was not to be rushed. To his cavalry commander he confided: "If they will let me alone I will fight this battle just as soon as it can be done, and will surely win it; but I will not throw the victory away . . . by moving till the thaw begins." He was as good as his word. Grant went so far as to appoint and sent out a successor to Thomas, but before he could arrive Thomas had struck.

The great two-day battle of Nashville was fought on December 15th and 16th. Thomas attacked and gradually turned Hood's left flank. Hood was forced to draw back his line: but even that did not save him. On the second day Hood's left was broken and the whole battleline dissolved in flight; 54 guns and 4,500 prisoners were captured, and the remainder fled to the rear with scarcely a semblance of order.

Forrest's cavalry had been absent during the battle, but returned in time to cover the retreat. It was the most decisive victory won by the Federals in the war, and Thomas had fought it with considerable skill. Unfortunately he did not follow up his victory with much push, and Hood was able to get back over the Tennessee with about 20,000 troops. Thomas did not pursue across the Tennessee, and Hood halted his army at Tuledo, 80 miles south-west of Tuscumbia, went into winter quarters, and

3 *B.H.S.P.*, ix, 522.

resigned his command of the army. Thus ended in utter ruin the most brilliantly conceived and daring campaign in the whole of the four years war.

COMMENTS.

Was Hood's a foolhardy venture, or was it deserving of success but dogged with bad luck? Schofield afterwards admitted, with a generosity unusual in military commanders: " The fortune of war was on the whole always in my favour." There is no doubt about Hood's bad luck, starting with his enforced delay at Tuscumbia. There is also no doubt that he ought to have gone far to destroy Schofield's army at Spring Hill. If this had happened Thomas could scarcely have withstood him at Nashville; and it is the almost unanimous opinion of the critics that Sherman would have been obliged to suspend his march to the sea, and return to Tennessee. If Hood was within an ace of such immense results how can he be fairly blamed for making the attempt? It seems to me that his critics are apt to judge military conduct by the upshot which is known to them, but was hidden to the participants at the time. Because Hood was eventually defeated they assert that defeat was " inevitable." I personally cannot see this inevitability. It is a facile and unconvincing form of criticism. War is a gamble. Risks must be taken. If Hood had played for safety he would have achieved nothing, and the war would have languished to its inevitable conclusion. It is especially encumbent on the weaker side to take risks, unless there is prospect of foreign intervention in its favour. This was no longer the case. Therefore Hood was justified. Into the vexed question of Thomas's generalship I do not purpose entering. Space prohibits it. That he was SLOW is universally conceded;* but was he also SURE? His numerous and clamant adherents insist that he was. Adherents of Grant and of Sherman assert that he was not even that. They say that he needlessly exposed Schofield to premature defeat by neglecting to concentrate in time; and that he muddled the battle of Nashville and by failure to pursue far and vigorously allowed the bulk of Hood's army to get away. All critics are, however, agreed that he possessed the unbounded, and even enthusiastic, confidence of his men.

Of Schofield all that need be said here is that he retrieved initial mistakes just in time, and that he fought the battle of Franklin with skill.

* Grant once described him as "slow beyond excuse."

Before passing on, I cannot withhold a word of tribute to this most maligned of Confederate commanders, this " one-legged hero " as he has been called; " that last and bravest champion of a desperate cause." Hood may be put down as one of the greatest failures among Southern generals; yet at one time his name was beginning to be uttered with dread in Northern territories. The key note to his failure was his physical condition. His three wounds had impaired not only his physical activity but his general efficiency.* Imperious by nature, the continual pain that he suffered at this period made him still more inaccessible and curt. In fact, he seems to have been a man of few friends. One may search the 48 volumes of the Southern Historical Society Papers without obtaining more than the most brief and fleeting references to him. None of his staff have served him as Badeau served Grant, and given us an intimate appreciation and picture of the man and his methods. For this and other reasons it is to be feared that an adequate biography of the man will never be written. But such a biography MUST be attempted. A secondary reason for his failure was his bad staff-work. His staff seems to have been inadequate and to have served him badly. It must be remembered that neither he nor his officers had received any professional training in such work.

We have spoken much of his failure, but contemporary documents show that for weeks he was considered dazzlingly successful. The number of desertions is a good test of the morale of an army, and it is noteworthy that during his advance into Tennessee the flow of desertion ceased almost entirely. Some Northern writers are more generous to him than his Southern friends. This is how Colonel H. Stone sums up his campaign: "Hood conceived and entered upon a campaign, unsurpassed for boldness, and, so long as pitted against Sherman, for success, by any undertaken by any Confederate General during the whole four years struggle."[4]

Hood's success was largely due to the speed and secrecy of his movements. The speed is obvious; as regards the secrecy there is not so much direct evidence, owing no doubt to the destruction of many papers; but such evidence as there is is supported by the indirect evidence that he always managed to mystify and surprise his opponents—one of the first attributes of generalship.

Hood was a man of one idea—to attack. He saw the impelling

* His health was so bad in November that he could not compile a report of operations for some time.

[4] M.H.S.M., iv, 482.

moral value of the offensive. With Napoleon he might say: " The moral is to the physical as three is to one." With Danton he might say: "L'audace, l'audace, toujours l'audace!" With Foch he might say: " A battle gained is one in which you refuse to acknowledge yourself defeated." Unfortunately for Hood, there is no absolute rule of war: success depends upon an infinity of factors, of which morale, though the most important, is only one.

Hood had not the mental stature nor vivid imagination of his great antagonistic. This is clearly evidenced in such of his correspondence as has come down to us. Even allowing for the fact that a seedy, one-armed man is not prone to writing voluminously, the contrast between them is striking. It may be ventured that if Hood was a man of but one idea, Sherman was a man of too many.

And so we leave him. His life after the war was still dogged with misfortune. Refusing a light sinecure post, he worked hard to support his wife and family. But he lost most of his money, he and his whole family were stricken with yellow fever, his wife and eldest son were struck down by it, and he himself, after a life of suffering, sorrow, and misfortune such as can have been the lot of but few, died on August 30th, 1879, at the early age of 48 years. In the words of a Northern historian: " General John Bell Hood, as a fighter and a man, was one of the truest and bravest that ever wore a uniform."

Sherman's March to the Sea.

After a long correspondence and a good deal of wobbling by Grant, Sherman at last received permission to make his march across Georgia to the sea. On November 16th his troops set out joyfully from Atlanta. Sherman's army was 62,000 strong, including a small force of cavalry under Kilpatrick. He carried several days' emergency rations, but calculated to live on the country. His order: " The army will forage liberally on the country" was interpreted as permission to loot. Sherman, indeed, exhibited his intention to " make Georgia howl " by destroying the country on a 60 mile wide band on his line of march. This march was in effect a peace march. The average day's march was 15 miles. Wheeler's cavalry and the Georgia militia offered practically no opposition, and on December 10th, Sherman appeared before the city of Savannah, having marched 300 miles in 24 days. Hardee commanded the defence force. 18,000 strong, but he did not intend to allow himself to be shut up in the city. Neither did Sherman intend to take the place by assault. To complete the investment and to gain access to the sea, Sherman sent a division to capture Fort McAllister at the mouth of the Ogeechee River, twelve miles to the south. After a brief engagement on December 13th the fort was captured, and simultaneously the vanguard of the Union fleet appeared. Next day Sherman met the admiral, and a plan of campaign was formed. Heavy naval guns were landed and preparations made for a bombardment. Before resorting to this, however, Sherman summoned the garrison to surrender. Hardee refused, but on the 20th decided to evacuate the city while yet there was time. That night he carried out his decision, and next morning the Union Army entered the capital city of Georgia. Sherman, with his ever-present sense of the dramatic, wired to the President: " I beg to present to you as a Christmas gift the city of Savannah."

Sherman's troops had thoroughly enjoyed the march. Shot-well puts it well. " This was the most halcyon period of their service and the one to which in after years their minds oftenest reverted with joyful recollections. There was little hardship in it. It was rather one bright patch of unclouded glory, the sunset of the war. There was fun everywhere, on the march, around the campfire, and in their tents. And it was attended by plenty. There was no hunger, no wounds, and no death. It held no sad memories. How in after years the faces of those men lighted up and their voices swelled to the chorus of the old tune of ' Marching through Georgia '! "5

The only criticism directed against Sherman has been that he allowed Hardee to escape from Savannah. Boynton says that Sherman allowed him to escape "without disclosing even a plausible excuse,"6 and Colonel Chisolm writes: " Having an overwhelming force his movement should have been a prompt and vigorous one to the rear of Savannah, and not a voyage to Hilton Head to borrow forces from General Foster."7

Comments.

The march to the sea caught the imagination of the people of the North even more than the capture of Atlanta. It formed a welcome " Christmas gift " and Sherman became the hero of the hour. In a large measure he deserved these plaudits. His superiors had not smiled upon his project, and he had only wrung a reluctant consent from Grant. " If it requires great moral courage under such gloomy conditions to launch an army

---

5 *The Civil War in America*, ii, 314.
6 *Sherman's Historical Raid*, p. 275.
7 *B. & L.*, iv, 680.

to an attack from a secure base, how much greater the effort and strength of will required to launch an army 'into the blue' knowing that the nearest point, Savannah, where he could hope to secure touch with his own side, was 300 miles distant."[8] Cox summarises the qualities required for this achievement very well: " The cool-headed, practical skill that carries out such a plan . . . is only possible to one who unites physical hardihood to mental grasp and unbending will."[9]

All this is incontrovertible; but we get into the region of controversy when we try to estimate what effect, if any, it had in shortening the war. It undoubtedly had a big moral effect upon the South at the time. Jefferson Davis admitted that "Sherman's campaign produced a bad effect on our people." On the other hand, it is at least arguable that if Sherman had done what Grant would have preferred, and settled with Hood first not only would the moral effect have been just as great, but, by transferring his army by land to join Grant, Lee might have been crushed in the early spring. It may therefore be the fact that so far from shortening the war, the march to the sea prolonged it. General Palfrey asserts that " Sherman's enormous waste (in Georgia) did not win any battle or cripple any army, and it is doubtful if it shortened the war one day."[10] General Alexander, on the other hand, considered that it was equal to the effect of a great victory in battle. Inasmuch as it led to numerous desertions from Lee's army, Alexander is probably right.

But it is unprofitable to speculate too far ahead: there is no finality to it. We are on firmer ground if we consider the immediate military implications of the march. Was Sherman justified on military grounds in turning his back on a hostile army in being, and pursuing a geographical or punitive objective? If he had kept to his one-time intention of giving Hood "a free pass" into Tennessee and then of combining with Thomas to crush him there it is doubtful if even a fraction of the Southern Army would have ever recrossed the Tennessee river. As it was, he left Thomas with an army only slightly stronger than Hood's, even when fully concentrated, if the immaturity of a large portion be taken into account, whereas his own 60,000 proved unnecessarily large for his own purpose. His justification for retaining so large a force, including the flower of his old army, is that

8 *Sherman*, by Liddell Hart.
9 *The March to the Sea*, p. 5.
10 *M.H.S.M.*, viii, 523.

Hood might have followed him. Indeed Sherman expected him to do so—another of his many faulty prognostications. Thus a total of over 120,000 men were required to restrain a hostile army of under 50,000. The reason for this was that Sherman had allowed Hood to occupy interior lines after Atlanta. The weakness of exterior lines when the enemy is aggressively minded is well illustrated by this campaign. Thus we come back again and again to Sherman's fundamental mistake of pursuing a geographical objective—the capture of Atlanta—rather than a military objective—the destruction of the hostile army. As one of his own Corps Commanders puts it: " It had to be left to two of Sherman's Corps, after the other four had gone on the march to the sea, to fight Hood . . . and overwhelm him. Why was this not done with a much larger force under Sherman at Atlanta? This is one of the questions for the future historian to discuss."[11] Future historians have for the most part left this question severely alone.

Modern Northern historians have a tendency to belittle the value to their cause of Sherman's march. It left behind it not only a trail of destruction but a bitterness of spirit in the minds of the vanquished that added enormously to the difficult problem of post-war pacification. Here are the recent opinions of eminent Northern historians, who cannot be suspected of Southern bias. " The army as it proceeded, having little or no fighting to do, devoted itself to organised plunder. . . . Along with the systematic business of foraging there was a shocking amount of downright plunder and vandalism. . . . It was a sorry chapter of the war. . . . Sherman's name became a byword at the South."[12]

" Sherman left a trail of smoking court-houses . . . and a population more bitterly intent on resistance than when his raid began."[13]

" Sherman's successful march to the sea would have been wormwood to the North without Thomas's victory at Nashville."[14]

Meade evidently also had his misgivings, for he wrote at this time: " I think it was expected Sherman's movement would draw Hood back to ·Georgia, but I anticipated just what he appears to be doing—a bold push for Kentucky, which if he succeeds in, will far out-balance any success that Sherman may have in going from Atlanta to the sea coast . . . I trust old

11 *Schofield*, p. 160.
12 *The Civil War and Reconstruction*, by Professor Randall (1937).
13 *The American Civil War*, by Professor C. R. Fish (1937).
14 *Hood's Tennessee Campaign*, by T. R. Hay (1929).

Thomas will come out all right, but the news is calculated to create anxiety."[15]

The last two extracts raise the question whether Sherman was justified in assuming that Thomas could dispose of Hood. Obviously, if he could not he was not justified either in turning his back on the Confederate Army of Tennessee. The balance of opinion of those who have given this subject close study seems to be that Sherman was *not* justified in assuming that Thomas could hold Hood, and I agree with them. By including all the troops (including many raw recruits and dismounted cavalry) in Thomas's scattered command, and by including Smith's Corps from the Missouri, quite a respectable total can be quoted. But Sherman departed with his 60,000 men long before Smith could arrive, leaving Hood locally in superior force, and had it not been for the bad weather, Hood would have advanced and overwhelmed Thomas before Smith could possibly be present. General Palfrey writes in M.H.S.M.: " There is no question, that if Hood had beaten Thomas, Sherman's course would have been a grave error, with disastrous consequences. The smothered disloyalty of Tennessee and Kentucky would have blazed out, a political revolution would have carried them over to the Confederacy. Hood's Army would have stood in a rich and friendly country proud to supply its needs, there was no other army to oppose it between the Alleghannies and the Mississippi, and it could have marched to the Ohio before meeting any hastily collected and organised force that could have been sent against it."[16] Palfrey then goes on to examine in detail the successive narrow shaves that Hood's opponents had, and concludes that by no process of reasoning could Sherman have divined that they would safely overcome them. " With so many and narrow escapes and with such small margin of time, it is idle to say that the result could have been forseen with any confidence by any human intellect. When any one accident would have changed the sequel everything worked together against Hood, as the stars in their courses worked against Sisera." The famous Northern historian Ropes supports this contention in strikingly similar language: " To transport the greater part of the Federal Army of the West far from the theatre of war, while the Confederate Army in that region was still a large, well organised, well commanded and formidable force, was certainly a most amazing step to take. It turned out all right,

[15] *Life and Letters of G. G. Meade*, p. 250.
[16] *Op. cit.*, viii, 519.

indeed; but no one can read the story of Hood's invasion of Tennessee in November and December without at times holding his breath.   It seems almost as if the goddess known as The Fortune of War from time to time interfered visibly to hinder and derange the operations of Hood and his lieutenants, and to further the combinations and movements of Thomas and his subordinates.   No one familiar with this campaign can honestly say that he thinks that such luck could fairly have been counted on by Grant and Sherman."17

It follows that it would be unsound to quote Sherman's successful march to the sea as an argument against the old military maxim that the true objective is the hostile army in the field.

CHAPTER XVI

Early's Valley Campaign.

WE left Grant and Lee, in Chapter VIII, facing one another before Petersburg. Lee had just managed to block the road to that city, but his right flank was open. Three days after the end of the Petersburg battle Grant attempted to turn to advantage this open flank. Beyond it two railroads fed Petersburg: the Weldon Railroad from the south and the Southside Railroad (to Lynchburg) from the west. Two cavalry divisions were sent to cut the latter, and two corps were sent to occupy the former. Thus it was hoped that the threat of starvation might induce Lee to abandon Petersburg. But the plan worked badly. The infantry effected nothing except to extend the front somewhat; the cavalry, after doing considerable damage to both the Southside and Danville Railroads, were caught by a superior force of Confederate cavalry on their return and lost many guns and prisoners. Thus, though the damage done to the railroads took several weeks to repair, the balance of advantage lay with the Southerners, for the double failure impaired still further the Union morale. Grant's offensive weapon was becoming blunted, in just the same way that Hood's offensive weapon had become blunted by the heavy casualties it had suffered.

After this abortive attempt, Grant settled down to "trench warfare." Both sides went underground. The Federals burrowed the deeper; in other words they started mining. There was nothing new about this. The novelty lay in the size of the mine. On July 30th no less than 8,000 pounds of powder were exploded under the hostile front line trench to the south-east of the town, and an enormous crater was formed, known ever since as "The Crater."*

The operation was a disastrous failure, costing the attackers 4,000 casualties, and the defenders about 1,000. Three features may be noted: (1) Lee rushed to the front and organised the counter-attack in person from a house (which still stands) only 600 yards behind the line; (2) the Northerners used black troops

---

* The lips of this crater can still be seen; they measure about 30 yards in diameter. (The Messines mines averaged 90 to 100 yards.)

in the attack for the first time; (3) As a result of the failure Burnside was replaced in the command of the attacking corps by General Parke. Apart from the extension of Grant's left flank to include the Weldon Railroad in August, the lines remained unchanged for the remainder of the summer.

Meanwhile, exciting news was coming in from the Shenandoah Valley, whither we must now direct our gaze.

JUBAL EARLY IN THE VALLEY. (*Map B.*)

It will be remembered that, immediately after Coldharbor, Lee had, with characteristic daring, denuded himself of over one-third of his army, sending first Breckinridge's Division and then Early's 2nd Corps to the valley. The immediate aim was to drive back Hunter, who was rapidly sweeping south on Lynchburg, a vital Southern centre. Early's secondary aim was, having disposed of Hunter, to make a bold demonstration against Washington.

On June 13th Early set out. The distance to Lynchburg was 140 miles. Two days earlier Hunter with an army of 18,000 men had reached Lexington, under 50 miles from Lynchburg. Between him and this important railway junction and food depot lay Breckinridge's force of under 5,000 men. The prospect of Early arriving upon the scene in time was therefore of the remotest. But Early, realising the urgency, drove his men hard. In spite of the fact that they had not yet recovered from the fatigues of the recent fighting, he made them march 80 miles in 4 days, thus arriving at Charlottesville on the 17th. Here he commandeered some trains, and on them loaded his leading division (less horses). The same day this division reached Lynchburg, while the remainder marched along the line, in order to meet the returning empty trains. Jubal Early went on ahead and found Breckinridge in bed as the result of an accident, while the Northern Army was only a few miles outside the town. This was not a good beginning, but Early pushed on in person to the front line, formed a rapid plan, and rushed up his leading troops into the line. Next day, the 18th, Hunter started to attack; but discovering that Early was now present in strength he drew off at nightfall. Though he outnumbered the Confederate force he then beat a precipitate retreat. To make matters worse, instead of retiring down the Valley, he fell back to the west, towards the Kanawha valley, thus opening the Shenandoah Valley to his opponent. He gave out as one excuse that he was getting short of ammunition. As to this, Early aptly remarks that such a shortage was peculiar so soon in a campaign which was designed to take him right up to Richmond. The fact is, Hunter seems to have lost his head, and to have been badly outgeneralled by his opponent. Thus, at a minimum cost in bloodshed, though at the cost of considerable physical exertion, the Confederate force had gained a notable victory. "Sweat saves blood." Jubal Early pursued "with unmitigated pertinacity," covering 60 miles in three days. At the end of that time, seeing that Hunter was rendered innocuous for the time being, he returned to the Valley. Here he received permission from Lee to give up the Washington project if he thought desirable and return to Richmond. But Early decided to persevere with it, and without more ado started on his famous march down the Valley. Marching rapidly he reached Staunton on June 27th, and Winchester on July 2nd. Sigel, who was in command of the troops in the lower Valley, retreated before him to Harper's Ferry, where contact was gained on July 4th. Meanwhile, Grant was reporting from Petersburg: "Early's Corps is now here." The surprise, thanks to Early's rapid movements, had been complete.

But the Southern commander, merely demonstrating at Harper's Ferry, sideslipped to his left and crossed the Potomac at Shepherdstown on the 5th. His whole army, about 15,000 strong, was thus on hostile territory, threatening the capital before a single man had been put in motion to defend it. (See Sketch Map 20.) The sudden and unexpected appearance of this powerful and compact host to the north-west of the capital naturally created extreme alarm in the North. The President called for volunteers to help in repelling the invaders, and Hunter was hurriedly recalled to the Valley. He, however, moved by the circuitous route of the Ohio and could not be expected to arrive for some days. What made matters worse was that for many of those critical days no news was received from him. Lastly, Grant was appealed to for help by the President, who even suggested that he should come with the bulk of his army. Grant alone appears to have kept a cool head. He quietly replied to Lincoln that "it would have a bad effect for me to leave here."[1] He did, however, send by water Rickett's division of the VI Corps and some dismounted cavalry. The remainder of the Corps would follow "if necessary." Ricketts embarked at City Point on July 6th.

Meantime a scratch force of less than 6,000 men, under General Wallace, moved out from Baltimore to the Monocacy river, just

[1] This and other quotations in this chapter are, unless otherwise stated, taken from O.R., vol. 37, part ii.

to the east of Frederick. Here on the 8th it was reinforced by Ricketts's division, 3,300 strong. Next day Early occupied Frederick and attacked Wallace. After a fierce action the Union troops, after losing very heavily, fell back on Baltimore. thus uncovering the capital once more. Jubal Early promptly continued his march, and on the morning of the 11th appeared before the fortifications of Washington, whilst his cavalry spread far and wide through Maryland, threatening Baltimore and collecting ransom and booty from various towns. The Confederate troops were tired but elated. The fortifications of the capital seemed, however, to be occupied in strength, and Early hesitated to attack them. This hesitation was fatal; for that very morning the remainder of Wright's VI Corps was disembarking at the city wharf, whence it was rushed up to the defences. Washington was saved. On the night of the 12th Early regretfully fell back.

There has been much discussion as to whether the Confederates could have captured the capital. The probability is that it could have been accomplished on the 11th, but that withdrawal would have been necessary within a few hours. Even a few hours would, however, have at any rate allowed of the Treasury being seized, and the moral effect of that, not only in the North but throughout the world, would have been enormous: it might even have caused the North to crack, for its morale was then at its lowest. So near and yet so far! But it is hard to blame such an enterprising commander as Jubal Early for not being a trifle more enterprising still. Lee had never expected him to capture the city; a demonstration was alone contemplated, and Early was hardly prepared for his good luck.

Even so, the effects of the raid had already been far-reaching. But if they were to be maintained it was essential that the invaders should be enabled to withdraw successfully. This was the problem that now confronted the Southern commander. The situation was an interesting one. Early's position looked precarious. A further division from the XIX Corps was on its way to Washington from Louisiana, and arrived on the 13th. It was originally intended for Richmond, but on reaching Fort Monroe was pushed forward to the Capital. Wright was pursuing with 14,000 troops. Early had a broad and unfordable river behind him, and somewhere beyond it (he did not know where) Hunter's force was advancing to hem him in. To retire by the way he had come would clearly be dangerous, and he elected to attempt a crossing to the east of Harper's Ferry. By a couple of rapid night marches he succeeded in getting clear of his antagonists, and on the morning of the 14th (complete with his enormous booty) reached the Potomac at White's Ford, opposite Leesburg, where he encamped that night. So far so good. Wright was a day's march behind, and so long as he remained on the north side of the river, Early decided to hold his ground. That same day Hunter crossed the Potomac at Harper's Ferry in the opposite direction, and encamped on the northern side! This palpable lack of co-ordinarion between the two pursuing armies is typical of two such forces that are operating on exterior lines, and is highly reminiscent of the lack of co-ordination that allowed Stonewall Jackson to escape south after his battle of Winchester.

The Union also suffered from a complete absence of a unified command at Washington. The assistant Secretary of War wrote feelingly on this point to Grant on July 12th: "General Halleck will not give orders except as he receives them; the President will give none, and until you direct positively and explicitly what is to be done, everything will go on in the deplorable and fatal way in which it has gone on for the past week." Grant's response is contained in a letter of the 14th to Halleck: "If the enemy has left Maryland he should have upon his heels veterans, men on horseback, and everything that can be got to follow to eat out Virginia clean and clear, as far as they go, so that crows flying over it for the balance of this season will have to carry their provender with them."*

Ultimately Wright crossed the river and joined up with Hunter; but by that time the Confederates were safely across the Blue Ridge and encamped at Berryville. Thence after some manoeuvring Early fell back to Strasburg on the 22nd and was followed cautiously by Wright. For ten days Grant had been in a painful state of indecision, issuing contradictory instructions from day to day, and wobbling woefully between two schemes: (1) that Wright should pursue up the Valley, and (2) that he should be recalled to Richmond before Early had time to rejoin Lee. For Grant feared that Lee might repeat his successful strategy of the Seven Days. The initiative had completely passed into the hands of the Confederates, as it had done during that campaign. These wobbles by Grant placed Halleck in an awkward and perplexing position, and it is impossible not to feel sympathy with him. The result of all this was that the pursuit of Early proved, in the words of the Assistant War Secretary: "An egregious blunder."

* Sheridan is usually credited with the authorship of this simile, but as he made use of it several weeks later it is evident that he was borrowing it from Grant.

Eventually (July 23rd) Grant gave a definite order: The VI Corps was recalled to Richmond, and the XIX Corps was to remain at Washington.

The comments on this sparkling affair are so obvious that we need not dwell upon them. With a minimum expenditure of blood a maximum of advantages had been obtained. The success was due, on the one side, to the driving power and readiness to take risks on the part of the Confederate commander, and to the marching powers of "Jackson's foot-cavalry," as his old corps was called, and on the other to the ineffectiveness and confusion resulting from divided commands and divided counsels. As for the moral effects, a Northern writer, Pond, says: "So bold a march revived for a time the failing fortunes of the South."[2]

MARYLAND AGAIN!

Grant, in recalling Wright, naturally assumed that Early's raid having been repulsed the raiders would retire up the Valley and rejoin Lee. But here he made a great mistake. No sooner had Early heard of the recall of Wright than he sprang forward once more. Leaving Strasburg on the very day after his arrival there he, on July 24th, pounced upon Crook (who had succeeded Hunter) at Kernstown. Crook was holding the same position that Shields had held against Jackson in 1861. The battle was short and decisive; Crook, utterly defeated, fell back in confusion, with a loss of over 1,000, and did not halt till reaching Bunker Hill, 16 miles to the north. The Confederate loss was slight, and Early pursued vigorously. The effects of this victory were immediate and striking. Not only was Wright's return to Richmond countermanded, but the remainder of the XIX Corps was sent to reinforce Washington. Shortly afterwards two fresh cavalry divisions were also despatched. Crook continued to fall back in haste, and on the 26th crossed the Potomac. Early was once more master of the prized Valley; the fat was once more in the fire. Wild rumours reached the Government at Washington, and there was again a confusion of counsel. Grant from his distant headquarters at City Point could not possibly control the situation. All he could do for the moment was to implore somewhat vaguely that "someone in Washington should give orders and make dispositions of all the forces within reach of the line of the Potomac."

On July 29th Wright's and Crook's forces united at Harper's Ferry. On the same day, Early commenced his second raid

[2] *The Shenandoah Valley in 1864*, p. 93.

into Maryland. This time it was chiefly confined to the cavalry. Stung, as he says, by some unnecessary destruction in the Valley, Early determined on reprisals. With this in view he ordered his cavalry to seize Chambersburg, and if a ransom demanded was not paid to burn the town. These instructions were carried out to the letter. The town did not pay and was burned. This was on the 30th. "The panic which had marked Early's previous incursion broke out afresh, and the people flew in all directions before McCausland's advance. In simply sensational effect, Early's second incursion had been as remarkable as the first, for he had caused almost as great a stir with two cavalry brigades and four guns as if he had used his entire army."[3] As a matter of fact Early had also crossed with his main body, occupying Williamsport and Sharpsburg in order to increase the illusion that a serious effort was intended; but he only remained two days in Maryland.

In order to protect the capital Wright was withdrawn across the Potomac and took up position on the Monocacy once more. Thither Grant himself proceeded in the hope of creating some sort of order out of the reigning chaos.

Meanwhile McCausland was effecting his withdrawal from Maryland. After threatening Cumberland, 60 miles to the west of Martinsburg (Sketch Map 20), he recrossed the river between that place and Hancock. Averell pursued with his cavalry, caught him up at Moorefield, 30 miles to the west of Winchester, surprised his camp at dawn and completely routed him, capturing all his guns. This defeat had a serious effect upon the morale and efficiency of the Southern cavalry thence forward.

As a result of Grant's visit, the various forces defending Washington were formed into "The Army of the Shenandoah," consisting of three corps, VI (Wright), XIX (Emory), and VIII (Crook), the latter being Hunter's old command. The cavalry consisted of the divisions of Merritt, Wilson, and Averell, and was commanded by Torbert. The army commander eventually appointed was Philip H. Sheridan, who thus achieved independent command at the early age of 33—the same age as Hood. The gross strength of the army when fully constituted was about 54,000. But owing to necessary detachments, Sheridan never had quite that number with him in the field. Against this army Early could put at first perhaps 13,000 men; but the exact strength of Southern formations is always difficult to ascertain.

Grant's orders for the new army deserve quotation: "What we

[3] *Pond, op. cit.*, p. 101.

want is prompt and active movements after the enemy," he wrote;
Sheridan was "to put himself south of the enemy and follow
him to the death. Wherever the enemy goes let our troops go
also. Once started up the Valley they ought to be followed till
we get possession of the Virginia Central Railroad." The Valley
was also to be ravaged so that "nothing should be left to invite
the enemy to return." We shall see presently how Sheridan
observed these orders. Lincoln evidently had misgivings on the
subject for he wrote to Grant: "I repeat to you, it will neither
be done nor attempted unless you watch it every day and hour
to force it."

After occupying the Harper's Ferry bridgehead for some
days, Sheridan advanced towards Winchester on August 10th.
Early fell back before him to Strasburg, while Sheridan followed
him to Cedar Creek, three miles to the north. But on the 14th,
news reached him from Grant that two Southern divisions were
advancing down the Luray valley to join Early. Grant instructed
Sheridan to " be cautious, and act now on the defensive, until
movements here (Richmond) force them to detach to send this
way." Now as it happened, Sheridan was at that moment
ideally situated to deal with the enemy in detail, for he possessed
interior lines, and Anderson (who was in command of the reinforcements) was bound to approach via Front Royal, owing to
the impassable Massanutton Mountain on his left. But Grant's
despatch put a damper on any such enterprise: indeed, Sheridan
decided to retreat to Berryville. Forty-eight hours later Grant
by implication rescinded his defensive order, stating that only
ONE division had gone to Early, not two. But this did not cause
Sheridan to suspend his retreat. On the 15th the retreat started.
Early pursued rapidly, and so hustled the rearguard that Sheridan
continued to fall right back to his bridgehead at Harper's Ferry.
Here Anderson, with Kershaw's Division, joined the Confederate
Army, and here for the next few days Early with a force less than
half that of his opponent, danced about audaciously in front of
him, first threatening to attack his position, then threatening
another invasion of Maryland by Shepherdstown. It was an
amazing example of bluff; and it was as successful as bluff nearly
always is in war. For war is a game of poker, in which the higher
the stakes the easier it is to bluff successfully. Grant's despatches
to Sheridan were steadily altering in tone: the gist of them being
that only one division had reinforced Early, and that Sheridan
must be prepared to take the offensive when the opportunity
presented itself. But Sheridan strove to prove that Early was

MAP 20

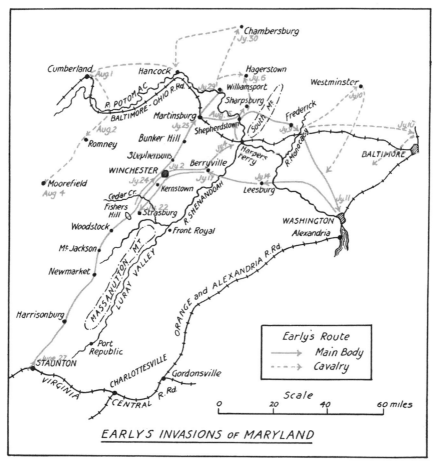

Chambersburg
Jy.30

Cumberland
Aug.1
Hancock
Hagerstown
Jy.6
Williamsport
Westminster
Jy.10
R. POTOMAC
BALTIMORE - OHIO R. Rd.
Jy.29
Sharpsburg
Martinsburg
Aug.3
Frederick
South Mt.
Aug.2
Jy.25
Shepherdstown
BALTIMORE
Romney
Bunker Hill
Jy.10
Stephensons
Harpers Ferry
WINCHESTER
Jy.2
Berryville
R.Monocacy
Moorefield
Aug 4
Jy.24
Jy.17
Jy.14
Leesburg
Kernstown
Cedar Cr.
R. SHENANDOAH
Jy.11
Fishers Hill
Jy.22
Strasburg
WASHINGTON
Woodstock
Front Royal
Alexandria
Mc.Jackson
MASSANUTTON MT.
LURAY VALLEY
Newmarket
ORANGE and ALEXANDRIA R.Rd.
Harrisonburg
Port Republic
June 27
STAUNTON
CHARLOTTESVILLE
Gordonsville
VIRGINIA
CENTRAL R. Rd.

Early's Route
→ Main Body
- - → Cavalry

Scale
0   20   40   60 miles

EARLY'S INVASIONS OF MARYLAND

still being reinforced. Hence he would not budge from his position, even when Early left only a single division in his front and moved with the remainder of his army to the north. The only action Sheridan took was to prepare to fall back across the river himself. " I have thought it best to be very prudent," he explained to Grant.

But the Government did not see it in this light, and for the third time in six weeks alarm began to spread through the North. For here was Jubal Early once again to the north-west of the capital, with a great army of 40,000 men retreating before him and shutting itself up in a defensive bridghead! No wonder murmurs began to arise, and suggestions to be made that the new commander was not the man for the job. There seems to be considerable justification for these complaints. On August 17th, Sheridan wrote to Grant: "I have therefore taken position at Berryville, which will enable me to get on their rear if they should get strong enough to push north." Yet, when a few days later Early did this very thing Sheridan, so far from " getting on their rear," wrote to Halleck that if the enemy crossed the Potomac he would have to fall back across it, too. This was in the face of a strong hint from the cavalry general Wilson that he should seize the opportunity of Early's splitting of his forces to "make a strong attack on the two divisions still on your front." On this a Northern writer comments: " It is difficult to conceive of conditions more favourable to success than those which existed on the 25th and 26th of August, when he could have placed an army nearly if not quite three times as strong as Early's across the latter's line of retreat without endangering his own. Such an opportunity is one seldom presented to a General."4 In view of the complaints against Sheridan's lack of enterprise, it was fortunate for him that Early returned on the 26th to his old position at Bunker Hill, for Sheridan now ventured to advance to his old lines at Berryville, but very cautiously, taking a week to do it.

Meantime, Early's cavalry had again destroyed the Baltimore Ohio Railroad, and caused considerable panic in Western Virginia. During all this time the Confederates were busy reaping and carrying away the crops in the lower Valley, a point of great importance to them. All these things tended to increase the concern which Sheridan's inactivity had caused. Probably Grant had forgotten the exact terms of his despatch to Halleck that Sheridan should act on the defensive " till movements here force

4 *M.H.S.M.*, vi, 39

them to detach to send this way," for his later despatches clearly implied that Sheridan was at any time at liberty to take the offensive, and Sheridan must have realized that the ban on offensive action had been raised. He was, however, prolific in excuses for not taking the offensive.

On September 14th Kershaw's division, after one abortive attempt, left to rejoin Lee, thereby reducing Early's infantry, according to his own reckoning, to 8,500 muskets for duty, whilst his cavalry were under 2,000. It is difficult to check these figures, which, however, seem on the small side. The two armies were left facing one another between Winchester and Berryville. The Confederate army was now little more than one-third that of the Union; but so far from curbing Early's audacity this disparity in numbers seemed rather to increase it. For on September 17th he advanced with two divisions towards Martinsburg where the Northern cavalry were reported to be trying to repair the railway.

Meanwhile, there was an important happening in the Union camp—no less than a personal visit from the Commander-in-chief. The occasion for it was the increased pressure that was being put upon Grant to get the threat to the Baltimore Ohio Railroad and canal removed; the cut in both was causing serious inconvenience. Grant therefore himself formed a plan of attack and took it with him. But on arrival at Sheridan's headquarters he found that the latter had already decided to attack, having learnt of Anderson's departure. Hearing further on the 18th that Early had moved two divisions north on the previous day to cut the railway at Martinsburg, Sheridan decided to fall upon the remainder before it could be reinforced, expecting (according to Swinton) to catch it *"in flagrante delicto."*

BATTLE OF THE OPEQUON (OR WINCHESTER), SEPTEMBER 19TH

Ramseur's Division was holding a position astride the Winchester Berryville road, two miles in front of the former town. At 5 a.m. the Union cavalry, followed by the whole Union army, burst upon it. Ramseur's fate seemed sealed, for the remaining three divisions were miles away—two at Stephensons, 6 miles north of Winchester, and one on the return march from Bunker Hill, 8 miles still further north. But the execution of the Northern plan fell short of the conception. In front of the position the road ran through a defile over two miles long. Instead of deploying the army on the far side of this defile, Sheridan marched it through in a single column. As a natural result there was considerable congestion and delay in getting it deployed. It was noon before it was ready to advance in line. This delay enabled the absent divisions (which had started back on the previous day) to approach the battlefield. They arrived on it in the nick of time. Still, though they fought well, they were steadily driven back by the vastly superior numbers of the Northerners (generally computed as at least three to one), and at 5 p.m., Early, fearing that his retreat would be cut by the Union cavalry, ordered a general retreat. Early had " shown great vigour and skill in fighting the battle," writes an opponent, and he had inflicted greater losses than he had sustained, but the defeat was a sad blow to the splendid morale that his army had previously enjoyed, and a corresponding enhancement of that of the Union Army.

The defeated army fell back to its old position just south of Strasburg at Fisher's Hill. Sheridan followed up and attacked this position on the 22nd. The right flank was very strong, overlooking and being protected by the Shenandoah; but the left flank was weak, resting on a wood on the slopes of Little North Mountain. The position was also too extensive for Early's reduced numbers, and he intended to retire that night. But before he could do so he was attacked, his left flank was turned and the whole army quickly dissolved in flight. Sheridan seems to have contemplated attacking the right flank, in which case he would probably have suffered defeat, but Crook persuaded him to attack the left instead. Sixteen guns were lost and Sheridan pursued with great drive, shouting to his men: " Forward, forward everything! Don't stop."

The cohesion and morale of the Confederate army appeared to be quite shattered by this heavy blow, and it retired with scarcely a stand as far as Port Republic, closely followed by its opponents. On September 28th the Union cavalry raided Staunton and damaged the Virginia Central Railroad and laid waste as much country as it could.

OCTOBER IN THE VALLEY

Jubal Early being finished with, and the Northerners once more in possession of the Valley, the question now arose: What next? On this point there was a difference of opinion between the Commander-in-Chief and his subordinate. Grant wished the victorious Army of the Shenandoah to continue its advance either eastwards to cut the Virginia Central Railroad at Charlottesville, or southwards to Lynchburg. But Sheridan raised objections to these projects. He preferred to consider the campaign closed on the occupation of Harrisonburg; he proposed to devastate the Valley, as ordered, and then return to Richmond. Grant gave way, and the Army on October 1st commenced its withdrawal down the Valley, methodically laying waste the country as it went.

In the discussions that we have just summarised there was one striking omission—the action of the enemy. But Early was the last man to sit down under such an insult. Moreover, he had just been again reinforced by Kershaw's Division and by Rosser's Cavalry Brigade. As soon, then, as the Union Army started its withdrawal (on October 5th) the Confederate army moved forward. On October 10th Sheridan halted at Cedar Creek, and Early stopped short at Newmarket, 35 miles to the south. The Confederate cavalry had suffered a reverse in the course of this advance, still further lowering its morale, which had just started to revive.

Fresh differences of opinion began to develop between Grant and Sheridan. Though he had given way to his subordinate, Grant kept recurring to his pet project of a cut at the Gordonsville railroad. Halleck also disagreed with Sheridan. In consequence, the latter was called to Washington for conference. But before he went, Early sprung another of his surprises. He was believed to be lying somewhere at the southern end of the Valley, but all the time he was, as we have seen, at Newmarket. The VI Corps was on its way to join Grant; there had even been talk of sending the XIX Corps, too. But events were now to take a dramatic turn. On October 13th the irrepressible Early suddenly appeared before Cedar Creek, attacked the outposts and inflicted about 300 casualties. Sheridan had already halted the VI Corps, since Grant wished him to advance again. The sudden apparition of Early now caused him hurriedly to recall it to his own army. On top of this came another disturbing incident. A Confederate signal message was intercepted by his own men, in the following startling terms: " To Lieut.-General Early: Be ready to move as soon as my forces join you, and we can crush him if he finds out I have joined you." It was signed " Longstreet."

This might be a " fake " message, but to be on the safe side Sheridan cancelled a projected raid by his cavalry. Satisfied that his position was now unassailable, Sheridan then repaired to Washington for the conference, and returned on the 18th as far as Winchester. Next morning, hearing sounds of gunfire to the south he continued his journey, and was soon met by a stream of fugitives who assured him that " the army was broken up, in full retreat, and that all was lost." Early had evidently been on the war-path again!

We must now go back a few hours, and into the hostile camp in order to discover the reason for this astonishing state of affairs.

BATTLE OF CEDAR CREEK, OCTOBER 19th.

It should first be explained that the intercepted message was indeed a fake—written out by Early himself. He hoped it would have the effect of inducing Sheridan to fall back further; but as it failed in this purpose he decided to assume the offensive.

Jubal Early was occupying the scene of his old defeat at Fisher's Hill. From the sharp ridge on which it stands the ground beyond Strasburg where the hostile army was in position can easily be seen. A still better view can be obtained from the top of Three Top Mountain, which lies just across the river to the right. Gordon, whom we have met before (and who has written a splendid account of the battle) made a careful reconnaissance from the mountain top, as a result of which he was entrusted with two divisions, and ordered to make a wide sweeping movement to the right and attack the enemy's left flank. This movement involved a long and intricate night march and the fording in two places of the Shenandoah.* And now occurred what was in some respects the most remarkable battle of the war.

All went according to plan on the Confederate side. While two divisions approached from the front Gordon led his column successfully through the night and at 5 a.m. his troops crashed into the unsuspecting enemy in an operation that a Northern writer describes as " one of the most daring and brilliant attacks recorded in history." Panic ran through the Union Camp and the whole of two corps were soon streaming to the rear. By 10 a.m. the Southerners had driven the enemy back 4 miles, captured 1,300 men and 24 guns. The VI Corps, however, now barred the way, and the question arose, should the Confederates attack again, or make good the ground they had won? Though there are contrary accounts of this battle, it seems that both Early and Gordon wished to resume the attack, but the troops were exhausted with their great exertions and half famished; many of them were regaling themselves with the food found in the captured camp. The resulting disorganisation rendered an immediate resumption of the attack impracticable. Early therefore gave orders to fortify the position won. On the other side Wright had

* So excellent is Gordon's description that it is still possible to follow in the tracks of his memorable march.

made arrangements for a counter attack to take place at noon, when at about 11 a.m. Sheridan arrived, having ridden 11 miles in about two hours. To judge by his own account he seems to have spent the greater part of the ensuing five hours riding along in front of his troops, hat in hand. He was everywhere received with cheers and enthusiasm, and when at 4 p.m. he gave the order to attack his troops went forward with splendid dash. The Confederate line held for some time, but at dusk a breach was made, and the whole line fell back. To add to their bad fortune two wagons jammed on a bridge over the Tumbling Run, a tiny brook just in front of Fisher's Hill, thereby causing not only the recapture of the Union guns, but of 24 Confederate guns as well. On the other hand the Northerners had suffered 5,700 casualties, including 1,400 prisoners whom Early succeeded in carrying off, nearly twice that of their opponents. The pursuit was not continued and the Confederates halted at Mount Jackson. When the story of the victory and of Sheridan's ride from Winchester got about the North rang with his praises; but it would seem that a large share of the praise ought to go to Wright, who fought a very fine battle with great coolness.

Cedar Creek, though a defeat for the South, proved beneficial, inasmuch as it prevented the projected transference of troops from the Valley to Richmond. It was now realised that Early was always dangerous, even in defeat, and that Sheridan's army could not be weakened with safety. It might be supposed that after his victory Sheridan could and would prosecute the project so dear to Grant's heart—that of advancing to the Virginia Central Railroad. Grant yet again suggested it: " If it is possible to follow up, after your great victory, until you reach the Central Road, do it, even if you have to live on half rations." But Sheridan again made difficulties. He had so thoroughly destroyed supplies in the Valley that he feared to make the attempt. He was "hoist with his own petard."

So far from advancing, Sheridan on November 9th withdrew to Kernstown. Whereupon the tireless Early for the fifth time, in that memorable campaign, advanced through Strasburg. On the 12th there were cavalry fights, which showed that Sheridan was still in force. Early therefore retired once more to Newmarket. But his audacious advance had the effect of detaining the whole of the Union army in the Valley till mid-December.

Shortly afterwards Kershaw's Division was returned to Lee. On hearing of it Grant again returned to the project of an advance to the Central Railroad, this time with the cavalry only. But a cavalry reconnaissance up the Valley disclosed that Early was still in force at Newmarket. Nothing was therefore attempted for the time being. Indeed, the next considerable move came from Early who sent two cavalry brigades to destroy the Baltimore Railroad at New Creek, 12 miles south of Cumberland. This was succesfully accomplished, and 500 of the garrison and 5 guns were captured. In the aggregate, as the result of Early's raids, the North was deprived of the use of the Baltimore Ohio Railroad for a period of three months. Nothing further of note occurred in the Valley that year, so Early had at least the satisfaction of striking the last blow. In December both armies were drastically reduced, and the remainder went into winter quarters: the North round Harrisonburg and the South round Staunton.

COMMENTS

Jubal Early's Valley campaign achieved for the South the following advantages: It secured for them the 1864 harvest of the fertile Valley, and also a portion of the Maryland harvest; it diverted two corps and two cavalry divisions from the Petersburg front for several weeks; it temporarily raised the morale of the South and depressed that of the North; it denied to the North the use of the important Baltimore Ohio Railroad for three months; it inflicted considerably greater casualties than it incurred and acquired immense booty; and finally it contained three times its own strength in the Valley for several critical months. Had these troops been available at Richmond, Grant would probably have been able to achieve a decision in the 1864 campaign.

On the liability side, it destroyed its own cavalry arm, weakened its artillery owing to the big loss in guns, and in the end impaired its own morale.

Viewed as a whole, perhaps the most striking fact is that, with the exception of the sixteen days, September 24th to October 10th, the Confederates held the whole of the Valley as far north as Newmarket, while from July 3rd to September 20th they held all but a tiny patch of the northern Valley as well (less the six days July 20th to 26th), and this was accomplished in the face of a hostile army that for the most part outnumbered their own by at least two and sometimes three to one. The credit for this remarkable achievement must be accorded almost entirely to the Confederate commander. General Lee, apart from his original instructions, interfered practically not at all with his subordinate, whom he trusted implicitly, even after he had suffered two defeats. The narrative should have made it clear to what Early owed his success. It was his own boldness, activity, quick-wittedness, driving power, and willingness to take risks that produced these results.

I cannot refrain from quoting the following tribute to him paid by Colonel Wm. Allen in *Southern Historical Society Papers:* " As time goes on . . . history will do justice to the vigour which drove Hunter almost in panic out of the Valley, to the audacity and celerity—only comparable with that of Stonewall Jackson—which carried 15,000 men in less than three weeks from Salem to the suburbs of Washington and spread consternation in the North; to the skill which extricated his army in safety from the multitude (of foes); to the hard blows which demolished Wallace and Crook; to the splendid game of bluff which for six weeks kept 50,000 men cooped up in a corner of the Valley; to the indomitable courage and tenacity which would never accept defeat, but struggled on against overwhelming numbers and resources, almost snatching victory from fate itself, until his cause and country sank exhausted in the unequal strife.5

Taking it as a whole it is open to question whether Early's Valley campaign was not the most brilliant of the whole war, not excepting that of Stonewall Jackson.

An instructive aftermath of Early's failure is the attitude adopted by President Davis and by General Lee. In spite of considerable pressure they declined to make him a scapegoat. Lee wrote to his lieutenant: " I have weakened myself very much to strengthen you. It was done with the expectation of enabling you to gain such success that you could return the troops, if not rejoin yourself. I know you have endeavoured to gain that success, and believe you have done all in your power to ensure it. You must not be discouraged. . . ." And the President replied in the following terms to the Governor of Virginia who had asked that Early should be dismissed: " General Early could no doubt in many instances show wherein he might have changed his operations to advantage, but this does not prove that another would have foreseen what he did not."

In conclusion, it should be noted that though Early was a strict disciplinarian and prevented loot and excesses in Maryland, he became increasingly out of touch with and unpopular among his troops in proportion as his fortune deserted him.

In Sheridan's conduct of the operations it is difficult to find much to admire. In his Memoirs he is prolific with reasons for his cautious attitude (what commander is not?) but the cold facts

5 *Op. cit.*, ii, 281.

are a damning indictment. It may be advanced that his activity was restricted by Grant's defensive instructions of August 12th. This would be plausible were it not for the fact that throughout the campaign, and even when Grant was urging him forward, he continued to dig his toes in stubbornly. Seldom is one general more contemptuous of his opponent than was Early of Sheridan. To use his own words: he considered he was " without enterprise and possessed an excessive caution which amounted to timidity." But Sheridan had showed himself a dashing and enterprising cavalry commander in the past, and was to do it still more in the near future. How then are we to account for this absence in operation of those qualities which Sheridan was known to possess? I think the explanation must be that—to use the jargon of psychology—he was suffering from an inferiority complex. Consider the position in which he found himself when he took over the command. It was his first independent command of all arms; he was suddenly entrusted with a large army, 50,000 strong. He was a young man, a mere 33 years of age, and was confronted by one of the veteran commanders in the Southern camp, a general who had immensely enhanced his already great reputation in the last few weeks, in command of a compact army of veterans who were carrying all before them, flushed with success and of the highest state of morale. Small wonder if this young and untried commander distrusted his own ability to defeat such an army, especially as its numbers were grossly exaggerated. Even after it had suffered defeat it had sprung up surprisingly fresh in the next round. So Sheridan, like Joe Johnston, preferred to fall back, waiting for an opportunity to strike. Eventually such an opportunity occurred and he took it. Ramseur's division had been left isolated at Winchester. Sheridan was quick to spring at it. But the very strength of the force that he employed against it—more than ten to one—proved his undoing, for as we have seen, his 40,000 men took six hours to deploy, thus allowing the remainder of the Southern army to come to Ramseur's support. A single corps would probably have done the work better. But a still better course would have been to keep to his original plan and place his whole army astride Early's line of retreat. This he could easily have done, and had he done so it is hard to see how Early could have avoided losing the bulk of his guns and the whole of his train. But Sheridan went for small game and accordingly won a small success.

The battle of Fisher's Hill was skilfully conducted by him, and he showed splendid drive in speeding the pursuit. This was easily the best piece of work he did in the whole campaign—even though his plan was pressed upon him by a subordinate.

The battle of Cedar Creek is more difficult to assess owing to the conflicting witness of four of the chief actors in it—Sheridan, Keifer (a divisional commander), Early, and Gordon. As far as Sheridan is concerned the question is, was he justified in holding up Wright's attack for over four hours? The delay of course increased the weight of the attack when it did come; but it also increased the power of the Confederate defence. At noon it would have caught a large number of the Confederates disorganised with plunder and exhausted by their tremendous exertions. The four hours' respite enabled them to recover somewhat. To discuss the matter properly it would be necessary to go into tactical details, with which this book is not concerned.

Sheridan exposes himself to severe criticism for obstructing Grant's express orders, that he should push forward against Charlottesville in October. He complained of the difficulty of crossing the Blue Ridge, but in his final report he afterwards wrote: "The Blue Ridge can be crossed almost everywhere by infantry or cavalry." A move which was perfectly feasible in October was therefore delayed till March. Major Huntington's comment is: "Grant's judgment was sound, while Sheridan's action practically nullified his victories in the field. It seems not unlikely that if he had complied with Grant's instructions immediately after the battle of Fisher's Hill, Richmond would have fallen in September or October 1864, instead of April 1865."[6]

This is severe criticism, but that it is merited no impartial investigator can doubt.

To sum up: This campaign is an admirable example of the maxim that in war the policy of "safety first" leads to no results. In four months Sheridan, with a vastly superior army, had only attacked the enemy in one operation, and at the end of the campaign that enemy was still in possession of nearly half the Shenandoah Valley, with an intact (though dispirited) army. In short, Sheridan as an independent Army Commander must be set down a failure.

[6] *M.H.S.M.* vi, 5–7.

CHAPTER XVII

The Autumn and Winter at Petersburg.

WHILE the foregoing exciting events had been taking place in the Valley the *tempo* of operations was noticeably slowing down at Petersburg. What we now call " trench warfare " had set in; but the peculiar point about it was that, unlike the Great War, each side maintained an " open flank " throughout. In July this open flank rested to the south-east of Petersburg. Throughout the succeeding months Grant endeavoured to extend it westwards. We have seen how in August he succeeded in extending it to embrace the important Weldon railway. This necessitated the transference of stores from railroad to wagons several miles to the south of Petersburg, and their transport by road along the Boydtown Plank road to Lee's army. Apart from this, Early's activity in the Valley kept Grant quiet at Richmond.

At the end of September Grant launched a skilful double offensive. Two corps were secretly transferred to the north of the James and attacked and carried Fort Harrison, near the river south-east of Richmond. On the 29th the fort was captured, and next day the crucial attack was made to the south of Petersburg. Grant hoped that the attack on Fort Harrison would induce Lee to denude the southern end of his line. But the Confederate commander did not fall into the trap and when the V Corps attempted a turning movement round Lee's right flank Hill's Corps replied promptly with a counter-attack. However, considerable ground was gained, and the line now reached to the south-west of Petersburg. But the vital Boydtown Plank road remained in Confederate hands, their right flank now resting on Hatchers Run. (Sketch Map 22.)

On October 27th Grant made yet another attempt to extend his lines, and if possible seize the Southside Railroad. Over 30,000 infantry and a cavalry division were employed in this ambitious undertaking. But it was foiled by the vigilance of Hill, who again counter-attacked with spirit, and Hancock's II Corps only avoided being cut up by a hasty retreat. Simultaneously Butler demonstrated on the north bank of the James, but he was brilliantly repulsed by Longstreet, who had just resumed command of his old corps.*

Apart from doing further damage to the Weldon Railroad in December, nothing of note occurred for the next three months. On February 5th Grant made yet another attempt to extend his lines. It was carried out by Warren's V Corps and part of the II Corps, now commanded by Humphreys (Meade's old Chief of Staff). Again Lee was ready for him; again the ubiquitous Hill counter-attacked, and again the ground won was but slight. After this Grant gave up all idea of active operations till the spring weather should dry up the water-logged ground. It affords, therefore, a convenient occasion to review the situation of the two armies and to consider future prospects at the opening of spring.

THE POSITION AT THE OPENING OF SPRING, 1865.

On February 9th Lee had at last been appointed General-in-Chief of all the Confederate armies. But he still regarded himself as subordinate to the President in a military capacity, and in any case had little time to influence the course of events. In fact, his only notable action, outside Virginia, was to bring back J. E. Johnston to command the remnants of Hood's army, which had now collected in North Carolina. Breckinridge at the same time succeeded Seddon as Secretary for War.

The Army of Northern Virginia was now in a sorry situation. Outnumbered by 2½ to 1 it lacked almost everything: armament, munitions, rails to make good the damage done to the railroads, food, clothing, forage for horses. The latter led to the army being practically immobile during the winter months; while the lack of food and clothing led to extreme privation, which in turn led to desertion. The move in this direction was speeded by the sense of despair that was spreading over the whole community, among the civilians more than among the soldiers. But letters from home impaired what morale the soldiers still had, in much the same way as happened in the German army in 1918. Lee's only asset was the fact that he possessed interior lines. Tactically he had interior lines against Grant, and was always able to move troops in time to the threatened point; strategically he held, with Johnston's army, interior lines—a matter that we will deal with in due course. His use of interior lines tactically has drawn warm praise from the Northern writer Swinton. "The success of the Confederate tactics was wonderful; each movement, save that to the Weldon railroad . . . ended in a

* At the same time a IVth Corps was formed out of Hoke's and Johnston's divisions, and Anderson appointed the Commander.

check, generally accompanied by one or more thousand prisoners. The aggregate of captures made by the enemy in these successive swoops is astonishing."[1]

But time was now on the side of the North. Up till August it had been the other way about, and that month was the nadir of Union hopes—not the eve of Gettysburg, as is usually supposed. Before Gettysburg there was no very active peace treaty party in the North. But in July 1864 the Union was plunged in gloom, and in August Lincoln, according to the historian Rhodes, " would undoubtedly have made peace on the basis of reunion, saying nothing about slavery."[2] Lincoln, indeed, at this time despaired of winning the Presidential election. But the successes of Sherman at Atlanta, Sheridan in the Valley, and Farragut in Mobile Bay restored the waning morale of the North, and the will to victory of its inhabitants.

Thus it was seen that time was, after all, on the side of the North; from which it followed that Grant's policy of attrition was justified. For in war, as in business, nothing succeeds like success. But consider what the verdict on Grant would have been if peace had been made in August 1864!

Yet, how had the situation changed! The morale of the Army of the Potomac had recovered, and from the other main theatres came encouraging news. Sherman was marching north from Savannah, and was already nearly half way to Petersburg. Sheridan was advancing up the Valley once more, in response to positive orders from Grant, and on March 2nd he utterly dispersed the miserable " scratch of an army " with which Early attempted to withstand him at Waynesborough. The unfortunate Early only managed to escape with his personal staff; but in a typical way he yet lived to get in the last blow, for collecting a small band he suddenly threw himself on Sheridan's flank and rear at Gordonsville!

The Union armies were steadily concentrating on Richmond and nothing, it would seem, could now avert the impending doom of Lee's army. Grant could now sleep quietly in his bed.

COMMENTS

"The farce of 60,000 enveloping 140,000 was continued for nine months."[3] This, in its hyperbolical way, is a natural criticism on Grant's policy during those months. It has always seemed to me one of the curiosities of the war, that the two armies should for so long maintain open flanks in the way that they did. Why

[1] *Campaign of the Army of the Potomac*, p. 552.
[2] *History of the Civil War*, p. 335.
[3] *Has General Grant Genius?* by Private Jones, p. 115.

was Grant content to remain in that unsatisfactory position during all that time?

But was he content? What was his policy?

It should be a simple matter, at this distance of time, to answer the question. But it is not. It is difficult for the simple reason that no two experts give exactly the same answer! When doctors disagree who shall decide? Here are quotations from some of the leading experts:

General Fuller: "To hold fast to Lee so that Sherman's manœuvre may continue."

General Edmonds: "To starve Lee into evacuation."

General Maurice: "To keep Lee tied to the defence of Richmond."

Swinton: "The capture of Petersburg."

Steele: "To get possession of the two railroads."

Humphreys is not so concise: Grant occupied entrenchments "which the army might be withdrawn from at any time, leaving a sufficient force to hold them, and move to intercept the railroads and attack Lee's army in unexpected quarters, south or even north of the James."

As for Badeau, he makes no serious attempt to define Grant's plan of campaign at all!

Amid this confusion of views we must fend for ourselves. It may assist in the quest if we set down the possible alternatives before Grant. At first sight they appear to be four in number:—

1. *To capture Richmond*, either by driving out Lee or by surrounding him in the place.

2. *To defeat Lee's army*, either by surrounding it, or by forcing it into the open and then attacking it.

3. *To hold Lee's army to Petersburg* (" pin him " is the fashionable term) while the war is won elsewhere.

4. *To play with Lee's army* until the other armies converge on Richmond.

Analysing these in turn, we see that if course 1 or 2 was his object, Grant should have boldly marched round Lee's rear, much as Sherman did to Hood's army at Atlanta. If on the other hand he favoured courses 3 or 4 he should not have threatened Lee's railroads and lines of communication, as it might lead him to evacuate his lines and join forces with the other armies.

What follows? Simply this: because Grant did not seriously and consistently attempt to surround Richmond courses 1 and 2 are ruled out; because he threatened Lee's communications courses 3 and 4 are ruled out. We therefore are left with the surprising conclusion that Grant cannot seriously have intended any of these four courses! There is no one policy to which he consistently held. In other words we are left with only one possible solution—*he wobbled.* His attempt at the Weldon Railroad is described by Freeman as " an afterthought "; his final attempt to cut the Southside Railroad is cancelled out by the daily fear (which he afterwards admitted) that Lee would slip out of Petersburg some night. What inconsistency! If he desired courses 1 or 2 why did he not bend Sheridan to his will in the autumn, and insist on his attacking Gordonsville and closing Lee's back door? Lee has been accused of showing weakness and leniency to an obstinate subordinate, but he never countenanced anything more glaringly at variance with his wishes than was Sheridan's attitude to Grant. If, finally, he favoured course 4 why did he hasten to defeat Lee in March before Sherman's army had time to arrive?

I am forced to the rather tame conclusion that Grant had no clear-cut policy, but that he realised that time was on his side, and that his attrition policy was right in theory; but that as he had practically been forbidden by the President to pursue it any further he decided merely to whittle away time, contenting himself with an occasional operation in order to keep his army occupied, and to keep the Government and people quiet and encourage their will to victory. If this was really his secret aim, though it cannot be called a very heroic one, it cannot be denied that it was sound and led unerringly to ultimate victory.

Of Lee's conduct during the autumn and winter there is not so much room for speculation, nor for comment. We have ample evidence that he foresaw the end long before it came. Only four days after his arrival at Petersburg he foresaw the loss of the Weldon Railroad and asked the Government to prepare to supply the army by the Danville Railroad alone. But the Government neglected to take the necessary steps. It is difficult to see what he could have done during those trying months that he neglected to do. An attempt has been made to saddle him with the responsibility for the inadequate supply service. But this was outside his province. It was vested, through the Government, in the Commissary General, whom Swinton describes as "a man of notorious ignorance and incompetence." In the last weeks he was replaced, but it was then too late to repair the damage. In any case, that question belongs to the final chapter.

Lee was continually urging, even nagging, the Government to improve matters. Beyond that he did not consider that he could go.

CHAPTER XVIII

The March Through the Carolinas.

WE left Sherman and his army enjoying a well-earned rest at Savannah. While the troops were engaged in their Christmas festivities Sherman and Grant were corresponding on the future course of action. Grant had originally ordered Sherman to take ship for Richmond before he attacked Savannah, and Sherman was preparing reluctantly to comply when Grant changed his mind. Sherman gave his views as follows. He would march north and "strike for the Charleston and Wilmington Railroad. . . . Then I would favour an attack on Wilmington. . . . I would then favour a movement direct on Raleigh. The game is then up with Lee, unless he comes out of Richmond, avoids you and fights me, in which case I would reckon on your being on his heels." Grant eventually gave his approval, and on January 21st wrote: " From about Richmond I will watch Lee closely, and if he detaches much more. or attempts to evacuate, will pitch in. In the meantime, should you be brought to a halt anywhere, I can send two corps of 30,000 effective men to your support from the troops about Richmond. A force of 28,000 or 30,000 men will co-operate from New Berne or Wilmington or both." The last sentence refers to Schofield's army of the Ohio which was being transferred to the sea coast via Pittsburg and Washington and thence by boat. After an unsuccessful attempt in December, a force of two divisions captured Fort Fisher on Wilmington harbour in mid-January. Thus the last remaining port was closed to Southern ships, and on February 21st Wilmington itself fell to General Cox. (Map A.)

Meanwhile Sherman had commenced his march through the Carolinas. There is no occasion to describe it in detail. For the greater part of the way opposition was of the slightest, and the elements were more a hindrance than the enemy. Sherman at first aimed at a point midway between Charleston and Augusta, two important towns. Beauregard, who was now in command, was thus left in suspense as to which to defend, and eventually left half his force at Charleston under Hardee keeping the remainder under his own hand at Augusta. But Sherman marched between the two, the effect being the evacuation of both cities.

Hardee struck north for Cheraw, 50 miles north of Florence, while Beauregard made for Charlotte. Columbia thus fell an easy prize to Sherman on February 17th. For the burning of that town the Confederates tried to saddle Sherman with the responsibility; but though the story is obscure and involved, it is clear that Sherman was in no way responsible. He seems, however, to have exulted in the fact. A few weeks later Lyman overheard him say: " Columbia! Pretty much all burned; and burned *good!* " On March 3rd Sherman reached Cheraw and on the 11th Fayetteville, having negotiated some appalling country with consummate skill. Hardee had fallen back before him to Smithfield where he joined up with Beauregard. Here Johnston assumed command of the army, then about 22,000 strong, but daily increasing. At Fayetteville Sherman wrote a remarkable letter to Stanton in which he said: " The utter demolition of all the railroad system of South Carolina and the utter destruction of the enemy's arsenals at Columbia, Cheraw and Fayetteville are the principles of the movement. . . . Let Lee hold on to Richmond and we will destroy his country, and then of what use is Richmond? "[1]   Sherman appeared to be reverting to his old idea of destruction, as practised in Georgia, rather than co-operation of his army with that of Grant in a military sense, such as his letter to Grant of December 24th had seemed to indicate. But perhaps it was a reflection of his letter to Grant on the eve of his setting out: " I expect Davis will move Heaven and earth to catch me, for success to my column is fatal to his dream of empire. Richmond is not more vital to his cause than Columbia and the heart of South Carolina."

On March 15th Sherman resumed his march on Goldsborough on a broad front, his left column passing through Bentonville. But Johnston had concentrated his army, now about 27,000 strong, at that spot, and on the 19th he fell upon the flank column, Slocum's corps, as it passed. He achieved a partial success but Union reinforcements came up in the nick of time. Next day the bulk of Sherman's army had reached the battlefield, but Johnston reverted to the defensive, and as Sherman declined to attack, an impasse resulted. On the 21st Sherman was presented with a splendid opportunity to break through on to the enemy's line of communications owing to a surprise attack by Mower's division.* But he preferred not to take the risk. " By his

[1] This and other quotations in this chapter are from *O.R.*, vol. 47, parts ii and iii.

* It is fair to point out that Johnston claims to have eventually repulsed Mower's attack.

restraint," writes Liddell Hart, "Sherman forfeited a tactical crown, but gained a strategic base." But if he had attacked with his whole army (a thing he never did in his whole career) he would not only have won a tactical crown but gained a strategic base also; for Schofield, advancing from Newburn, was already in Goldsborough. Johnston retreated north, and next day Sherman joined Schofield in Goldsborough. Thus had Sherman completed a great march of 425 miles in 51 days, "the greatest march in modern history," and one to which the march through Georgia was child's play. The campaign had now reached a supremely interesting strategical stage, and the reader is requested to study Sketch Map 21 rather closely. It would seem that Grant's patient far-flung plans were approaching fruition. Four great armies were now gathered about the decisive point: at Petersburg Grant himself with 120,000 men appeared to have got a stranglehold on Lee's 50,000; at Goldsborough Sherman with 85,000 was opposed by Johnston's 40,000 at Smithfield. Now a few distances: From the lines south of Petersburg to Goldsborough, in a straight line, 125 miles; to Smithfield the same distance. Petersburg to Danville 120 miles; Smithfield to Danville 85 miles; Goldsborough to Danville 120 miles.

Running right across the front between the two groups of armies was the River Roanoke, a formidable obstacle on the east, not so formidable on the west. A direct but very much damaged railroad ran from Goldsborough to Grant's army; a roundabout but only slightly damaged railroad from Smithfield to Lee's army. Roads were good in the neighbourhood of Goldsborough but probably getting worse as the Roanoke was approached. Under these conditions, what was the right policy for the Union armies? The student might consider this problem before reading further. . . .

Sherman considered the answer to be that his army should march north and combine with Grant to beat Lee. Grant, on the other hand, considered that he could now defeat Lee single-handed *provided that Johnston was in the meantime kept away*. Now, Sherman could join hands with Grant in under a fortnight; but in a still shorter time Johnston could join Lee, to the north of Danville, unless impeded. There can therefore be no doubt that Grant was right in prescribing this duty to Sherman.

The mission that confronted Sherman on his arrival at Goldsborough therefore was to prevent Johnston from joining Lee. This mission could be carried out in one, or a combination, of three ways. (1) He might defeat Johnston so thoroughly in battle as to disintegrate his army, thus making any question of helping Lee out of the question. (2) He might drive Johnston away from Lee. (3) He might interpose his own army between Johnston and Lee. Should Johnston retire along the railroad to Greenborough, Sherman's cavalry should be able to cut the railroad to Danville in his rear—a combination of courses (2) and (3).

Any of these courses would entail a forward move by his own

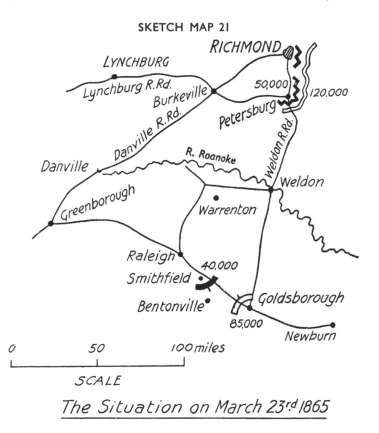

SKETCH MAP 21

The Situation on March 23rd 1865

army. It was becoming evident that at any moment Lee might abandon Richmond and attempt to join Johnston. Prompt action was therefore indicated, provided Sherman's troops were capable of it. Of this there can be no doubt whatever. Sherman's own statements fully bear it out. According to him, they were in excellent health and spirits, the army was in superb order " and the trains almost as fresh as when we started from Atlanta "; there was no shortage of food and as long as they kept on the move no difficulty was anticipated in this connection; no shortage of munitions; the troops, who had been averaging nine miles a day, were not unduly fatigued; there was therefore no paramount need for even the shortest halt at Goldsborough. Johnston had been pushed back, and the military maxim is that once on the run the enemy should be kept on the run. Sherman himself had no doubt of his ability to keep Johnston on the run; for on the day after Goldsborough he wrote to Grant: " I am satisfied that Johnston's army was so roughly handled yesterday that we could march right on to Raleigh. . . ."

Sherman, however, decided to suspend the march for eighteen days. The reasons for this decision will be examined later. His troops therefore settled down at Goldsborough and for the next seventeen days they did not see an enemy. It was the period of the profoundest peace that they had ever experienced.*

Meanwhile Sherman, having put some " ginger " into the collection of stores at Goldsborough, went by sea to City Point to consult Grant. There the two had an interview, the exact nature of which will never be known, for neither made a record of it at the time, and there were no witnesses. According to Schofield, who should know, Sherman's object was to persuade Grant to adopt his own point of view, namely that he should march direct on Petersburg, in order to take part in the final battle. Apart from the perfectly sound military reasons against this, Grant had a natural desire to prove that the Army of the Potomac could finish its duel with the Army of Northern Virginia unaided; in fact, he admits as much with perfect candour in his Memoirs. No doubt this was the subject of their conversation, and it probably ended in Grant asking when Sherman would be ready to participate in his mission against Johnston, and in Sherman answering, April 10th. There is no evidence that Grant tried to get this date put forward, but that he deliberately hoodwinked Sherman as to the imminence of his coming offensive is improbable. However that may be, it is evident that Sherman did not achieve his purpose at City Point, for the plan that he prepared on his return envisaged an attempt to interpose between the two Confederate armies. Sherman had now nearly 90,000 men, so was almost as strong as Lee and Johnston combined and he believed himself stronger; so he prepared to advance in full

* As an example of the halcyon period through which they were passing, it was considered an appropriate time to issue the following General Order: "N.C.O.'s in charge of squads will see that the men wash their hands and faces daily; that they comb and brush their heads; that their hair is kept short."

confidence. But before his preparations were complete the reason for his march had ceased to exist. Lee had surrendered to Grant, and Sherman was left with the task of settling with Johnston. This he started out to do on March 10th and reached Raleigh on the 13th, Johnston falling back before him to Greenborough. From there Johnston sued for peace, and on the 27th his army laid down its arms without further fighting. Thus General William Tecumseh Sherman passes out of our story without having had the crowning glory of taking a hand in the final defeat of Robert E. Lee.

COMMENTS.

The interest in this march centres in its concluding phases. Until Sherman met Johnston he had committed not a single mistake; his movements had been brilliant and flawless. But the conclusion of the march was marked by two flagrant errors of judgment on his part—errors that have been slurred over by the critics and mercifully screened from the public view by Grant's action in destroying Lee's army, and thus bringing the war to an end.

The first of these errors was Sherman's failure to take advantage of the wonderful opportunity to defeat Johnston at Bentonville, whose line of retreat was practically cut by Mower's division when Sherman recalled the latter. Sherman himself admitted afterwards that he had committed an error, so there is no need to enlarge on the point. His reason was apparently an excess of prudence. He wished to unite with Schofield's 26,000 men before engaging Johnston decisively in battle. Thus he was not mentally prepared to seize Fortune when she presented herself. Napoleon's hackneyed phrase comes irresistibly to mind: " Fortune is a woman; . . ."

Sherman's second error was in failing to pursue Johnston after the battle. " Touch once gained should never be lost " is a sound maxim. Why did Sherman disregard it in this case? To Grant on the 22nd he explained his inaction as follows: " We have now been out six weeks . . . our men ' dirty ragged and saucy ' and we must rest and fix up a little." Note that he does not claim that his men were short of food or ammunition, the only adequate excuse for refraining from pursuit. The fact is, Sherman liked to take his campaigns in stages, with a pause to " wash and brush up " in the intervals. He felt that his men deserved an easy at this stage, and doubtless they fully deserved one; but this attitude of mind is hardly that of a conquering general, who pays no regard to the supposed "deserts" of his troops if they militate against success in the field.

So Johnston was able to lick his wounds in peace and given nearly three weeks in which to drill his miscellaneous collection of units into a homogeneous army—a task for which none was better fitted than himself. Further, as Johnston himself points out, the pause was advantageous to him, "for it gave time for the arrival of several thousand men. . . . It also enabled the chief commissary to provide for a march by collecting supplies."[2] Sherman would have found Johnston's army a very different nut to crack in April from what it was in March. The lesson is obvious: You should not give your army a pause to rest before considering whether that pause may not confer even greater benefits on your opponent. Three times, now, had Sherman given his opponents an opportunity to set their house in order, and to recover from a rebuff. Meanwhile, Sherman spent precious days at City Point taking tea with the President and Mrs. Lincoln, and receiving the plaudits of Grant's generals. Only Lincoln himself seems to have disapproved of Sherman's inaction, but the broad hints thrown out by him that Sherman's right place at this decisive stage of the war was with his army seem to have fallen on deaf ears.

As to why Grant acquiesced in Sherman's inaction while he himself was launching his final attack upon Lee we will consider later. All that need be pointed out here is that the three weeks respite granted to Johnston should have enabled him, if he wished, to leave a cavalry screen at Raleigh and join Lee in the neighbour-hood of Burkeville—while Sherman's troops were junketting in Goldsborough. Finally we come to the consideration of the question, What was the real reason why Sherman halted for so long at Goldsborough, thus missing participation in the last phase of the war? Most of his biographers accept the statement that a move forward before April 10th was impracticable, and leave it at that. But when we investigate the impediments which prevented an earlier move we encounter some curious facts. As I have pointed out, there was no insuperable impediment to following up Johnston and not halting at Goldsborough at all. But assuming for the sake of argument that such a halt was considered essential, was eighteen days necessary? "We want stores and nothing else," wired Sherman to Newbern. What was the nature of these essential stores? Apart from building up a food reserve, it is difficult to ascertain; but the first trains

[2] *Narrative of Military Operations*, p. 394.

to be loaded up contained " shoes, socks, shirts and pants to make the men comfortable." Shoes, by all means; but " pants to make the men comfortable " hardly seems an adequate reason for holding up the advance of a victorious army just when it has gained contact with the enemy. Sherman's army was in rags; still more so were those of Lee and of Johnston; but such a plea never prevented these armies from moving. The matter of boots is more serious. It is difficult to say how many men were bare footed, certainly under 20,000. Unpleasant, but Southern armies were accustomed to marching in this condition; and if it were considered undesirable to demand such hardship from Northern troops, the barefooted men could have been temporarily left behind at Goldsborough, and still Sherman would have ample men with which to follow up Johnston's still more dirty and ragged and " saucy " men.

To take the matter a stage further; let us assume that Sherman did not at first appreciate the need for gripping on to Johnston at once. But surely the news that Grant was attacking should have caused him to quicken up his programme? The silence on the part of Grant from April 1st to 6th should have told Sherman that he must be on the move; and if on the move, then on a *forward* move. On April 6th he learnt definitely that Petersburg had fallen and that Lee was in retreat to the west. But he still stuck to his pre-arranged date for moving. Even when on the 8th he received two messages from Grant ordering him to " push on " and " push Johnston " he adhered to the old date. On the very day of his arrival at Goldsborough he had indicated April 10th as the date for the resumption of the offensive, and to that date, though events moved fast and conditions changed, he stuck like a limpet. That very fact has been adduced by his biographer as " a side light into his insight into the ' Q ' side of strategy," and that " he fulfilled his calculation to the day." Rather the reverse is the case. His calculation was not particularly impressive, for as he himself admits: " We find the country here . . . with more corn and forage than I expected." And again: " Our railroads have worked double what I calculated." Why then did he stick to his original period of seventeen days to replenish? As far back as March 31st his Quartermaster reported: " There are twelve days' rations for the whole army now in this town (Goldsborough), and the clothing to refit the army is here, or will be here to-day." Sherman in effect corroborates this on the same day: " We only await the loading of our wagons, and patching up and mending made necessary." Yet he did not move for ten days more.   Ten days seems rather a long period to pack wagons, while Grant's army was pursuing Lee's to its doom.

The conclusion is inescapable that either Sherman was hopelessly blind to the realities of the situation or else he had become so accustomed to making rigid plans in advance, and to carrying them out, that he could not rapidly adapt himself to new and unforeseen circumstances.   For months he had been planning his own movements with scant consideration for those of the enemy, and now the enemy had sprung a march on him!   That he had been for some time wedded to the idea of a halt at Goldsborough is indirectly borne out by a passage in a letter written on the day of his arrival: " I have constantly held out to the officers and men to bear patiently the want of clothing and other necessaries, for at Goldsborough awaited us everything."   Perhaps that is the real clue to the halt.   He had made a promise, and he would not break his word.   As to his blindness as to the imminence of the end; on April 7th, even after hearing of Lee's hasty retreat, he is writing to his base: " The army is so much interested in mails and small parcels that we will need such a line as. . . ." Mails and small parcels, and Lee within forty-eight hours of surrender!

It is no answer to this criticism to point out that Johnston did not in fact attempt to join up with Lee, and that therefore Sherman was justified in sitting still also.   Johnston had a 35-mile start of Sherman, a two days' march; and the reason why he did not move to join Lee is a mystery.   Probably Lee sent him some message that was captured by the Union cavalry; he certainly received none.   But Sherman had no right to count on this.   The conclusion, therefore, is that Sherman's last campaign, after an auspicious start, petered out dismally, owing to his failure to clinch the victory at Bentonville, to his failure to follow up Johnston's retiring army after the battle, and to his failure to resume the grip on Johnston when he learnt that Lee was on the move.

As for the contention that his march and devastations had an indirect influence on Lee's defeat, such an eminent historian as Ropes finds that Sherman was " entirely mistaken in thinking that to devastate the state of S. Carolina would have a direct and immediate bearing on Grant's campaign in Virginia."[3]

There remains but to note Sherman's reaction to Grant's order to " push Johnston " while Lee was retreating.   It will be remembered that, foreseeing such a contingency, Grant had enjoined him to prevent the junction of the two Confederate

[3] *M.H.S.M.* x, 149.

armies; yet Sherman now wrote to Grant: " I may take a course round Johnston for the purpose of turning him *north*. . . . I don't want to race all the way back through Georgia and South Carolina. It is to our interest to let Lee and Johnston come together, just as a billiard player would move the balls when he has them in a nice place." It is not known what Grant thought of this singular picture of a game of billiards, involving the gift of interior lines to the enemy, nor how he viewed the projected absolute reversal of his own policy; for by the time he received the letter he had brought the war to a conclusion—in a manner that we must now set forth.

CHAPTER XIX

Appomattox.

THE situation within the Confederate lines at Petersburg grew increasingly gloomy as March progressed. First came the news of Early's defeat, and the capture of Charlottesville by Sheridan; then the news of Sherman's steady approach, culminating in the ominous tidings that he had reached Goldsborough and joined forces with Schofield. Lee had little doubt that Sherman would continue his march and join up with Grant. Such a contingency had to be avoided somehow, or else Lee must abandon Richmond and join forces with Johnston.

Lee made his plans; and on March 25th delivered the first offensive blow he had launched at Grant since the Wilderness. Fort Stedman was the point fixed for the attack. For years to come there was to be great discussion as to the reason for this offensive. It was eventually cleared up by the publication of Lee's *Confidential Despatches* in 1915. In a despatch to the President dated March 26th, Lee gives a perfectly comprehensible and sound reason. If the attack were successful, he explains to the President, " General Grant would at least be obliged so to curtail his lines that upon the approach of General Sherman I might be able to hold our position with a portion of the troops, and with a select body unite with General Johnston and give him battle. If successful I would then be able to return to my position."[1] In other words, Lee envisaged an application of the science of interior lines, which would have afforded great interest to the military student. Unfortunately for the student, the attack on Fort Stedman failed disastrously, after an initial success, the attackers losing nearly 5,000 men to the defenders 1,000. (Sketch Map 22.)

Before describing Grant's reply, which was swift, we must glance briefly at the strategical situation. Grant was still intent on hemming in Lee, and with this in view had ordered Sheridan to capture Lynchburg, while Thomas was to advance eastwards from Knoxville. But Sheridan again disobeyed his orders, and from Charlottesville went straight to Richmond, while Thomas exhibited his usual slowness. Stoneman's cavalry did, however,

[1] *Op. cit.*, p. 341.

MAP 22

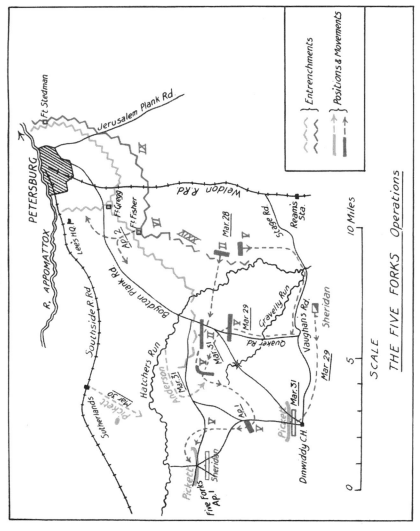

THE FIVE FORKS Operations

Entrenchments
Positions & Movements

SCALE
0   5   10 Miles

PETERSBURG
Ft. Stedman
Jerusalem Plank Rd.
R. APPOMATTOX
Lee's HQ.
Ft. Gregg
Ft. Fisher
IX
VI
Southside R. Rd.
AP.1
AP.2
XXX
Boydton Plank Rd.
Weldon R. Rd.
II Mar. 28
V
Stage Rd.
Reams Sta.
Hatchers Run
Anderson Mar. 31
Pickett Mar. 30
Sutherlands
V
Mar. 31 II
V
Mar. 29
Gravelly Run
Quaker Rd.
Vaughan's Rd.
Sheridan
Mar. 29
AP.1
V
V
Pickett Mar. 31
Dinwiddy C.H.
Pickett
Five Forks
AP.1 Sheridan
V

push on to Lynchburg and were destroying the railroad there when the campaign came to an end.

Meanwhile Grant had already planned the blow which, four days after Fort Stedman, he proceeded to carry out. It may best be given in his own words to Sherman. After explaining that Sheridan with a force of 9,000 cavalry was to cut the Southside Railroad and destroy it on both sides of Burkeville, he goes on: "From that point I shall probably leave it to his discretion either to return to this army . . . or to go and join you. . . . When this movement commences I shall move out by my left, with all the force I can, holding present entrenched lines. I shall start with no distinct views, further than holding Lee's forces from following Sheridan. But I shall be along myself, and will take advantage of anything that turns up. If Lee detaches I will attack; or if he comes out of his lines I will endeavour to repulse him, and follow it up to the best advantage." This passage deserves close study, not least for the light it throws on Grant's propensity—shared by all the great commanders—for making his plan elastic and adaptable: he refrains from making a formal cut-and-dried plan which is to be adhered to whatever the enemy may do; but is content to define the main object and to leave the working out of details to be decided, and if necessary modified, in accordance with the action of the enemy. All this is in glaring contrast to the method of his great lieutenant. Sherman was prone to make far-flung plans, to fix on distant objectives, irrespective of what action the enemy might take, and to endeavour to carry them out with precision and punctuality as to place and time. In this he was generally strikingly successful. His detailed plans for his final campaign (never carried out) are a striking example of this precision. But the student should be on his guard against approving of such a course. It was successful in Sherman's case largely because of his preponderance in numbers and strength over his opponents; but such a situation cannot be reckoned upon in war, and the more elastic methods of Grant and of Lee are the sounder.

To return to Grant's plan. Even before the attack on Fort Stedman, he had decided on it. He gives his reason in a letter to Sheridan on March 21st: "There is now such a possibility, if not probability, of Lee and Johnston attempting to unite that I feel extremely desirous not only of cutting the lines of communications between them but. . . ."[2] His method of carrying this out involved a general side-slip of all his forces to the left, and a

[2] O.R., vol. 46, iii, 67.

thinning out of the line. Further, the V supported by the II Corps was to operate to the west of the lines, forming a kind of stepping stone between Sheridan's cavalry and the remainder of the army. (Sketch Map 22.)

The move commenced on March 29th. Sheridan made a wide detour to the south and reached DinwiddieC.H. safely. Warren's V Corps also made a detour via Vaughan's Road and northwards up the Quaker Road. Here it was attacked, somewhat to its surprise, but had not much difficulty in driving off the attackers.

So far all had gone well and this encouraged Grant to enlarge his operation. He therefore wrote to Sheridan: " I now feel like ending the matter, if it is possible to do so, before going back. I do not, therefore, want you to cut loose at once and go after the enemy's railroads at present. In the morning push around the enemy if you can, and get on to his right rear." But rain fell heavily all night, converting the roads into quagmires. On the morning of the 30th Grant was therefore strongly urged by his staff to postpone the operation, and he actually issued orders to that effect. This was not to the liking of Sheridan, who rode over to Grant's headquarters and persuaded the General-in-Chief to allow the operation to continue. Owing to the rain, however, little progress was made that day, but on the 31st the advance was resumed. The II Corps gained contact with the extreme right flank of the Confederate entrenchments, while further to the west the cavalry was advancing northwards towards Five Forks, and the V Corps northwards towards the White Oak Road, just beyond the Confederate entrenchments. Without warning, a double blow suddenly fell upon both cavalry and infantry. Sheridan was driven right back to Dinwiddie by a superior force of cavalry and infantry, while Warren's two leading divisions were struck heavily in front and left flank and driven headlong back upon the third, with a loss of nearly 2,000 men. Whence had come this sudden blow? To answer it we must return to the Confederate camp.

Lee had got wind of Grant's proposed operation in the nick of time. His reply to it was characteristic of the man. In spite of the great loss he had just sustained at Fort Stedman, and the resulting lowering of the morale in his troops, Lee instantly decided on a counter-offensive, cost what it might. But how to find the troops? On a front of 38 miles (10 of it being water) the defenders had an average density of 1,140 men per mile; the line was perilously thin. Pickett's division, 5,000 strong, was however in reserve on the north of the river. This, together with the cavalry, was brought south by train and moved to the extreme right. It was this force (with part of Johnston's division) that drove back Sheridan's cavalry, 8,500 against 9,000. But Lee was not content with this; discovering that the left flank of the Northern infantry was " in the air " he determined to roll it up. A scratch force of four brigades, coming from three different divisions, all under the command of Anderson, was therefore launched to the attack just as Warren was advancing, with the result that we have already seen. A force 6,500 strong had driven back two divisions of the V Corps, 9,000 strong. The third division " stopped the rot " and restored the situation, but this sudden and unexpected double blow, one of the most brilliant in Lee's military career, created extreme alarm in the Union camp. For the time being all thought of the great offensive was dropped. Sheridan was isolated; Sheridan was in danger; Sheridan must be saved! Such was the paramount consideration; and all through the ensuing night wires hummed, while messengers spurred backwards and forwards along the woodland tracks, all directed to the same object—the saving of Sheridan. The unfortunate Warren received eight successive messages from Meade during this night, each contradicting or to some extent modifying the previous one. Thanks to the proceedings of the Warren Court of Inquiry we know the details of Five Forks better than almost any battle in the war. The result of these comings and goings was the battle of Five Forks, fought next day, April 1st—a battle of such great interest and importance that it must be accorded a section all to itself.

THE BATTLE OF FIVE FORKS, APRIL 1ST. (*Sketch Map* 22.)

One division of the V Corps had been sent to Sheridan's help during the night. The remaining two were told to push south-west against the rear of the enemy confronting Sheridan. Grant wished this done during the night, but conditions were difficult and Warren decided not to attempt the movement in the night but to wait till he received word at dawn that his other division had joined up with Sheridan. Warren has been blamed for this delay; but in any case he would have been too late to intercept Pickett who, seeing that he was isolated and confronted by superior forces, very wisely retreated in the night to Five Forks. Here he hastily entrenched a position and awaited events.

Sheridan followed up the retreating Confederates and at 2 p.m. came in touch with the new position at Five Forks. Meanwhile

Warren had been placed by Grant under the command of Sheridan, who now formed a plan for a combined attack on Pickett. His own cavalry were to hold the front and demonstrate on the left flank while Warren mounted an oblique attack against the hostile left with two divisions in line and one in second line. In order to effect surprise, Warren was ordered to form up his corps under cover, opposite the supposed hostile flank but without getting a glimpse of it. Warren did this with great care and at 4 p.m. he advanced to the attack. Unfortunately the location of the Confederate position had been wrongly reported, with the result that the right-hand division, followed by the third, overlapped the position and went marching past it into the blue, the wooded country hiding their error from them. Warren, spotting the error that had been made, galloped after them, and eventually succeeded in swinging them round through three-quarters of a circle to the left. By this time they were right behind the hostile position, with the result that when they did advance they struck Pickett in the rear. Meanwhile Sheridan, " the very incarnation of battle," was fighting like a demon with Warren's second division against Pickett's left, while his cavalry was threatening the hostile right. Almost surrounded, Pickett's men broke and fled, losing over three thousand prisoners. The victory was complete, and its completeness was due to an error in locating the enemy's position—surely an ironic occurrence!

COMMENTS ON FIVE FORKS.

Would Sheridan have won Five Forks if he had not wrongly located the enemy's position? It is impossible to say, but what is certain is that his victory would not have been nearly so complete, with the result that Grant might not have been encouraged, as he was, to risk a general assault—and history might have been changed! This reflection leads one to agree with Lyman who, writing at the time, refers to " the totally undeserved prominence given to Sheridan."[3]

Sheridan had become Grant's "blue-eyed boy." When informing the cavalry leader that Warren was placed under him, Grant had thrown out a pretty broad hint that Sheridan could relieve him of command if unsatisfied with him. This Sheridan did on the evening of the battle, on the grounds that " he did not exert himself to get up his corps as rapidly as he might have done . . . " "and that he did not exert himself to inspire his troops with confidence." All that need be said about the unfortunate affair is that

[3] *Meade's Headquarters*, p. 358.

Warren, after frequent applications, was granted a Court of Inquiry in 1880 and that the Court found substantially in his favour, a verdict that is accepted by practically all historians.

Sheridan was undoubtedly hasty in taking this action. He was impulsive by nature, and it is to be noted that his impulsiveness was instrumental in inducing Grant to persevere with the operation on March 30th. His relations *vis-à-vis* Grant may be compared to those of Gallieni *vis-à-vis* Joffre at the inception of the battle of the Marne. Though Sheridan had failed as an independent army commander, his energy and drive in the Appomattox campaign is very much to be admired. 52

Grant had left City Point and had taken up quarters nearer the line for the operations, which he conducted in person. This led to the same complications that had been in evidence in the Wilderness, for most (but not all) orders went through Meade, which delayed matters, besides converting Meade's headquarters into a glorified post office. Grant may have been influenced by the knowledge that Meade was not on good terms with Sheridan —an example of the importance of the personal factor. Grant's refusal to make detailed plans too far ahead, as shown by his letter to Sherman, is to be commended. As Badeau puts it, " Grant was always ready to conform to the changing actualities as they occurred." The Commander-in-Chief built up his plan, stone by stone, on the gradually unfolding actualities. We shall presently see how he laid another stone as the result of the battle of Five Forks.

Lee never displayed greater judgment and sureness of touch than in his dispositions to counter Grant's obviously impending offensive. His possession of interior lines stood him in good stead, enabling him to concentrate troops in time to the threatened point. He has however been criticised for encouraging Pickett to stand at Five Forks in an isolated position. With the advantage of knowing the ensuing course of events we can afford to condemn him, but it must be remembered that a weaker force *must* take risks and put up a certain amount of bluff. For months Lee had been bluffing with success, and the bluff in this last case had been surprisingly successful at first, and but for Sheridan's lucky error it might have continued to be successful. But Lee was approaching the end of his tether. In order to produce his counter-attacking force he had had to deplete his front to beyond the edge of risk: only 16,000 infantry were now holding 20 miles of front on the south of the river. The end was drawing near! Even the cautious and pessimistic Meade said at this time: " I do not see what Lee can do." Nor could Lee himself, and he told the President so.

THE RETREAT TO APPOMATTOX.

At 9 p.m. on April 1st Grant received the good tidings of the battle of Five Forks. Quietly folding up the message form he turned to Meade and said: " Very well then; I want Wright and Parke to assault to-morrow morning at 4 o'clock." Only a dozen words ushered in the decisive move of Grant's career and of the whole war!

The attack took place as ordered, at dawn on April 2nd. On the right the IX Corps could make little progress but Wright's VI Corps smashed right through the Confederate lines between Forts Fisher and Gregg and advanced straight upon Lee's headquarters (Sketch Map 22). The Southern commander, who had summoned Field's division from the north of the river, was lying in bed conferring with Longstreet when a staff officer burst in with the alarming news that the enemy had broken the line. Lee dashed to the door; in the dim half light a line of riflemen could be seen approaching. General A. P. Hill, who was with Lee, sprang to horse and galloped off to ascertain if it were friend or foe. A moment later he was shot dead. It was the enemy! There was only one thing to be done, and Lee did it. Collecting what troops he could he manned the inner line of the defences. The enemy was brought to a stand; but a wedge had been formed in the middle of the Confederate army, Pickett, Johnston, Anderson and the cavalry were all outside the wedge and their fate was unknown.

The situation was grave in the extreme, but Lee remained outwardly calm. Quickly coming to the conclusion that the only chance of saving his army was an immediate retreat, he penned a letter to the President to that effect. Jefferson Davis was in St. Paul's, Richmond, when the dire intelligence arrived. A messenger came to his pew, just as the minister was uttering the prayer for the President of the Confederate States. Davis quietly got up and walked out of the church.* and that evening he and his government had left Richmond for Danville by train, never to return.

That night the Army of Northern Virginia silently and skilfully evacuated the lines that they had held so stoutly for over nine months, and filed off to the west. Marching all night, and making for Amelia Court House (Sketch Map 23) they had put 16 miles

* The pew he occupied can still be identified.

MAP 23

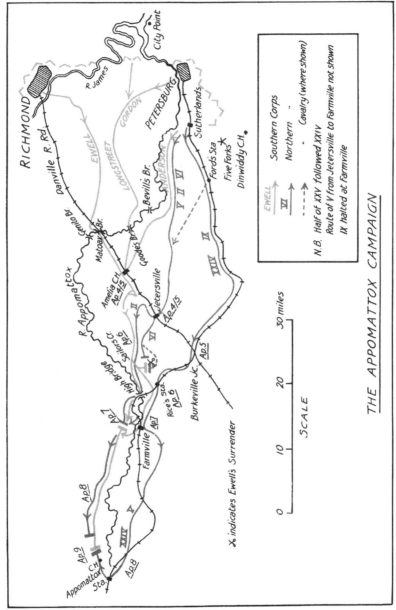

RICHMOND

City Point

R. James

PETERSBURG

EWELL

LONGSTREET

GORDON

ANDERSON

Sutherlands

Fords Sta.

Five Forks

Dinwiddy C.H.

Danville R. Rd.

Bevill's Br.

V II VI

XXIV

IX

Genito Br.

Mattoax Br.

Goode's Br.

Amelia C.H.
Ap.4/5

Jetersville
Ap.4/5

R. Appomattox

II

VI
Ap.6

High Bridge

Sailor's Cr.

Ap.5

Burkeville Jc.

Rice's Sta.
Ap.6

Ap.7

Ap.7

Farmville

Ap.8

Ap.9

C.H.
XXIV

Ap.8

Appomattox
Sta.

SCALE

0   10   20   30 miles

X indicates Ewell's Surrender

EWELL   Southern Corps

                Northern   "

                Cavalry (where shown)

VI

N.B. Half of XXV followed XXIV
Route of V from Jetersville to Farmville not shown
IX halted at Farmville

THE APPOMATTOX CAMPAIGN

between them and their opponents by the morning of the 3rd. Lee was making for Danville, via Amelia Court House and Burkeville, hoping to join up with Johnston. The latter, however, received no instructions to approach Lee, and remained stationary at Smithfield. Anderson's troops and the remnants of Pickett's marched by Sutherland Station and the south side of the Appomattox, making also for Amelia Court House.

On the morning of April 3rd the Union troops entered unopposed into Richmond and Petersburg. But Grant set but little store now by the occupation of the capital that he had been striving for so long. His objective was not a geographical one. Lee's army was on the move. " The rebel armies are now the only strategic points," Grant wrote to Sherman. And to Sheridan he explained: " The first object of present movement will be to intercept Lee's army and the second to secure Burkeville." Acting on his own maxim, Grant now launched nearly his whole army to the pursuit. Strictly speaking it was more a race than a pursuit—a race for the Danville Railroad. The cavalry and the V Corps headed for Jetersville, followed later by II and VI, while XXIV and IX took the line of the Southside Railroad direct for Burkeville. It was thus a move on three parallel lines, the Confederate army taking the northernmost one.

April 4th.

Longstreet had made for Bevill's Bridge, but finding it flooded, he crossed by Goode's Bridge and reached Amelia Court House on the morning of the 4th, followed by Gordon and Anderson. Ewell, failing to cross by Genito Bridge, used the railroad bridge at Matoax, and did not arrive till the 5th. In the afternoon of the 4th Sheridan's cavalry and the V Corps reached Jetersville. It was just possible for Lee to brush them aside before the II and VI Corps could come up. But a ghastly discovery was made at Amelia Court House. The food that he had expected to find there was not forthcoming and all that day and much of the 5th had to be consumed in scouring the country for food for the famishing Army of Northern Virginia. This allowed II and VI to close up, and XXIV to reach Burkeville. The road to Danville via Burkeville was thus effectually and doubly blocked. Lee's only chance of escape now was to make for Farmville.

But his intelligence service had almost completely broken down, and he was unaware that his road was blocked. Consequently he ordered the retreat to be continued through Jetersville, the wagon trains to take a more northerly route.

APRIL 5TH.

Late in the morning the Confederate army resumed its retreat, the foraging wagons having returned almost empty. Seven miles down the road to Jetersville it came to an abrupt halt: the enemy was entrenched right across the road. Lee rode forward and reconnoitred. The position was, he learnt, held by cavalry, but infantry was close at hand. Should he attack? Regretfully he decided against it. This decision of his was afterwards criticised by Sheridan; and doubtless Lee's admirers would have liked to see one final blow from Lee's strong right arm. But it is now clear that it would have had no chance of success. Lee probably was influenced chiefly by the knowledge that his men had lost most of their offensive and manoeuvring power. Tired, dispirited and famished men can hold a defensive position resolutely; but it is a very different matter to expect them to manœuvre and attack. Lee's right arm was no longer strong. In the light of actuality Lee was right; for the V Corps was present with the cavalry, the II Corps was just arriving and the VI Corps was only a few miles away. An attack on Sheridan could have had only one issue.

Lee had to make a fresh plan. Obviously the Danville Railroad was now denied to him. There remained only the Lynchburg line. There should be some supplies on it at Farmville. Lee therefore decided to make for that town, hoping thence to strike south for Danville across country. But the enemy now had the interior lines. If they chose to anticipate his move, and make straight for Danville they were bound to arrive first. Lee's only hope was to shake off contact by a night march. If he could get to Farmville clear ahead of the enemy and slip off to the south before his change of direction was spotted, there was a sporting chance that the enemy would go blindly groping for him towards Lynchburg. Farmville to Danville in a straight line is 75 miles; Smithfield, where Johnston lay, to Danville is 90 miles. Did Lee call upon Johnston to make for that town? If he did, Johnston never received the order; in fact he received nothing direct from Lee during the whole retreat as far as I can ascertain. Meanwhile Grant was showing his best form. He had divined his opponent's intention. Writing to Sherman on the 5th he said: " All indications now are that Lee will attempt to reach Danville with the remnant of his force. If you can possibly do so push on." And next day his plan took still more definite shape: " Push Johnston at the same time, and let us finish this job all at once." There speaks the true Grant—the paramount idea with which he had taken up the office of General-in-Chief remained paramount, to finish the job in one mighty sweep, combining as many as possible of his far-flung forces. His dream was coming true, before even he was properly aware of it! He now exerted his best driving force. The cavalry marched and fought with ardour and dash; some of the infantry, notably the XXIV Corps, marched even better. All were imbued with Grant's spirit of victory.

APRIL 6TH.

At dawn the cavalry and the three corps of the Union right wing advanced towards Amelia, only to find that Lee had slipped them. Evidently he had gone west, and thither the direction of the march was changed, whilst the left column continued along the railway towards Rice's Station, which it reached that night. On the extreme right the V Corps did not gain contact, but the II Corps caught up the rearguard, Gordon's Corps, and inflicted heavy losses on it, capturing 1,700 prisoners. Further to the left the VI Corps was still more successful against Ewell and Anderson, in conjunction with the cavalry, who got round their rear at Sailor's Creek. Ultimately practically the whole of these corps were captured or dispersed, Ewell being included among the 4,300 prisoners. Nearly one-half of Lee's army had been destroyed on this fatal April 6th.

During these direful events Longstreet's corps, which formed the vanguard, had been sitting down near Rice's Station, waiting for the remainder to close up. But the other three corps were in a state of disintegration. Let a Northern writer picture the scene. " The Confederates began the retreat with but one ration, and when no supplies were met at Amelia Court House they were reduced to such scant stores as could be collected from the poor and almost exhausted region through which they passed. Those men were fortunate who had in their pockets a few handfuls of corn which they might parch by the wayside. . . . While the sufferings of the men were thus severe, those of the horses and mules were even keener; for of forage there was none, and the grass had not yet sprouted. . . . Dark divisions, sinking in the woods for a few hours' repose, would hear suddenly the boom of hostile guns and the clatter of the hoofs of the ubiquitous cavalry. Thus pressed upon on all sides, driven like sheep before prowling wolves, with blazing wagons in front and rear, amid hunger, fatigue and sleeplessness, continuing day after day, they fared toward the setting sun."[4]

4 *Campaigns of the Army of the Potomac*, p. 613.

With an army in such a plight, with a staff depleted and worn out (one of his staff had no sleep for seventy-two hours), it would be idle to look for tactical or strategical lessons in Lee's conduct of affairs.   Sheep driven by wolves cannot make plans in advance; when Lee was asked where certain supplies should be brought to on the railroad he replied that he could not specify the exact point.   This was the simple and exact truth; conditions were beyond his control, the future was utterly unforeseeable.   It would therefore be pointless for me to dwell in detail upon the following few days.

It was now clear that Lee could not strike south from Farmville. He therefore ordered his army to cross to the north bank, Gordon by High Bridge and Longstreet by Farmville, and both were to destroy the bridges.   By this means the wearied army might get a few hours' respite, after which the retreat might be continued for the time being in the Lynchburg direction.   Lee himself spent the night in Farmville.

APRIL 7TH.

Longstreet carried out his part of the order, crossing to the north bank at Farmville and burning the bridges, but Gordon after crossing High Bridge, did not succeed in burning the road bridge in time; Humphreys's II Corps, driving on with great dash, seized the bridge and continued the pursuit.   About three miles north of Farmville Gordon halted and there he was joined by Longstreet.   The Army of Northern Virginia was once more concentrated, and Humphreys did not dare attack it unsupported. But Lee's hopes of a brief respite had been frustrated, the Appomattox was no longer a protection, and another night march became necessary.   Danville was still the ultimate objective, but that was utterly impossible unless food could be picked up on the railroad.   Appomattox looked the obvious place, and thither the steps of the Confederate army were now directed.

Late that night Lee received a letter from Grant suggesting that the time had come for surrender.   Lee replied that that time had not arrived, but requested details of Grant's terms.   Grant, who had probably been induced to send this letter from remarks dropped by the captured Ewell, spent the night at Farmville, only a few miles from his opponent.

APRIL 8TH.

Lee had again slipped away in the night.   Grant directed the II and VI Corps to pursue in his tracks, while the cavalry, followed

by the XXIV and V Corps, made for Appomattox Station. The
cavalry after a 30-mile march reached the station that evening,
just in time to hold up the Confederate vanguard and to capture
four trains of supplies. Ord's XXIV Corps surpassed itself, and
marching all night reached the scene at 10 a.m. next day. All
was over " bar the shouting."

During the day two further letters passed between Grant and
Lee, and that night Lee held his last council of war. The conclusion come to was that an attempt should be made by Gordon to
break through the cavalry next morning, but that if hostile infantry
should be found to have come to their support it would be useless
to carry on the struggle any longer.

APRIL 9TH.

In accordance with the above plan, Gordon's Corps advanced
to attack the cavalry in the early hours of the morning. The
attack was delivered " with wonderful impetuosity," the enemy
was flung back and even two guns were captured. But the
cavalry fell back on to infantry—fatal sign! " I have fought my
corps to a frazzle," reported the intrepid Gordon. " Then,"
said Lee, " there is nothing left me to do but to go and see General
Grant! " The war was over! But it is perhaps appropriate that
the last blow should have been struck by Lee.

The two commanders met face to face at Appomattox Court
House, in a memorable scene that did honour to both of these
great-hearted men. Honourable terms were granted, and 28,356
men were paroled, of whom only about 8,000 infantry and 2,400
cavalry still held arms.

Though it was some weeks before all the scattered Confederate
forces had lain down their arms, the surrender of the Army of
Northern Virginia marked the virtual end of the War.

COMMENTS.

When a tool, say a chisel, falls to pieces in the hands of the
man who is using it, it is idle to criticise the design he is attempting
to cut out. Lee's tool fell to pieces in his hand; therefore it
would be profitless to criticise his tactical dispositions during
that painful operation.

But there are two points of criticism that have been advanced,
and that demand examination here. The first is that Lee delayed
unduly the evacuation of Richmond. Various reasons have been
suggested for this. General Maurice writes: " I believe that Lee
did not leave Petersburg earlier because he knew that to do so

would be a measure of despair." But I see no grounds for rejecting the reason given by Lee himself. This was a simple one: his horses were so weak from lack of forage that they were incapable of hauling the wagons until the roads dried up somewhat. As to what the horses were capable of doing, that is of course a matter of opinion. But it is notable that Grant formed exactly the same estimate of his own animals, which were in much better condition than Lee's as they were not stinted in forage. On March 16th he wrote to Sheridan: " The roads are entirely impassable." And Lyman, Meade's Staff Officer, writes on March 2nd, that the ground is " saturated and rotten, no more passable to either party till about April 1st." That seems to dispose of the first criticism. But it may be pointed out that apart from the inability to move there was a strong military (in addition to political) reason for holding on. Burkeville was the vital focal point, connecting the railway systems of the west and the south. At all costs it must be held. The Richmond-Petersburg position, backed by two railroads, formed an admirable bridgehead for this purpose. For nine months Grant had directed his gaze to this point, but the Confederate defence system had kept him away from it.

The second criticism is that Lee made no adequate arrangements to feed his army. This is based largely on the fact that no rations reached the army at Amelia Court House. There has been a good deal of controversy on this point. It is dealt with in detail in appendix 2, vol. IV, of Freeman's *Lee.* The upshot seems to be that Lee gave orders to one of his staff that Richmond should be asked to send rations to that point, but that in the confusion and hurry of the move the message never got delivered. This may imply criticism of Lee's staff, but hardly of Lee himself. It must be remembered that the Commissary-General resided at Richmond, 20 miles from Lee's headquarters, and received his instructions from the War Minister, not from Lee.

A further criticism, which I have not heard stressed, might be that Lee should not have delayed his march in the effort to save his train. A Southern general was heard to exclaim on the day of the surrender: " Saving the wagons lost the army! " But it is easy to be wise after the event. When a starving army is struggling to escape from its pursuers it cannot afford to abandon what little food it has. In short, there seems to be no valid and useful criticism that can be launched against Lee for his conduct of the retreat.

To Grant and to his sprightly subordinate Sheridan is primarily

due the surrender at Appomattox. Grant never showed to
greater advantage than he did in this campaign. It was the
moment for which he had been patiently waiting and working.
When it came he, like Napoleon, kept his eye steadily fixed on
one point—the enemy. The time for manœuvre, for finesse, was
over. To strike, and to go on striking was now the *mot d'ordre*.
To Sherman he wired in words conveying a palpable hint that
Sherman also should make up his mind to strike: " The rebel
armies are now the only strategic points." To Meade and to
Sheridan his constant refrain was: " Push on, do not allow the
enemy breathing space! " On the evening of the 6th he was up
almost in the battle line, ahead of Meade. That day he wrote
him: " If we press him with vigour for a couple of days more
I do not believe he will get off with more than 5,000 men," a
remarkably accurate prophesy. As for Sheridan, he needed no
urging. I have had occasion to criticise pretty freely his conduct
as an independent army commander. But now, as a subordinate,
he was in his element. His fiery nature inspired his horsemen,
who swarmed everywhere, dashing without warning into the
hapless Confederate trains, burning the wagons, cutting off
stragglers, and creating alarm on all sides. The credit for cutting
off the Confederate army at Appomattox must go entirely to him.
No order to that effect seems to have come to him from Grant,
it was entirely his own conception; Grant merely backed him up
with infantry. It looks as if the General-in-Chief lost some of
his ardour for pursuit on the 8th. He was intent on his correspondence with Lee, and wrote to Sheridan: " I think Lee will
surrender to-day." Sheridan however expressed a contrary opinion
—and continued to pursue. Sheridan was right, Grant was
wrong. No wonder the former afterwards became the idol of the
North.

CHAPTER XX

Lee, Grant and Sherman.

AND now it only remains to assess the military abilities of three great men. For great men they all three were, without a shadow of doubt. But how far were they great military leaders? Ah, there's the rub! Controversy will rage over the subject till the crack of doom, for war is an inexact science, information is never complete and opinions on the conduct of operations will always differ. All that can be attempted here is to consider the light thrown on the subject by the 1864-5 Campaign.

General William Tecumseh Sherman displayed imagination, resource, versatility, broadness of conception, and genuine powers of leadership in this campaign. These are all fundamental traits of the great commander. Unfortunately he also exhibited two failings—that of pursuing a geographical rather than a military objective, and that of avoiding risk—which between them more than neutralised his assets as the commander of an army. To take the first. His campaign had three phases, in each of which he pursued a geographical end. In the first, this end was Atlanta; thereby he allowed Hood to escape and to " live to fight another day," which, as we have seen, he did to some purpose. In the second, it was Savannah; thereby he allowed Hardee to escape, and to live to give him a severe fright at Bentonville. In the third, it was Goldsborough; thereby he allowed Johnston to escape out of his clutches and to augment and reorganise his army at leisure till it reached the formidable strength of 45,000 men.

Sherman's second failing—the avoidance of risk—enabled Johnston to escape at Resaca, Hood to escape at Atlanta, French at Allatoona, and Johnston once more at Bentonville. It is a formidable list.

Hear what two of his corps commanders have to say on this point. Stanley writes: " General Sherman never fought a battle, though he had a thousand chances. Partial affairs called battles he fought, but it was always by a fragment of his army. He never had the moral courage to order his whole army into an engagement."[1] This is strong language, but it is corroborated by Schofield, who has an interesting theory to account for it: "Sherman's own knowledge of his own impulsive nature made him unduly distrustful of his own judgment, when under great responsibilities or emergencies. . . . He lacked the element of confident boldness or audacity in action which is necessary to gain the greatest results."[2] Possibly Sherman realised this in retrospect, for he made a speech shortly after the war in which he affirmed that "You cannot attain great success in war without taking great risks."

Against all this we can set Sherman's courage in breaking loose from his communications in the march through Georgia and his cheerful perseverance, foresight and calculation exhibited during the march through the Carolinas. He thoroughly deserves all, or nearly all, the eulogies showered upon him for these achievements, but they do not go very far to wipe out the debit balance.

It has been frequently and confidently asserted that these marches and devastations hastened the end of the war, and it is of importance to examine this contention and to assess the degree of truth in it. Unfortunately the investigation is beset with difficulties. To clear the ground: it is evident that neither of these marches had any *direct* influence on the Confederate collapse, which was the military defeat of the Army of Northern Virginia. Let Schofield again be our witness. "Sherman's destruction of military supplies and railroads . . . did not materially hasten the collapse of the Rebellion, which was due to Grant's capture of Lee's army."[3] To establish how far Sherman's operations had an *indirect* effect we must analyse the causes which led to the defeat of Lee. Now almost any action or movement on the part of a given body is the resultant of two or more forces acting upon that body in differing intensity or direction. This could be illustrated by a geometrical figure in the case of the retreat and defeat of Lee's army, if we could be sure we knew *all* the factors. We do know one of them—it is the factor of desertion. Now desertion grew alarmingly in the last months of the war, and it is generally agreed that Sherman's two triumphant marches had much to do with it. But how much? That is a question that can never be exactly answered. The motives of a man

[1] *Personal Memoirs*, by General D. S. Stanley, p. 182.
[2] *Schofield*, p. 341.
[3] *Schofield*, p. 314. Lest it should be supposed that Schofield is a hostile witness this is his opinion of Sherman as a general: "Sherman's campaigns stand alone without a parallel in military history . . . in most respects among the highest examples of the art of war."

remain locked in his heart. But here also they can be represented in geometrical or diagrammatical fashion. Draw an oblong figure to represent a soldier. Imagine that a group of forces are pushing him to the RIGHT, that is, to march against the enemy; and another group pushing him to the left, that is, to retreat or desert. Those pushing him to the right can be sub-grouped into *inherited forces*, such as inborn courage and stability of character, and *acquired forces* such as discipline, enthusiasm for the cause and for the leaders, confidence in ultimate victory, etc. The forces pushing him to the left or desertion can be sub-grouped into (a) *hostile action*, i.e. bullets, shells and cold steel; (b) *mental action*, i.e. hostile propaganda, solicitude for family, etc.; (c) *shortage of food, munitions or numbers*. Now, which of all these were due to Sherman's marches? It is evident that no items under headings (*a*) and (*c*) were, in the case of Lee's army, due to action by Sherman. There remains heading (*b*). Obviously solicitude for family affected those who lived in the Carolinas and Georgia, but it is difficult to compute how many of Lee's army deserted from this cause. Suppose we put it so high as 10,000. Then we find that the action of Sherman's army, 60,000, and later 90,000, strong, neutralised 10,000 of the Confederate forces at the decisive point. It seems a heavy outlay of capital to produce this result. It is no answer to say that Sherman also neutralised 40,000 of Johnston's army (even if that were true, Sherman's efficiency factor would only be about 50 per cent!), for Johnston's army would not have been within reach of Lee's had not Sherman marched into North Carolina. Had it not been for Sherman's curious inertia or blindness (which ever it may have been) his army might have had a direct influence on the ending of the war; but his rigid adherence to a timed programme denied to him a participation in the final triumph.

One thing is certain: Sherman's marches had no appreciable effect upon Lee's surrender. The semi-starvation of the Army of Northern Virginia was not caused by them: there was still enough food in the unoccupied regions to sustain it. It was the disastrous floods which ruined the railway between Danville and Greenborough that led to virtual starvation in Lee's army. It was the loss by stragglers and deserters, the direct result of Grant's implacable pursuit, that brought about the collapse. The verdict of Rope's is incontrovertible: " Sherman was . . . entirely mistaken in thinking that to devastate the state of South Carolina would have a direct and immediate bearing on Grant's campaign in Virginia." The war was won in Virginia in April, and it would in all probability have been won there, and then, had Sherman's men not rifled a house nor burnt a barn in the whole of the Confederacy. It is important to establish this point lest future commanders should be encouraged to emulate Sherman's unfortunate example.

I have purposely refrained from dwelling upon the details of the devastations, with which the names of Sherman and Sheridan are so closely connected. Perhaps the doctrine on which they were based is most clearly expressed by Sheridan as reported by Bismarck's biographer: " The proper strategy consists in the first place in inflicting as telling blows as possible upon the enemy's army, and then in causing the inhabitants so much suffering that they must long for peace, and force their government to demand it. The people must be left with nothing but their eyes to weep with over the war." The German Kaiser has sometimes been credited with this elegant expression. James T. Adams, who quotes this, considers that " it is not unlikely that the Germans developed their own theory of war and ' frightfulness ' from a study of the policy of some of the Northerners in the Civil War."[4] All that need be pointed out here is that, whatever military claims may be made for such a policy, it had in the long run unfortunate effects, causing such an intensity of animosity in the South as to delay by at least a decade that true unification of the country—the object for which the Northerners went to war. It would be unfortunate if this conception of Sherman and Sheridan should be accepted as a sound military maxim.

We pass on to the General-in-Chief of the Union armies. The chief criticism directed against Grant is that he was a butcher, regardless of the lives of his men. Though widely held, I can find no substance in this criticism. It is true that Grant, in common with all other generals at the time, did not realise the stopping power of the rifle in the hands of veteran troops behind the comparative security of entrenchments—until it was put to the proof. That was done at Coldharbor, and thereafter Grant carefully refrained from attacking entrenchments till the final and successful attack. It is true that he announced at Spottsylvania " I propose to fight it out on this line if it takes all summer," but he did not carry out his intention, and a man should be judged by his acts, not by his words.

A better-founded criticism would be that he failed to exploit situations that by his skill he had created. This was notably the case on the approach to the North Anna, the crossing of the

---

[4] *America's Tragedy*, p. 341.

Pamunkey and the crossing of the James. Of this latter his latest biographer is severe in his criticism: a " contemptible failure," he bluntly calls it.[5]

The fact that he was content to sit down before Petersburg for nine months, with an open flank, is also unimpressive. The curious phenomenon of this open flank has already been alluded to. Various reasons may be advanced for it: solicitude for his base, City Point; in the early summer mistrust of the offensive ability of his army after Coldharbor and Petersburg; in the late summer shortage of troops owing to the heavy detachments to Washington (an ample justification for Early's campaign). All sound reasons, but one cannot help feeling that Lee, in the same position, would have shown more audacity, and a greater readiness to take risks—the most essential pre-requisite for success in war.

It is doubtful whether Grant accurately appreciated the " time factor." Time was in favour of the South in '64, yet after Petersburg Grant marked time: it was in favour of the North in '65, yet he hastened to clinch the matter before Sherman appeared ready to co-operate. The " time factor " would thus indicate that the taking of risk was more justified in '64 than in '65, yet Grant reversed these values. There can be no doubt that, though he did not admit it, Grant in his heart of hearts feared Lee. In this attitude he was encouraged by the pessimistic Meade. It was Sheridan more than anyone who eventually dispelled this fear.

On the positive side, Grant's most striking quality as a general was his broadness of conception and singleness of aim. He kept one vision before him throughout—that of the slow strangling of the chief Confederate army, to which all resources direct and indirect were to be devoted. The curious fact that at the eleventh hour he apparently lost patience and struck before Sherman from the south, and Thomas from the south-west, were ready to play their part, is in a sense to his credit: it showed that he had after all an elastic, open and receptive mind and that he was ready to seize an unexpected opportunity that presented itself, even though it meant departing from his carefully prepared programme. It is difficult to envisage Sherman acting thus had he been in Grant's shoes. But, properly regarded, Grant's seven words to Sheridan, " I NOW FEEL LIKE ENDING THE MATTER," can be placed among the most tremendous utterances of military history, ranking with Wellington's apocryphal " Up Guards and at 'em! " and with Caesar's " I have crossed the Rubicon! "

5 *Ulysses S. Grant*, by R. R. McCormick, p. 188.

Little has been said in this book regarding Grant's moral qualities. The historian must here trust to the utterances of contemporaries. Chesterfield said that no man is a hero to his own valet, and it is a fact that a general is seldom a hero to his immediate subordinates, who are better placed than anyone to form a just judgment. Thus, anything *good* that the subordinate utters is likely to be true. I will therefore quote from Meade's letters to his wife, which may be presumed to represent his true opinion. " Grant is of a very sanguine temperament, and sees everything favourable in a strong light, and makes light of all obstacles." " Grant is not a mighty genius, but he is a good soldier, of great force of character, honest, and upright, certainly not influenced by others, and particularly a simple and guileless disposition." Another subordinate describes his predominant qualities as: " truth, courage, modesty, generosity, loyalty."[6] These two opinions give us what is probably a fairly accurate picture of the man. From the purely military point of view, the quality most to be admired is his perception that the true objective in war is the destruction of the enemy's main army. Clausewitz placed as the principal object in war " to conquer and destroy the enemy's armed forces." Clausewitz was right, and Grant knew it. There is no short cut to victory; there is no roundabout way by which the clash of arms, the " dread arbitrament " of battle can be avoided. Prepare the ground and make favourable the conditions by all means for that final crossing of swords, but the ultimate decision will be reached in the field. Sherman might help to prepare the ground, but it was Grant who struck the blow.

For many years after the war General Robert E. Lee was the recipient of nothing but indiscriminating praise. The inevitable reaction followed, one of the most eminent of the attackers of the Lee tradition being General Fuller. Criticisms from such a source must receive close and careful attention. There seem to be four main heads to the indictment.

(1) That Lee " failed to be a grand strategist." This is undoubtedly true. Compared with Grant he had a parochial outlook. He took up arms in defence of his native state of Virginia, and he never seems to have exhibited much interest outside that state. Such a friendly writer as R. S. Henry admits as much: " Even of Robert E. Lee . . . it might be said with truth that the country

---

[6] *Personal Recollections*, by General G. M. Dodge, p. 129.

he defended was Virginia."[7] Perhaps this accounts for his lack of ambition, and his reluctance to extend his command beyond the boundaries of his own State. Lee had not the spirit and urge of Pitt, who declared, " I know that I can save this country and that no one else can." Probably he had it in his power to be a grand strategist, but he never made the attempt.

(2) That he " possessed neither the character nor personality of a general-in-chief." In so far as this is true it springs from his aforementioned lack of ambition. We are told that he " could not impose his will on Davis." The answer is simple; it never occurred to him to try to do so. Such an attempt would to him appear a transgression of his duty, which was to carry out the behests of his Government unquestioningly and to the best of his ability. His conception of his office was akin to that of Douglas Haig rather than, shall we say, that of Joffre; and this attitude, needless to say, was perfectly correct.

(3) That he was too complaisant in dealing with inefficient subordinates. On the surface this may be allowed, but when it is remembered that he was dealing with a " new army " and when we bear in mind the reasons he gave for his complaisance (quoted on page 32), who shall say that he was wrong? It is to be noted that Grant also was lenient with inefficient subordinates. His only notable action in this connection was to remove Warren from the V Corps, and that was of very questionable expediency.

(4) That he failed as an administrator. The most formidable indictment under this head is made by Fuller in a passage which must be given in full. " On April 1st at Richmond or within easy call of this city, were stored up 4,000,000 rations of meat and 2,500,000 of bread, without counting considerable supplies of tea, coffee and sugar. Lee could have drawn on these immense supplies not only before the evacuation of Richmond but during it; this is made abundantly clear by Jefferson Davis; but he issued no orders concerning them, and when asked at what point on the railroad he would like supplies sent, he replied " that the military situation made it impossible to answer." The final dictum of history must be that whatever excellence Lee possessed as a strategist or a tactician, he was the worst Quartermaster-General in history."[8] As it would appear from the context that Fuller bases his conclusion on the foregoing episode, it will be worth while examining the statements of fact on which it is based.

In the first place General Fuller's figures are at variance with

[7] *The Story of the Confederacy*, p. 416.
[8] *Grant and Lee*, p. 240.

those given by General St. John, the Commissary General, for April 1st, which read: " At Richmond, 300,000 rations bread and meat, and 350,000 reserve rations; at Lynchburg (the next nearest place) 180,000 rations bread and meat."   Second: those who study Appendix 2 to Volume IV of Freeman's *Lee* (written since the publication of Fuller's book) will probably agree that Lee *did* cause orders to be issued, though they did not reach the department concerned.   Third: the date when he was asked at what point he would like the supplies sent was not, as might be inferred from the context, April 1st or 2nd, but April 6th, when the situation had rapidly and materially deteriorated, and when it was literally impossible to give any instructions for supplies with any probability that they could be exactly carried out.   To give precise orders under such circumstances would be worse than useless. The officer charged with the stores, on finding that he could not carry out his instructions would probably halt the supplies until he could obtain fresh orders, instead of acting promptly and on his own initiative, which was the right course to take.   Fourth: the exact words used by Jefferson Davis were, " General Lee replied *in substance* that the military situation made it impossible to answer."   Davis wrote several years later when no doubt his memory of what he was told had become foreshortened.   What Lee actually said was probably much as follows: " The situation is now beyond my control.   Those people have obtained the initiative, their cavalry are roaming the country; nothing is safe anywhere.   It would therefore be misleading for me to give precise orders which probably could not be carried out.   You must therefore act on your own initiative; my staff will give you the military situation regarding the enemy, so far as we know it. For myself, I aim at reaching Farmville to-night and thereafter working towards Danville.   Do the best you can on those lines." Could even the best Quartermaster-General in history do better than that under the circumstances?

If the indictment is extended further back, it should be remembered that he had no power or control over the old Commissary-General, who was described by Swinton as " a man of notorious ignorance and incompetence."   One of the first steps that Lee took on becoming General-in-Chief was to have him replaced by St. John.   " Regarding the commissary," writes Dr. Freeman, " [Lee] might as well not have spoken at all, because Mr. Davis held to Northrop until it was too late to save the army from the despair that hunger always breeds."   After that there is no more to be said.

Let us consider Lee next as a strategist and as a tactician. Perhaps his most striking feature is his audacity, combined with a willingness to take risks. " There is always hazard in military movements," he once wrote in a striking phrase, " but we must decide between the *positive* loss of inaction and the risk of action." This seems an echo of Wolfe's dictum: " In war something must be allowed to chance and fortune, seeing that it is in its nature hazardous and an option of difficulties." In this campaign Lee showed audacity and took risks conspicuously, in attacking Grant at the Wilderness, in detaching Early when in the midst of a desperate defensive with inferior numbers, and at Five Forks where he denuded his line beyond the edge of risk in order to deal a counter blow.

This brings us to his next attribute in the field, namely his belief in the virtue of the offensive, even in the form of the offensive-defensive, and his realisation that the pure defensive leads nowhere. Even when defending, it is notable that in nearly every battle, right up to the very last day of the war, Lee got in the last blow. " We must deal him a blow," was his reiterated cry. His reputation as a defensive general rests chiefly on his use of field fortifications, his skilful siting of them and his eye for country. Both in attack and defence he aimed always at " concentration at the decisive spot," and was for ever declaring its virtues in his correspondence with the President. His relations with Davis and the Government were always good—some would say they were too good and that if he had made more of a nuisance of himself he would have got more out of them. In this respect it is probable that his innate humility of spirit cost him and his army a good deal.

In the case of Lee pre-eminently it is impossible to divorce the general from the man. His essential greatness will always reside in the grandeur of his character and personality. All his immediate subordinates (with the possible exception of Longstreet who behaved abominably towards him at times) had the highest regard for him. I will conclude with a few assessments of the man from outside their ranks

A regimental officer at the North Anna, who had just seen Lee pass in a carriage, wrote of it: " I felt a new man all over."[9] Then his men: after the surrender at Appomattox, " as he rode along the lines, hundreds of his devoted veterans pressed around the noble chief, trying to take his hand, touch his person, or even lay a hand upon his horse, thus exhibiting for him their great

9 *Three Years in the Confederate Artillery*, p. 275.

affection. The General then, with head bare and tears flowing freely down his manly cheeks, bade adieu to his army." General Maurice's comment is, " Many a victorious general has been welcomed home by the plaudits of his grateful countrymen, but I know of only one instance in history of the people flocking to cheer a defeated general." Next comes the assessment of a Northern general: " Cautious, magnanimous and bold, a very thunderbolt in war, he was self contained in victory but greatest in defeat."[10] And now a foreign general. Lord Wolseley wrote: " I have only known two heroes in my life, and General R. E. Lee is one of them . . . . I believe that when time has calmed down the angry passions of the North, General Lee will be accepted in the United States as the greatest general you have ever had."[11] Finally here is the estimate of a distinguished Northern historian, J. F. Rhodes: " How was the South able to resist so long? . . . The paramount factor was Robert E. Lee." The cumulative effect of these and similar tributes is decisive; the student must feel that the military leader *par excellence* to whom he must pay homage is Robert E. Lee.

This book has been full of criticism. If it were not so it could never have been written. It is the penalty of greatness that it attracts to itself the fierce searchlight of criticism. But to err is human; no man is infallible; and, as Schiller says, " Let no man measure by a scale of perfection the meagre product of reality."

Thus we take leave of three great Americans. It is impossible to define greatness, but we know it when we see it; and seldom has it been seen in such abundant measure in three so different persons as the tall and dignified Lee, the stocky and taciturn Grant, and the lanky and loquacious Sherman.

[10] General C. F. Adams in *Photographic History of the War*, vol. ix.
[11] *S.H.S.P.*, xii, 232.

CHRONOLOGICAL TABLE

1864	THE EAST		THE WEST		OTHER EVENTS
	RICHMOND	THE VALLEY			
MAY	WILDERNESS Campaign	Newmarket	ATLANTA Campaign Resaca Cassville		Red River Expedition ends
JUNE	Coldharbor James River PETERSBURG Siege	Piedmont EARLY'S Campaign Kenesaw Mt.			
JULY	The Crater	Washington Maryland	Atlanta		
AUGUST	Weldon R. Rd.				Mobile Bay
SEPTEMBER	Fort Harrison	Opeqnon	Jonesborough TENNESSEE Campaign		Invasion of Missouri
OCTOBER		Cedar Creek	Allatoona		
NOVEMBER			Franklin	March through GEORGIA	Retreat from Missouri Lincoln re-elected
DECEMBER		Staunton	Nashville	Savannah	
1865 JANUARY					
FEBRUARY	Lee made G.-in-C.			March through CAROLINAS Columbia	Breckenridge succeeds Bragg Wilmington falls
MARCH	Fort Stedman	Waynesboro		Goldsborough	
APRIL	Five Forks Appomattox			Surrender of Johnston	Selma captured

ENDNOTES

(*Note numbers below are keyed to those found in the outside margins of the text.*)

1. This greatly exaggerates the dependence of the Confederate army on captured ammunition. From the very start of the war the South was able to supply its troops adequately with ammunition and by the latter part of 1863 was fully self-sufficient in this respect.

2. This is more myth than fact. Northern soldiers possessed as much "martial spirit" as Southern and the great majority of them also were "countrymen." The views expressed here by Burne were widely held by American historians at the time he wrote.

3. Confederate cavalry superiority, which as a general thing did exist during the first half of the war, derived mainly from superior leadership, better organization, and more effective use by Confederate commanders. Moreover, Southern cavalry, especially in the West, tended much more than Northern to be armed and to fight as mounted infantry. Paradoxically, this gave them an advantage, with Nathan Bedford Forrest's "critter company" being the most notable example.

4. Actually Texas was cut off from the rest of the Confederacy for all practical purposes prior to the capture of Vicksburg, and the opening up of the Mississippi by its capture had virtually no effect on the subsequent course of the war. The alleged great importance of Grant's taking of Vicksburg remains one of the hoary but entrenched myths of the Civil War. Grant would have contributed more to Union victory by retaining as prisoners the thirty thousand–plus Confederate troops he captured there instead of paroling them.

5. By "moral" Burne means "morale." Through much of the book he uses "moral" in the same way, yet in the latter part he employs the word "morale."

6. "FitzLee's Cavalry" is a reference to General Fitzhugh Lee, a nephew of Robert E. Lee.

7. "Newmarket" should be New Market. Here and elsewhere Burne habitually contracts place names that consist of two words into one word.

8. "Great War" is a reference to what now is commonly called World War I. It was standard usage in Britain prior to World War II.

9. For Atkinson, see Bibliographical Note, pp. xxvi.

10. Le Cateau refers to a battle in France in 1914 in which the well-directed rifle fire of British regulars repulsed a German attack.

11. Verdun and Passchendaele refer to World War I battles in which the Germans in the former and the British in the latter persisted in making attacks long after it should have been obvious that they could not succeed.

12. "A.D.C." means aide-de-camp, a staff officer.

13. This is a reference to the placing of Marshal Foch in command of the French and British armies in France as a consequence of the defeats suffered by them in the German offensive in the spring of 1918.

14. This statement is somewhat misleading in that Burnside repelled an ill-conceived attempt by Longstreet's forces to take Knoxville by storming its fortifications on November 29, 1863. Longstreet then withdrew into the eastern part of East Tennessee where he remained during the winter and early spring of 1864.

15. During the Mexican War Sherman remained in the United States and saw no service whatsoever in Mexico.

16. Burne errs here. A close reading of Sherman's reply, which was dated April 10, 1864, reveals that in spite of its slangy statement that he was to "knock Joe Johnston"—an expression that could mean so many things that it means nothing—Sherman conceived his primary mission as being to prevent Johnston sending reinforcements to Lee and to take Atlanta, which he proposed to do by cutting its railroad communications. On this subject, see Albert Castel, *Decision in the West: The Atlanta Campaign of 1864* (Lawrence: University Press of Kansas, 1992), 90–91.

17. Crewe is a town in north-central England, which, apart from being a railroad hub, bore little comparison to Atlanta, having in the 1930s a population of about 45,000, whereas Atlanta had close to 300,000 inhabitants. Burne also was ill-informed about Atlanta in 1864. Despite the fall of Chattanooga the railroads that radiated from the city remained highly important to the Confederate transportation system, and, although it did not have, contrary to Burne's statement, "large steel foundries," it had a rolling mill and numerous factories and shops engaged in producing war materiel. Its capture by Sherman would be a severe blow to the Confederacy both physically and psychologically.

18. Grant did not visit Sherman, whose headquarters then were in Nashville, on April 17. He did write Sherman on April 19, in response to Sherman's April 10 letter, and as the passage here quoted demonstrates, he too regarded Sherman's prime mission as being to prevent Johnston from reinforcing Lee in Virginia. Both Grant and Sherman expected Grant to win the war by defeating Lee, with the

consequence that Sherman viewed, as he informed one of his generals on April 24, 1864, his campaign in Georgia as "secondary" and Grant's offensive in Virginia as the "principal one" (see Castel, *Decision in the West,* 91).

19. The Army of the Potomac, not Sherman's army, was "the best equipped and supplied army in the Union." During the Atlanta Campaign there were times when many of Sherman's troops were short of rations and their animals were starving, and by the end of the campaign large numbers of them were in ragged, threadbare uniforms and even barefoot.

20. Burne is correct in his figure for the number of troops of all arms in Sherman's army at outset of the Atlanta Campaign, but with regard to Johnston's army he overstates its strength. It had approximately 60,000 men prior to being reinforced by Polk's army (or corps as it became de facto), and at most 75,000 after all of Polk's troops arrived in Georgia. In the next-to-last sentence on page 75, Burne gives the correct figure for Johnston's strength before being reinforced by Polk.

21. Despite what Johnston claimed in his memoirs, which Burne unfortunately took at face value, Johnston's orders and correspondence during early May 1864, as found in the *Official Records,* make it clear that he was unaware of Snake Creek Gap, or if aware of it did not realize the potential danger it posed, with the result that he gave no orders for it to "be watched." Likewise he did not adequately guard Dug Gap, and as a consequence a Union division nearly penetrated it. Johnston expected Sherman to try to outflank him by moving on Rome, Georgia, and hence had his attention fixated on that threat, mentally blinding him to other, closer ones.

22. The main, in fact, sole, reason Sherman changed his plan to send McPherson to strike at Rome was that as the date for beginning the campaign against Johnston drew near Sherman realized that four divisions that he expected to form part of McPherson's army would not be able to join it in time, with the result that McPherson would be too weak to carry out such a venture without undue risk. Hence he adopted a proposal that had been made to him by Thomas to have the Army of the Cumberland move around Johnston's left flank, pass through Snake Creek Gap, and seize Resaca, thereby blocking Johnston's line of supply and retreat. Unfortunately, though, he made two fatal changes in this plan: (1) the army of the Tennessee, not the Army of the Cumberland, would execute the Snake Creek Gap maneuver; and (2) since it was only one-third as strong as the Army of the Cumberland, instead of taking up a blocking position at Resaca, it would merely cut the railroad there, then with-

draw back to Snake Creek Gap from where it would attack Johnston in the flank as he retreated to Resaca, which he would have to do in order to restore his supply line.

23. Here Burne, probably following Liddell Hart, is mistaken. Sending Thomas's Army of the Cumberland through Snake Creek Gap would not have involved "crossing two armies over each other." Furthermore, Thomas's army, numbering 60,000, would have been strong enough to have blocked Johnston's retreat, and so presumably Sherman would not have been so foolish as to order it to return to Snake Creek Gap after reaching Resaca.

24. Johnston did not realize that Resaca was threatened until after McPherson approached Resaca and then withdrew to Snake Creek Gap. For a detailed critique of the Snake Creek Gap maneuver, see Castel, *Decision in the West*, 181–85, 567–68.

25. A Union force did appear on the Canton road and on Hood's left flank and rear, but it did not consist of Butterfield's division of the XX Corps. Instead it was composed of two divisions of cavalry that Sherman had ordered to cut the railroad south of Cassville. In calling off the attack Hood acted correctly, for the only prudent assumption that he could make was that enemy infantry were following the cavalry. Far from being "excellent," Lieutenant Mackall's diary contains passages that he inserted into it long after the war at Johnston's behest for the purpose of discrediting Hood, which he succeeded in doing by arranging to have this diary published in the *Official Records*. This forgery was exposed by Richard M. McMurry, "The Mackall Journal and Its Antecedents," *Civil War History* 20 (1974): 311–28.

26. Hood's statement that there was a Federal force on the Canton road is even more fully corroborated by the diary of one of his staff officers, Colonel Taylor Beatty—a diary that, unlike Mackall's, does not contain postwar falsehoods. On this, see Richard M. McMurry, *John Bell Hood and the War for Southern Independence* (Lexington: University of Kentucky Press, 1982), 107–8, and pertinent endnotes.

27. Burne's judgment that the Confederate second position at Cassville was untenable owing to it being enfiladed by Union artillery fire is confirmed by other sources, both Union and Confederate, than Captain Morris, whose statement on the subject appears in Hood's *Advance and Retreat* (see Castel, *Decision in the West*, 203–6).

28. Contrary to what is stated here, Sherman assaulted the Confederate position at New Hope Church on May 25, only to be repulsed. Then on May 27, he tried to turn the Confederate right but again failed in the Battle of Pickett's Mill. On May 28, the Confederates made a blundering attack on McPherson at Dallas, an action

the main effect of which was to reinforce Sherman in his decision, already made, to return to the railroad, thus abandoning the attempt to reach the Chattahoochee by this route. Quite possibly the errors in Burne's account of the operations at New Hope Church and Dallas resulted from his relying on Sherman's *Memoirs*, which falsely blames the defeat at New Hope Church on the slowness of the Army of the Cumberland and does not even mention Pickett's Mill while describing the much lesser fight at Dallas.

29. Sherman may have ordered his troops to take twenty days rations with them but this did not necessarily mean that they did so. Less than a week after crossing the Etowah many of them were going hungry and their animals were starving, the consequence of Sherman's inadequate wagon train and difficulties in distributing food and forage in a veritable wilderness with few and miserable roads.

30. The ratio of strength between Sherman and Johnston prior to the arrival of Blair's corps probably was closer to 3 to 2, for the Confederates also had suffered heavy casualties and were losing large numbers of men from illness, exhaustion, and (increasingly) desertion.

31. The rains ceased on June 22. A movement around the Confederate flank did not "involve leaving the railway," as Burne himself admits on page 93, where he states that the "danger of Johnston taking advantage of Sherman's flank movement to push forward down the railway and cut him off from his base was little more than theoretical." The Union attack at Kennesaw (the correct spelling) was not directed against that height per se but against lesser elevations to the south of it. The attack took some Confederate units by surprise but most of them were ready and eagerly waiting for it, as it was exactly what they hoped the Yankees would do.

32. This is one of the weakest sections of the book, if not the weakest, probably the consequence of Burne not having taken sufficient time in his research to achieve an adequate knowledge of the operations of both armies during this phase of the campaign, as witness his numerous factual errors. He is right in saying that Sherman "formed too precise a picture of what the enemy would do" but should have added that Sherman habitually did this and, what was worse, adhered to his preconceived picture long after it should have been evident to him that it was unrealistic. Contrary to what he contends, Liddell Hart was perfectly correct (for a rare change) in maintaining that an attempt by Sherman to reach the Chattahoochee by making a flank movement toward it from the New Hope Church–Dallas area almost certainly would have failed; as indicated in note 29, Sherman's supply situation alone would have made such a movement virtually suicidal. Sherman was not influenced to be overly

concerned about the safety of his railroad supply line by the "cautious Thomas": Sherman *always* was "nervous" about that, and Thomas both before and after the June 27 attack at Kennesaw—an attack he did not favor, as did all of Sherman's top generals—advocated doing what Sherman finally did do, namely flank Johnston from his Kennesaw position. As for Johnston, there is "little to criticise," given his basic policy of reacting to Sherman's moves rather than trying to force Sherman to react to his moves. He did, however, fight more than one offensive battle, that of Seven Pines, during his career. Thus at Resaca he twice assailed Sherman's left flank in an attempt to cut Sherman off from Snake Creek Gap; only bad luck prevented him from attacking at Cassville; after Pickett's Mill he ordered Hood to try to turn the Union left but Hood found this unfeasible; and at Bentonville in March 1865 he fell on half of Sherman's army with most of his own, an action Burne briefly describes on pages 175–76. On the other hand, Johnston did not "mount Hood's attack on the 22nd" of June; Hood attacked on his own initiative and Johnston did not even know of the attack until after it had taken place.

33. Bragg did not return to Richmond with a report on Johnston. Instead Bragg sent Davis telegrams and a letter from Atlanta in which he reported unfavorably on Johnston and urged that Hood be named to replace him. Davis had already decided to remove Johnston from command but was undecided as to whether he should be replaced by Hardee or by Hood. Bragg's messages possibly caused him to choose Hood because they contained false assertions about Hardee, whom Bragg (not without some cause) hated.

34. Soult was one of Napoleon's marshals and commanded a small army assigned to the defense of southern France, which Wellington had invaded from Spain in 1814. Since Soult's army was hopelessly inferior in size, quality, and morale to his own, Wellington's move on Toulouse was risky only in theory.

35. As he does throughout his account of the Atlanta Campaign, Burne here overstates the strength of Johnston's army (but he comes closer to the actual strength than most historians dealing with this subject before and since). By mid-July, Johnston's army had dwindled to about 55,000 troops, and although Burne is correct in pointing out the difficulty of judging the morale of an entire army, it is significant that following the retreat from Kennesaw the number of Confederate deserters increased greatly.

36. Logically the so-called Army of the Ohio should have been reinforced by a corps from the Army of the Cumberland, but this was impracticable because all of the corps commanders in that army were senior in rank to Schofield.

37. By "Texas Wars of 1856" Burne means U.S. army operations then in Texas against hostile Indians. Hood was not wounded at the Battle of Gaine's Mill in the arm or anywhere else.

38. Hood knew that Thomas's forces were across Peachtree Creek; hence his plan called for driving them into a pocket formed by the confluence of Peachtree Creek and the Chattahoochee River, where he hoped to smash them. That Hood intended to strike the Federals as they were crossing Peachtree is another embedded historical myth that Burne, with his primary interest in strategic aspects, can be forgiven falling victim to, especially since historians to this day persist in repeating it.

39. McPherson's death was not "an irreparable loss to the Northerners"; neither was he "one of their best commanders." Howard proved to be a more than adequate replacement as commander of the Army of the Tennessee, whose administration and general efficiency he greatly improved, whereas McPherson was excessively cautious, so much so that Sherman would have been justified in removing him from his post—something, however, he never considered doing. McPherson's caution, though, served the Union army well on July 22, for it was owing to it that the two divisions of the XVI Corps were in position to counter Hardee's attack against what otherwise would have been a totally open Federal flank and rear.

40. Schofield's corps was not attacked at all on July 22, and had it been, it would not have been by Smith's militia, which were posted at the southern end of the Confederate line.

41. On the whole, Burne's account of this battle is accurate and is superior to most previous and many subsequent accounts by other historians in that it notes that Lee's orders were to establish a defensive line behind which Stewart's Corps would pass to make a "turning movement" against the Union right flank and rear the following day. It was Lee's disobedience of these orders that turned Ezra Church into the bloody debacle for the Confederates that it became, yet most historians have blamed Hood for the debacle. He did not even know of Lee's attack until after it had been made and failed, and not until he learned of it did he send Hardee to take command of both Lee's and Stewart's Corps. Burne, however, errs in asserting that the Union troops used repeating rifles at Ezra Church. Perhaps a few did, but the vast majority were armed with single-shot muzzleloaders. These, obviously, sufficed.

42. Burne is right in stating that "Hood's weapon was becoming steadily blunter" and Sherman's "steadily sharper." But this had to do more with morale than a willingness to attack. When it came to that, Sherman's soldiers by this stage of the campaign were little, if

any, less reluctant to make frontal attacks against an entrenched enemy than Hood's men. In common with all veterans of all Civil War armies by 1864, they had discovered through both their experience and that of the foe that such attacks "did not pay" unless delivered in overwhelming force.

43. Sherman was not "put off by gloomy reports from Thomas" on July 22. Thomas sent Sherman no reports, gloomy or otherwise, on that day, and despite Sherman's claim in his *Memoirs* to the contrary, he did not order Thomas to "make a lodgement" in Atlanta unless an order he issued early in the morning of July 22 to Thomas (and also Schofield) to occupy the city, which he believed the Confederates were evacuating, be deemed such an order. Had Sherman instructed Thomas (and Schofield) to attack during the battle, the result probably would have been the destruction of Hood's army or, at the very least, the suspension of its attack on the Army of the Tennessee (see Castel, *Decision in the West*, 413–14).

44. Rodmans, not "heavy Parrott guns," were brought up for the bombardment of Atlanta.

45. Hood *hoped* but did not conclude that Sherman had "raised the siege." Moreover, he soon ascertained that most of Sherman's army was moving to the southwest of Atlanta. Other than redeploy his own army accordingly, though, he could not take any counteraction until he obtained reliable intelligence as to where Sherman intended to strike.

46. Burne errs badly here. Howard approached to within easy artillery range of Jonesboro (the correct spelling even though it is spelled with an "ough" in the *Official Records*) on the evening of August 30. The Confederates opposing him numbered only about 2,500, mostly cavalry, and hence made no attack. Neither did Howard; instead he entrenched on a range of hills one-half mile west of Jonesboro. On the afternoon of August 31, Hardee's and Lee's Corps, which Hood had ordered to Jonesboro on the night of August 30, attacked Howard but were easily repulsed. On the night of August 31, Lee, acting on instructions received from Hood the night before, returned to Atlanta for the purpose of guarding against an advance on the city from the south by Union forces operating to the north of Jonesboro. This would have been an excellent move by Sherman, but, as Burne demonstrates, Sherman was solely concerned with cutting the railroad and so did not think in such terms.

47. The reason Sherman failed to overwhelm and capture Hardee's Corps at Jonesboro on September 1 is that he did not order an attempt to do this until so late in the afternoon that he was able to bring only one corps (the XIV of the Army of the Cumberland) into

action. Moreover, he compounded this failure by not having Howard attack at all! Instead, he instructed Howard to send one of his corps, the XVII, to the south of Jonesboro to block Hardee's retreat. So fearful was the XVII Corps of being attacked in the open after its harrowing experience in the July 22 battle that it did not even reach the railroad but entrenched some distance from it. In stating that Sherman would have achieved a greater success "but for the hesitation of one of his corps commanders," Burne again allowed himself to be deceived by a false claim in Sherman's *Memoirs*.

48. The morale of Hardee's troops had little to do with his generalship, even though it was impeccable on September 1 at Jonesboro. Nearly all Confederate troops remained capable of fighting well on defense. Offense, as previously noted, was a very different matter.

49. To repeat what already has been stated in the Foreword, Burne's overall assessment of Sherman's, Johnston's, and Hood's performances in the Atlanta Campaign is superior to that of virtually all historians prior to him and a goodly number who have written since him, even up to the present. This more than compensates for the errors of detail in his descriptions and interpretations of the campaign.

50. By 1864 the North had abandoned almost totally the practice of forming new regiments and adopted that of replenishing existing units with recruits and conscripts. But by the summer of 1864 many veteran regiments had been disbanded because an insufficient percentage of their survivors agreed to re-enlist. This was especially true in the Army of the Potomac, the quality of which had already been badly impaired by the heavy losses of veteran troops it suffered during May and June of 1864.

51. The Messines mines were attempts by the British during World War I to break through the German lines by blowing them up with explosives placed beneath them by way of tunnels. Although not as ghastly a failure as "The Crater," they achieved no more substantive success.

52. Joffre was commander of the French army at the beginning of World War I in 1914. Gallieni, one of his top field commanders, failed badly in independent battles with the invading Germans but is credited with playing a key role, under Joffre's supervision, in defeating the Germans in the Battle of the Marne.

53. Haig, as commander of the British army in France during World War I, endeavored to accommodate military operations to the political-diplomatic objectives of his government. Joffre did not, which was a main reason why the French government eventually replaced him as top commander with Marshal Foch.

INDEX